Rekindling The Word:

In Search of Gospel Truth

Rekindling The Word:
In Search of Gospel Truth

Carsten Peter Thiede

E.J. DWYER

First Published in 1995

Gracewing
Fowler Wright Books
Southern Ave, Leominster
Herefordshire HR6 0QF
United Kingdom

Trinity Press International
P.O. Box 851
Valley Forge, PA 19482
U.S.A.

E. J. Dwyer
Unit 13 Perry Park
33 Maddox Street
Alexandria NSW 2015
Australia

National Library of Australia
Cataloging-in-Publication Data
Thiede, Carsten Peter

Rekindling the Word: In Search of Gospel
Truth/ ©
Carsten Peter Thiede

Includes bibliographical references.
Trinity Press International ISBN
1-56338-136-2
E J Dwyer ISBN 0-85574-254-2
Gracewing ISBN 0-85244-3358

1. Bible. N.T. - History of contemporary
events.
2. Bible. N.T. - Criticism, interpretation, etc.
3. Bible. N.T. - Manuscripts (Papyri).
1. Title.
226,06

Library of Congress
Cataloging-in-Publication Data
Thiede, Carsten Peter
Rekindling the Word: In Search of Gospel
Truth/ ©
Carsten Peter Thiede

Includes bibliographical references.
ISBN 1-56338-136-2 (pbk. alk. paper)
1. Bible. N.T. - Criticism, interpretation, etc.
2. Bible. N.T. - Manuscripts, Greek.
3. Bible. N.T. - Manuscripts (Papyri).
4. Bible. N.T. - Gospels - Authorship - Date
of authorship.
5. Magdalen papyrus.
6. Magdalen College (University of Oxford).
Library.
7. Dead Sea scrolls - Criticism,
interpretation. etc.
8. Qumran community.
1. Title.
BS2361.2
226.06 — dc20
95 - 38673
CIP

Typesetting by: 4is Print and Photography,
Dutton House Studio, Leominster HR6 8AQ

Printed in Great Britain by The Cromwell Press.
Broughton Gifford, Melksham, Wiltshire SN12 8PH

UK ISBN 0-85244-3358
US ISBN 1-56338-136-2
Australian ISBN 0-85574-254-2

I dedicate this book to my three year old daughter Emily
with a saying of Jesus from St Matthew's Gospel: 'Heaven
and Earth shall pass away, but my words shall not pass away'.

(St Matthew 24:35)

Contents

Bibliographical References

The following chapters, now published in this book in volume form, originally appeared as articles in the publications detailed below:

1. C.P. Thiede, *Jésus selon Matthieu. Les origines de l'évangile d'après le manuscrit p⁶⁴ d'Oxford*, Paris: F.-X. de Guibert (O.E.I.L.), 1995.

2. *Zeitschrift für Papyrologie und Epigraphik* 105, 1995, pp 13-20 + one plate

3. C.P. Thiede/ G. Masuch (eds.) *Wissenschaftstheorie und Wissenschaftspraxis. Reichweiten und Zukunftsperspektiven interdisziplinärer Forschung*, Paderborn, Bonfatius Verlag 1995.

4. *Renconditi, Parte Generale e Atti Ufficiali, Istituto Lombardo/Accademia di scienze e lettere*, Milano, vol. 126, 1992, pp 129-147.

5. C.P. Thiede, *Jésus selon Matthieu. Les origines de l'évangile d'après le manuscrit p⁶⁴ d'Oxford*, Paris: F.-X. de Guibert (O.E.I.L.), 1995.

6. 'Petrus', *Das große Bibellexikon*, vol. 3, Wuppertal/Zurich ²1990, pp. 1166-1169.

7. 'Rom, neutestamentliche Zeit (Archäologie)', *Das große Bibellexikon*, vol. 3, pp. 1298-1301.

8. 'Schrift, VII. Tachygraphie/Kurzschrift', *Das große Bibellexikon*, pp. 1401-1403.

9. C.P. Thiede, *Jésus selon Matthieu. Les origines de l'évangile d'après le manuscrit p⁶⁴ d'Oxford*, Paris: F.-X. de Guibert (O.E.I.L.), 1995.

10. *Journal for the Study of the New Testament* 26, 1986, pp 79-96.

11. *Inklings: Jahrbuch für Literatur und Aesthetik*, Band 12, 1994, pp 131-146.

12. C.P. Thiede/G. Masuch (eds.), *Wissenschaftstheorie und Wissenschaftspraxis*, Paderborn, Bonifatius Verlag 1995.

13. C.P. Thiede (ed.), *Das Petrusbild in der neueren Forschung*. Wuppertal/Zurich, R. Brockhaus Verlag 1987, pp. 221-229.

14. *Museum Helveticum* 47/1, 1990, pp.35-40.

15. *ibw journal* 32/1, 1994, pp. 13-19.

16. *Aegyptus* 74, 1994.

17. Bernhard Mayer (ed.), *Christen und Christliches in Qumran?* Regensburg, F. Pustet 1992, pp 57-72.

18. Bernhard Mayer (ed.), *Christen und Christliches in Qumran?* Regensburg, F. Pustet 1992, pp 239-245.

19. *Aegyptus* 74, 1994, pp 123-128.

Introduction

The debate about the 'Magdalen Papyrus' of St Matthew's Gospel and its redating to the first century has not abated since *The Times* made it headline news in their Christmas Eve issue 1994. It has also engendered new and lasting interest in an arcane subject, papyrology. As a Canadian scholar put it at the 21st Congress of the International Papyrologists' Association in Berlin last August, the furore and controversy caused by the original paper (reprinted in this volume) is the best thing that could have happened to papyrology. And people have been realizing that there is more to the study of New Testament origins than the outlandish but bestselling theories of Robert Eisenman, Michael Baigent, Richard Leigh or John Dominic Crossan, in short: that the study of the oldest manuscripts can contribute to a better understanding of these beginnings.

But papyri and papyrology cannot and do not function in isolation. Quite apart from the fact that the vast majority of ancient papyri are 'secular' (there are only some 100 New Testament papyri, among tens of thousands of known papyri worldwide), the results of applied papyrology within New Testament studies make sense only if and when they are used together with the contributions of other classical disciplines: history, archaeology, classical philology and literature, epigraphy, numismatics - to mention just the more important ones.

In a way, they are all part of what we might call 'Ancient History'. And, needless to say, the events told in the New Testament, the letters and historical documents of Early Christianity, are very much an integral part of 'ancient history'. The essays and papers reprinted in this book, previously published in British, French, Italian, Swiss and German journals or collections, try to do justice to this encompassing, interdisciplinary research. Naturally, most of them cover the different aspects of papyrology, from Egyptian discoveries to the Dead Sea Scrolls: *The Origin of the Gospels and the Magdalen Papyrus; Papyrus Magdalen Greek 17 (Gregory-Aland* p[64]*): A Reappraisal; The Origin and Tradition of Mark's Gospel in the Light of Recent Investigation; On the Development of Scroll and Codex in the Early Church; Dating Ancient Manuscripts: Why We Need to Work Together; Papyrus Bodmer L: The New-Testamental Papyrus Fragment* p[73]*; Greek Qumran Fragment 7Q5: Possibilities and Impossibilities; Fragment 7Q5: A Forensic Analysis in Jerusalem;* and *An Unnoticed Fragment from Qumran.*

These essays, including the first edition of a New Testament papyrus, demonstrate the variety of techniques and their application.   Most of them are consciously written (or translated) in a non-technical language: papyrology is no esoteric science. Its approaches, and above all its results, can be and should be accessible to any interested reader. The same, of course, applies to other fields: there is an essay on radiocarbon dating and a brief entry from an encyclopaedia in ancient shorthand writing, which both attempt to introduce readers to the complexities of their subjects in as uncomplex a language as possible.

The historical and archaeological background and the context of New Testament writings is described and analyzed in a further group of essays: *Archaeological Rome in New Testament Times; Babylon, 'the other place': Thoughts on the Whereabouts of Peter; Speaking in Tongues: On the Multilingualism of the Essenes and Early Christianity; Christianity and Qumran: Cave 7 in its Papyrological Context.* There is a paper on textual history and textual criticism: *A Pagan Reader of 2 Peter: Cosmic Conflagration in 2 Peter 3 and the* Octavius *of Minucius Felix.* Historiography as a vital tool of research is used in the article on *St Peter: A New Approach to a Biography.* And even literary criticism is given its due, in an essay on Dorothy L. Sayers and her timeless contribution to New Testament studies, *A Critic of the Critics: Dorothy L. Sayers and New Testament Research.*

If anything, all these texts are the papyrologist's and historian's argued appeal to take the sources seriously, to bid good-bye to presuppositions, schools of thought, ready-made paradigms and vested interests. The often amazing amount of first-hand evidence from New Testament times, the growing awareness of circumstantial evidence from the first and second centuries, and the refinement of the tools with which we may analyze them, constitute a stimulating and fascinating challenge. Taking the sources seriously also means appreciating them in their own right: comparing them to non-Christian, non-biblical texts is obligatory, but taking one's yardsticks from what 'the others' did may easily become misleading. As Richard Blackmore wrote in his *Paraphrase on the Book of Job*, in 1700:

> It may be considered farther that the eastern people differ something from us in their notions of eloquence. We condemn them for being too pompous, swelling and bombast; perhaps they despise us for being languid, spiritless and insipid. People are apt to form their notions of excellence from their own perfections, and their notions of things from objects with which they are most conversant. Our art of criticism is drawn from the writers of Rome and Athens, whom we make the standard of perfection. But why have not the Jews as much right to prescribe to them as they have to prescribe to the Jews?

In other words, we must do justice to idiosyncrasies, to the exceptions as much as to the rules (most of them based on philosophical assumptions, anyway), and we must be prepared to be surprised by the unforeseen and unforeseeable developments which may overturn long-held positions. Richard Blackmore, back in 1700, could not know that two hundred and fifty years later, valuable papyri would be found which, in conjunction with other manuscripts and supplementary evidence from other fields, make the New Testament the single best attested collection of texts from antiquity.

He could not know that a combination of textual evidence and archaeology, for example, would help us date the origins of Scripture - as in that famous passage of St John 5:2-3, 'Now there is in Jerusalem by the Sheep Gate a pool, in Hebrew called Bethesda, which has five porticoes. In these lay a multitude of invalids, blind, lame and paralyzed'. As archaeologists have shown, not only is this description of the pool correct, but the pool was destroyed by the Romans in AD 70. Since the author, telling a healing story in the past tense, makes it unmistakably clear that the pool still existed (and could be visited, if you like) at the time of writing, it follows logically and conclusively that this text was written before AD 70.

Identifying, editing and dating papyrus manuscripts may be seen as another way of getting close to the origins. Not always, though, is such certainty as in the case of St John 5:2 attainable and demonstrable. We are, as St Paul put it, seeing through a glass, darkly (1 Corinthians 13:12). More often than we may like it, results have remained elusive, and there is no guarantee that even the latest scanning microscopes and other forms of 'space age' equipment will supersede the apostle's admission: 'Now I know in part'.

The 'then' for which he hopes is beyond the reaches of human knowledge. Even so, our generation of scholars is in a unique position. Never before have there been so many concrete, visible and attainable objects, from papyri to coins, inscriptions, and works of art, to help us reconstruct the multi-coloured and many-faceted fresco of Early Christianity. And in this sense, the papers and essays assembled in this book may be a humble contribution to our endeavours along the road towards an increasingly real and realistic understanding of Jesus, his followers and their time.

Carsten Peter Thiede

1

The Origin of the Gospels and the Magdalen Papyrus[1]

When St Paul wrote at the end of his second letter to the Thessalonians (2 Thess. 3:17), 'I, Paul, write this greeting with my own hand. This is the mark in every letter of mine: it is the way I write', he was unconsciously underlining the importance of palaeography, since he made a point in stressing that the greeting was written in his own hand. It is obvious that the rest of this letter was written by someone else - by Timothy, Silvanus, Tertius, or by an unknown scribe.[2] This was common practice in antiquity. Paul, like others, would have dictated his letters, and only very short, very personal communications, such as his letter to Philemon or the second and third letters of St John, would have been likely to have been written by the sender in person. Here St Paul's intention is to authenticate his missives. His personal style, his characteristic, recognizable handwriting serve this purpose. From this it is clear that even the very first readers of what was to become the New Testament were used to the importance of different styles of handwriting. They appreciated comparative analysis, and they knew how to arrive at judgments of reliability.

Like St Paul's letters and the cultural, literary information contained in them, the papyrus fragments of St Matthew's gospel which I intend to discuss in this chapter are equally part and parcel of the textual tradition of classical literature. This is true regardless of their exact date and precise contents. In fact, some of the fascination and excitement caused by these fragments comes from the knowledge that they are a part of our cultural heritage, a legacy which, having been the preserve of a few specialists, has suddenly and unexpectedly emerged into the full glare of the media, public curiosity and renewed scholarly debate. Even in a thoroughly secularized society, the New Testament appears to be more attractive than works by, say, Seneca or Philo of Alexandria. Would a papyrus fragment of a novel by Petronius, a contemporary of St Paul's and St Matthew's, have made headlines in *The Times*? We do not have a single papyrus of one of the most important Greek authors of the second century, Lucian of Samosata. Yet should such a papyrus be discovered tomorrow, would we read about it on the front page of *The Times*, and would the consequences and controversies be debated week after week in 'Letters to the Editor'? Excitement, enthusiasm and polemical criticism are particularly rife when dealing with the New Testament and its textual tradition. It is because of this that I have taken this opportunity to explain some of the aspects surrounding the Magdalen papyrus, and I hope general readers will bear with me when I go into the technical details surrounding my work on the fragments. I hope that by the end of this chapter the importance of the Magdalen Papyrus will have emerged from the wealth of details.

Ancient manuscripts were not always held in high esteem. We all know the story of the antiquarian who, in 1778, bought a documentary papyrus scroll from some Egyptian peasants and then watched as they happily burnt five more scrolls, enjoying the aromatic fragrance of the smoke. When the first two papyri were given to the library of Basle in the late 1500s no-one paid any attention to them, and it was not until 1917, four and a half centuries later, that they were finally published. On the other hand, vast numbers of papyri have come to light since the end of the 19th century, and not all of them are of equal value even to the specialists. In Tony Harrison's somewhat extravagant play, 'The Trackers of Oxyrhynchus' (1990), there is a scene where the two great scholars Bernard Grenfell and Arthur Hunt, described as 'the Holmes and Watson of Oxford papyrology', are seen deciphering and cataloguing papyri:

Hunt: Petition concerning repayment of loan.
            Petition complaining of non-payment of loan.

Grenfell: Letter on beer tax to the ταραχευται 'mummifiers'

Hunt: But ταραχευται might mean 'salt-fish suppliers'.

Grenfell: It might! It might! It might! It might!
               God! I do wish some literature would come to
               light.[3]

Well, eventually literature did come to light, at Oxyrhynchus and elsewhere in Egypt. In fact, more than 90% of all papyri discovered so far were found or acquired in Egypt where they had been protected by the soil in an arid climate. Other sites of major finds, such as the caves of Nahal Hever or the Wadi Murabba'at and Qumran near the Dead Sea offered similar conditions. Elsewhere, unusual events and conditions played a protective and preserving role. At Pompeii, and above all at Herculaneum, where a whole library was vacuum-sealed under the lava and the ashes of the eruption of Vesuvius in AD 79. At Petra in Jordan, where in 1992 a Byzantine library was discovered under the rubble of a church destroyed by earthquake and fire. At Vindolanda near Hadrian's Wall, where hundreds of letters written on thin slivers of wood are being discovered. This last group of documents was only preserved because burning rubbish was extinguished by rain, and then a layer of mud covered the debris protecting everything - letters, tent pieces, a baby's boot, leather artefacts. All lay undiscovered until their rediscovery in 1973.

The papyrus of St. Matthew's gospel at Magdalen College Oxford and its counterparts, the two fragments kept at the Fundación San Llucas Evangelista in Barcelona, belong to the group of ancient manuscripts which are shrouded in mystery. We know that the Oxford document was bought at Luxor in Southern Egypt, on the River Nile, and we know this because the Reverend Charles Huleatt, who sent the three fragments to his old college in 1901, tells us so. But how did the papyri get to Luxor? Did the people who sold them to Huleatt find them at this site, the southern part of ancient Thebes? And if so, were they actually *written* where they were buried and ultimately rediscovered?

At this juncture, we encounter the first of many problems - the first two fallacies to arise in the debate about ancient papyri. The first fallacy is connected with the fact that the Magdalen papyrus contains fragmentary verses from chapter 26 of the

Gospel according to St Matthew, or, to put it differently, from a Christian text. Since we know of no centre of Christian activity in Egypt, outside Alexandria, in the first century, you are invited to assume that no first century Christian papyri can have existed in Egypt. It is because of this that when a German papyrologist appears on the scene and suggests that those fragments at Oxford and Barcelona were written in the first century, he is greeted by hordes of scholars who wave sticks at him and tell him that this cannot be true because everyone knows that Christian texts were not written in Egypt at such an early date. But the assumption that there were no Christian scribal centres in first century Egypt outside Alexandria is based on the circular argument that there are no first century papyri to document their existence. Therefore, when a first century papyrus apparently turns up, what happens to the theory about Christian centres of activity? Does the theory prevail over the evidence of the papyrus? Second, who is to know that the fragments from St Matthew's gospel did not originate in Alexandria, a place where first century Christian activities may be assumed, anyway? Third, what is there to tell us that these fragments were written in Egypt at all? Manuscripts from places as far as Rome were found at Egyptian sites.[4]

In other words, this assumption about the existence or non-existence of Christian centres in first century Egypt does not get us anywhere. Then there is the allied follow-up critique - that a copy of St Matthew's gospel found or at least preserved in southern Egypt and written at such an early date would suggest an incredibly rapid process of dissemination of this gospel throughout the Mediterranean basin. Yes, if we are right, the progress would indeed have been rapid, but why should this in any way surprise us? We know a lot about means and methods of communication in the Roman Empire. In favourable conditions, it would have taken a ship five days to link Corinth in Greece and Puteoli in Italy. Cato once managed to reach Africa from Rome in under three days. Thus, to put an extreme case for the sake of argument, a copy of St Matthew's gospel dispatched from Rome could have reached Alexandria three days later and been in Luxor within a week. If in addition we take into account that a number of the gospels would have been sent out immediately as a matter of course, and that copies of copies would have been produced for further distribution without delay, we face a sober scenario, namely that the spreading of the gospel, of any gospel, throughout the Mediterranean basin was in all probability anything but a protracted affair of years or decades. It happened within weeks and months. To put it differently, to assume the existence of a copy of Matthew's gospel linked with Luxor on the Nile and dated to the latter part of the first century is historically speaking neither outrageous nor controversial. Such a papyrus could have, and indeed should have been expected anyway, given what we know about the communication techniques of the period of which Early Christianity was an integral part.[5]

The second fallacy is connected with the format of the papyrus. When the Magdalen fragments reached Oxford, Arthur Hunt, at the time a fellow of Magdalen College, examined them, realized that they were fragments of a codex, and decided on that basis that they should be assigned to the late third, but 'with more probability to the fourth century'.[6] There are fallacies related to this second fallacy all around us. For example, one of the reasons why in the opinion of many New Testament scholars the famous Qumran fragment 7Q5 cannot be a fragment of the Gospel according to St Mark is the fact that it is a *scroll* fragment. Since the great Kurt Aland had decreed that the Christians had used the codex format from the beginning,[7] it is assumed that there simply could not have been early Christian scroll fragments. As in the case of our first fallacy, what do you do when such a purported scroll fragment turns up? Who wins - the theory or the papyrus[8]? Arthur Hunt and his colleague Bernard Grenfell were adamant. As far as they were concerned, it is the theory that wins. Thus, when they edited the Oxyrhynchus papyrus 35, a Latin codex fragment of an otherwise unknown *History of the Macedonian Wars* now at the British Library, they realized that for palaeographical reasons, from a comparative analysis of the handwriting, this codex must be first century. But since it is a vellum *codex*, they decided that it had to be assigned to the late third or fourth century.[9] These days, no-one doubts that this Latin codex fragment does belong to the first century.

It is interesting to note at this point that the British Library codex fragment is quite 'sensational' in its own right. It is a

unique document that on its own contradicts everything that
had been assumed regarding Roman writing techniques. The
scroll, and nothing but the scroll was the maxim; a codex just
would not fit. A reference to the Roman poet Martial helps to
clarify this matter. Martial, writing in the ninth decade of the
first century, praises his and his publishers friend Secundus'
unheard-of marketing enterprise - the introduction of a library
of classical works in the codex format.[10] The fragment from that
lost *History of the Macedonian Wars* may be the only surviving
example of this possibly short-lived venture. There may be an
analogy in the New Testament. In one of the so-called Pastoral
Epistles, 2 Timothy 4:13, the recipient of the letter is asked 'to
bring the *biblia* and above all the *membranas*'. *Biblia*, that means
'scrolls', of course, probably scrolls of Old Testament books in
Greek, from the 'Septuagint'.[11] But *membranas*? Colin Roberts
suggested that this referred to parchment note-books,[12] and he
remarks on this passage that 'the only Greek writer of the first
century AD to mention the parchment note-book' is 'St Paul'.
And the American New Testament scholar Philip Wesley
Comfort suggested that these *membranas* 'may have contained
copies of the various epistles Paul had previously written in the
form of parchment codexes.'[13] Furthermore, there seems to be
a consensus among scholars that 'the codex was unique to
Christianity until the end of the second century'.[14] This is not
quite correct, as we know from Martial and indeed from the
codex fragment of the Macedonian Wars at the British Library.
Frederic Kenyon put it a little more cautiously: 'Among all the
papyri discovered in Egypt which can be assigned to the second
century no single pagan [i.e. non-Christian] manuscript is in
codex form'.[15] It is of course another common fallacy that acts
to generalize the situation in Egypt for the whole of the Roman
Empire. But in any case, there is a general agreement that the
Christians introduced the codex, that it happened in the first
century, and that its precursors or first examples were used by
the author of 2 Timothy. It does not have to interest us here, in
the context of the Magdalen papyrus, why they did it. We may,
however, venture a suggestion regarding the turning point *when*
the change took place in a more official way. It seems to me that
the 'watershed' for the Christian change from scroll to codex is
the period of Jewish revolt against the Romans, AD 66-70. In

my re-edition of the Magdalen papyrus,[16] I suggest that this occurred immediately after the destruction of the Temple in Jerusalem, in AD 70, which signified the end of Jewish-Christian missionary activities among their fellow Jews and brought an end to strategic reasons for using the common scroll format. This is, of course, a rather careful and conservative evaluation of the evidence. It may be argued that the decisive break between Jews and (Jewish) Christians happened as early as AD 62, when James, 'the brother of the Lord', was stoned on behalf of the high priest Ananus and the Sanhedrin in the absence of the Roman procurator. Since James was the leader of the orthodox Jewish Christian 'wing' within the Jerusalem church, his illegal execution was a carefully orchestrated breaking of all existing links between Jews and Christians, coming from the Jewish side.[17]

Be this as it may, a summary of the evidence at this point would indicate that the existence of Christian codices, even in first century Egypt, was historically plausible if not downright necessary. There are no historical or technical arguments against the existence of such papyri. To put it differently, their existence must be assumed for historical reasons. The three papyrus scraps from Magdalen College Oxford and the two pieces at the Fundación San Llucas Evangelista in Barcelona, re-dated to the latter part of the first century, would fulfil this requirement. Numerically speaking, they are as unique as is the one and only secular Latin codex fragment from the first century in the British Library. But as we have seen, a document's unique status does not necessarily render an early date impossible. A simple question therefore remains. Is it a first-century papyrus?

It may be as well to remember here that the Magdalen papyrus has already had its date dramatically altered. Arthur Hunt had suggested a date of the late third or preferably the fourth century. Fifty years later Colin Roberts found that it should be assigned 'a date in the later second century',[18] and this new date found a general acceptance at the time; Roberts himself refers to corroborative verdicts by Bell, Skeat and Turner. Thus, the papyrus was suddenly some 150 years older. It happened before; can it have happened again? Roberts gave his reasons for his dramatic re-dating as follows. First of all, he asserted that the prejudice about the date of the codex format had to be abandoned, and secondly he pointed out that certain palaeographical characteristics - such as 'the minute omicron and the flat omega, common in third century hands, are absent'.[19] Roberts' procedure worked here on the basis of negative criteria - he rules out aspects that would favour a later, third century date and arrives at a safe date in the second century. It was not his intention here to establish a particularly early date for the fragment, but to correct a particularly late date. He knew, of course, as every papyrologist does, that the dating of ancient papyri is a notoriously difficult, complex and complicated process. Literary papyri are, as a rule, undated. The earliest dated Greek New Testament manuscript is a 9th century minuscule in St Petersburg.[20] The only palaeographical way to arrive at a date for an undated manuscript is comparison. Papyri with dates, such as private letters, official documents, marriage contracts and so forth, and texts that are datable, such as those from Herculaneum and Pompeii which must precede the destruction of these cities by the eruption of Vesuvius in AD 79, or from Qumran, which must be prior to AD 68 when the settlement and the area of the caves was overrun and occupied by the Roman 10th Legion, provide a yardstick for comparison. Simply put, the closer the test document resembles in general appearance and details of letters the document to which it is being compared, the more reliable is the date given to the undated manuscript. Ideally, one would like to work with papyri from the same region, so as to include aspects of local culture and education. But this is not always possible, and it is not even a prerequisite. I was accused, in *The Times*, of having based my re-dating 'on the misassumption that all scribes of the Jewish diaspora wrote in the same script'.[21] Notwithstanding the fact that I am not guilty of such misassumption, it may be a salutary reminder to quote the Oxford classicist Peter Parsons himself, who made the following comment in an analysis of the script on the stork vase from the Mola di Monte Gelato: 'Palaeographers debate whether different areas practised different sorts of script. For documentary hands there is indeed some evidence of local peculiarities.... For literary hands, the evidence itself ... is minimal. The Monte Gelato text adds interestingly to that evidence, and speaks for uniformity: I can see nothing in the script that would be surprising in Greco-Egyptian manuscripts of the same period'.[22] Thus, on this occasion, Parsons clearly felt free, and rightly so, when assessing the script to look for 'parallels from the other side of the Mediterranean'.[23.] What, then, is our comparative material? Any new suggestion makes sense only when new evidence has become available, texts not known or accessible to those who had previously dated the papyrus. The most important such group of manuscripts are the Greek texts from the Dead Sea: from Qumran, the Nahal Hever, the Wadi Murabba'at, and so forth. Everyone knows about Qumran; in Britain, the BBC *Everyman* series recently showed a programme entitled *Secrets of the Sea* which discussed many of the so-called secrets and problems of the Qumran scrolls, but signally failed to even mention the existence of Greek fragments in caves 4 and 7. I am not referring to the partly controversial identification of these twenty-five fragments, merely to their existence. They are, as the Jewish Qumran scholar Emanuel Tov and others have since pointed out, an indication of the multicultural society in which even the Qumran Essenes - like for example the Masada defenders who also wrote Greek among themselves - used to live.[24] They furthermore indicate that it was feasible to 'import' and collect non-Hebrew, non-Aramaic documents. The sixteen fragments from Cave 7 were first edited in 1962, nine years after Colin Roberts' edition of the Magdalen papyrus, and a year after Roca-Puic's first edition of the Barcelona scraps.[25] They remained pretty much unnoticed until they acquired worldwide notoriety in 1972, when the Spanish papyrologist José O'Callaghan suggested that at least two of them are remnants of New Testament texts. But in the 1962 edition, they had already been assigned dates uninfluenced by the later identification. It was none other than Colin Roberts who had suggested that they belonged to a style that ceased to be used in about AD 50. The six Greek texts from Cave 4 were first edited in 1992.[26] However, beyond the Qumran scrolls, other finds must also attract our attention. A striking case is the so-called Greek Minor Prophets Scrolls from the Nahal Hever. Parts of it were first published by Barthélemy in 1963, but the first complete, critical edition was finally made available in 1990.[27] Barthélemy himself and later commentators like Roberts, Würthwein, Schubart and Hanhart all opt for a date in the mid-first century AD.[28] Emanuel Tov, the editor of the new and complete edition, left the task of dating that scroll to Peter Parsons, who does not rule out the mid-first century AD date agreed upon by the others, but would like to prefer an even earlier date, in the later first century BC.[29]

These, then, are the notable new texts that have come to light since Colin Roberts first edited the Magdalen papyrus. Add to these the important collection of Herculaneum papyri, known since 1752 but only recently properly assessed and evaluated. In this case, it took until 1975 for a papyrologist to realize that the Herculaneum type of handwriting exists in certain Greek papyri found at Qumran.[30]

I had warned you that we would have to delve into details and technicalities. And I must ask you for a little more patience. As you will have realized, all those recent or relatively recent 'acquisitions' have one thing in common: they belong to the first century AD or, perhaps, even BC. A New Testament scholar happy with the *status quo* would not bother with a close analysis of these manuscripts - after all, there is the so-called 'biblical uncial' style of handwriting to which second and third century biblical papyri have been assigned and where they have rested in peace. Long forgotten is the mould-breaking work of one of the truly great papyrologists of our time, Herbert Hunger of Vienna University. Hunger had suggested as early as 1960 that something is amiss with our filing cabinet attitude to the categorization of biblical papyri. He demonstrated what he meant with an analysis of the codex Bodmer II, or Papyrus p^{66}, of St John's Gospel. Commonly assigned to c. 100 AD, it was re-dated by Hunger to the first quarter of the second century, a shift of some 75 years.[31] Hunger was not alone in his re-date of manuscripts - Young-Kyu Kim, a young scholar from Göttingen University, attempted to re-date the Pauline codex p^{46} to the later first century;[32] it remains an important if controversial foray into the possibilities and limitations of palaeography.[33] But let us remember the fallacies we discussed before. Does the fact that the second and third centuries have been accepted as a convenient dumping ground prevent us from looking at earlier material? It does and should not, of course. One should never forget that even Colin Roberts, when he dated the famous papyrus fragment of the Gospel according to St John, the p^{52} at the John Rylands University Library Manchester, took notice of first century parallels, such as a papyrus from Fayyum of AD 94, or London 2078, a private letter from the time of Domitian, AD 81-96.[34] In the end, the cautious side of his nature won over, and he decided in favour of the latest possible end of the range available to him, c. AD 125. Thus, once again - and it cannot be underlined too often - there is nothing untoward, illicit or unsociable in the serious investigation of a first century date for the Magdalen papyrus.

Obviously, one does not go into the investigation of a document telling oneself 'let's date that papyrus to the apostolic era'. In my case, it happened because I was studying the recent Qumran and Nahal Hever editions and noticed the striking resemblance of some of these scripts to the handwriting of the Magdalen and Barcelona fragments. And here I am facing the temptation to bore my readers stiff with a detailed description of identical or near-identical letters, sloping or upright styles, ligatures and lack of ligatures, and so on. I shall resist this temptation since all this can be studied at leisure in my more scholarly article on the papyrus which is included as chapter 2 in this volume.[35] Suffice it to say that there are not that many letters in the small Oxford and Barcelona fragments, but that six of them (*Alpha, Epsilon, Iota, Omicron, Rho* and *Nu*) bear a striking resemblance to the script of the Greek Minor Prophets Scroll from the Nahal Hever. One's initial surprise is, however, mitigated by the observation that two other letters, *Eta* and *Mu*, look distinctly different. But the edition of that Dead Sea Scroll makes it obvious that there were *two* scribes employed to write it, and the second scribe has the *Etas* and *Mus* that look exactly like those in the Magdalen papyrus. So this is what you might call a starting point: two Jewish scribes who wrote in the middle of the first century AD, perhaps even earlier, used the same writing as we find in the fragments from Matthew's gospel. The circumstantial evidence for the first century date increases further when we look at the Qumran caves. The highly characteristic *Eta* of the Matthew papyrus appears in an unidentified papyrus from Cave 7 which in turn is typical of the Herculaneum style. Two manuscripts from Cave 4 offer further evidence: there is a papyrus with passages from Leviticus,[36] and a leather scroll from the same Old Testament book in Greek.[37]

The letters are so close to those in the Matthew gospel papyrus
that a drawing supplied by Peter Parsons looks as though they
were taken straight out of the Oxford scraps rather than the
Qumran fragments.[38] How interesting it would be to go one step
further and suggest that they, the Oxford, Barcelona and
Qumran fragments, were written by the same scribe. Such
results are, generally speaking, possible. No-one contradicted
me, for example, when I showed in my first edition of the New
Testament papyrus Bodmer L, that it was written by the same
scribe who had written the codex Bodmer XVII, using a
different stylus.[39] But the resemblance between the Qumran
hands and the Matthew papyrus is not *that* close. Here, we have
scribes belonging to the same period and sharing the
characteristics of that period, and yet they are distinct
individuals. For example, the scribe of the Qumran leather
scroll prefers a slightly more sloping style and occasionally likes
to link his letters. Obviously, one might legitimately go on to ask
if anything comparable exists in Egyptian Greek papyri of the
first century. Even though this is surplus to requirements, as
fragments from the Matthew gospel may not even have come
from Egypt but only have been bought here, it would be nice to
show that the new evidence from the recent Dead Sea
publications can be substantiated by previously known papyri.
Just let me briefly draw your attention to a fragmentary papyrus
scroll found at Oxyrhynchus, P. Oxy. XXXI 2545. It is the oldest
known manuscript of the Greek comedian Aristophanes, and it
was dated by Eric Turner to the late first century BC or early
first century AD.[40] A comparison between this papyrus and the
Magdalen fragments reveals a closeness of detail in many letters
and a likeness in overall appearance. More comparative work
can and will be done, but let this be enough for the present
occasion.

To sum up, it seems that the Matthew gospel papyrus belongs
to a style for which the comparative evidence derives from the
mid-first century, beginning even earlier. Individual letters and
overall appearance point in this direction. Add to this that we
should have been aware, since Herbert Hunger, of the obvious
problems with the late dates ascribed to the so-called 'biblical
uncial' style, of which this is a precursor, and a first century date

for the Matthew gospel papyrus is a palaeographically admissible, if not a necessary suggestion.

Let us assume for a moment that all this is and will be granted. What does it mean? What are the consequences? Some of the headlines since Christmas have told you in no uncertain terms. 'Eyewitness record of the life of Christ' (*The Times*, 24 December 1994) and 'Step Closer to Jesus?' (*Time Magazine*, 23 January 1995) are just two examples. At this stage, let me admit that I did not start my work with the intention to re-date the Magdalen fragments at all. I was much more interested in the reconstruction of the text, since it was obvious that the first edition of 1953 had not been complete and was, for whatever reasons, inadequate in a number of ways. First and foremost therefore, my paper offers the first complete reconstruction of all six sides of the three scraps and corrects a few errors in the handlists of Greek New Testament editions. It also improves the Greek text of a verse - Matthew 26:22 - confirming a reading preferred by a few other, old papyri in such a way that the printed Greek text of our New Testament will have to be adapted accordingly. This change is of greater significance than it sounds, for it affects our understanding of the Greek written by the first Christians: the Magdalen fragments preserve an interesting, unrhetorical, simple but correct Greek which we also find - for example - in the early St John papyrus p^{52}. The syntax differs, and certain unnecessary words are omitted or, to put it more precisely, are not here and were added in later copies. It was only then that the necessity to look at the dating of the fragments became apparent to me. Could it be that it belonged in fact to the same period as the St John papyrus, i.e. to the beginning of the second century rather than to the end? The rest is known to you and was described above - with the result that it may be earlier still, by up to fifty years.

There is one additional feature of these fragments which emerges as being important for chronological and theological reasons: the Magdalen fragments contain abbreviations for the name *Jesus* and the word *Lord*. These so-called *nomina sacra*, holy names, are a particular invention of early Christianity. They single out words connected with God, Jesus, with the Sonship and Lordship of Jesus, with the Holy Spirit, and so forth. Probably, the basic words God, Jesus, Lord and Spirit were the first to be abbreviated like this, and many more were to follow. It may well be that the first Christians did this not only to document the special, holy status given to these words, but also to emulate the old Jewish practice of writing the unpronounceable name of God with the four consonants JHWH and to continue this usage even in their Greek manuscripts. At one stroke, therefore, the Christians would have achieved a visual way of showing that to them, Jesus was Lord and God.[41]

Now, Colin Roberts, the man who did so much to place early Christian papyri in their social and cultural contexts, had suggested as early as 1979 that this Christian practice of writing abbreviated *nomina sacra* cannot have been the isolated decision of an individual scribe,[42] for it was picked up too soon and spread too widely all over the Empire. Roberts adds, 'the system was too complex for the ordinary scribe to operate without rules or an authoritative exemplar'. He suggested that it was in fact developed by the Jerusalem church before AD 70 - that is, before that community fled and was temporarily dispersed before and after the Jewish Revolt of AD 66-70 which ended in the destruction of Jerusalem and the Temple. Alternatively, he suggests, the system could have been introduced by the church in Antioch at about the same time. Note that Roberts did not derive his conclusions from Jerusalem or Antioch papyri, but from observations made in so-called Egyptian papyri of the second and later centuries. He postulated a starting point for a very important papyrological innovation without the actual visual, tangible evidence - that is, without a first century, c. AD 70 papyrus to show for it. Sheer logic requires that he assumed the existence of such evidence, either lost or perhaps retrievable at some stage. The Magdalen papyrus from St Matthew's gospel may be this 'missing link'. With its three *nomina sacra*, its particular Greek and, above all, its palaeographical date as suggested by analysis, it appears to be the visual evidence for the very early beginnings of an authoritative Christian scribal tradition during the lifetime of disciples, apostles, contemporaries.

Here, at the very latest, any New Testament scholar worth his salt will begin to feel uncomfortable, or, alternatively, excited. Obviously, a codex copy of an original gospel presupposes the existence of the 'archetype', the first manuscript, at an even earlier date. Since it appears to be, at present, the majority position within New Testament studies that the Gospel according to St Matthew was written not by Matthew anyway, but within a community or on behalf of a committee at some stage during the eighties of the first century, the consequences of the re-dating of the Magdalen and Barcelona fragments may indeed be enormous. Only those who have assumed and argued, over the years, that Matthew was written before AD 70 anyway, scholars like John A.T. Robinson, Donald Guthrie, R.C. Butler, R.T. France, John Wenham, Bernard Orchard, Robert Gundry, Bo Reicke, Gerhard Maier, and many others,[43] would have been or would be confirmed in their own historical or critical conclusions by the new papyrus date. But let us keep in mind that it has always been possible to place the complete gospel of Matthew before the watershed year of AD 70, in a period of eyewitnesses and observers. The arguments for and against an early date are too numerous to be listed and discussed in the context of this essay, but they begin with the question of the destruction of the Temple in Jerusalem and the dispersion of the Christian community. Jesus did prophesy both events. Could Jesus have prophesied? Did he really say these things, or were they put into his mouth after the events, as so-called *vaticinia ex eventu*?

Whatever our own predilections, and whatever the range of further questions and arguments may be, we would do well to remember an admonition phrased by the New Testament scholar Graham Stanton of King's College London. In an article on 'Presuppositions in New Testament Criticism', he wrote: 'The interpreter must allow his own presuppositions and his own pre-understanding to be modified or even completely reshaped by the text itself. Unless this is allowed to happen, the interpreter will be unable to avoid projecting his own ideas on to the text. Exegesis guided rigidly by pre-understanding will be able to establish only what the interpreter already knows. There must be a constant dialogue between the interpreter and the text'.[44] Ideally, the new and additional insights gained from the papyrus at Magdalen College Oxford will put Stanton's challenge to the test. Let us indeed examine our presuppositions about the origins of the textual tradition of the New Testament, of the origins of the gospels and of the people behind them. Let us not be afraid of the consequence of an analysis which may well take us back to the early apostolic era. John A.T. Robinson, a liberal theologian if ever there was one and thus, if you like, untainted by the tag of fundamentalism or conservative prejudice, wrote about his book *Redating the New Testament* in 1976: 'It is an irritant and incentive to further exploration, and, I should like to think, to the opening up of new questions.' And he concluded: 'If the chronology of the documents and the pattern of the development should turn out to be anything like what I have suggested, then there will be scope for numerous new trajectories to be drawn and for the rewriting of many introductions to - and ultimately theologies of - the New Testament. For dates remain disturbingly fundamental data.'.[45] Robinson did not analyse a single papyrus in his seminal book: he arrived at his conclusions *via* a detailed investigation into textual, historical and sociological sources and pieces of circumstantial evidence. The Magdalen papyrus from St Matthew's gospel, and indeed a systematic re-investigation of other early New Testament papyri may prove to be a timely incentive to pick up Robinson's gauntlet and to get, in many a sense of the word, 'a step closer to Jesus'.

NOTES

1   Paper delivered at the Hellenic Culture Week, Royal Holloway College, London University/Association of Greek-Orthodox Communities of Great Britain, 28 January 1995.

2   Cf also Romans 16:22; 1 Corinthians 16:21; Galatians 6:11; Colossians 4:18; 1 Peter 5:12.

3   T. Harrison, *The Trackers of Oxyrhynchus*, London 1990, 12-13.

4   Cf E.J. Epp, 'New Testament Papyrus Manuscripts and Letter-Carrying in Greco-Roman Times', in B.A. Pearson, ed., *The Future of Early Christianity. Essays in Honor of Helmut Koester,* Minneapolis 1991, 35-36. Epp argues on the basis of a wide array of evidence, that the Egyptian New Testament papyri do, in fact, represent text-types from the *entire* Mediterranean region. Cf R. Riesner, *Die Frühzeit des Apostels Paulus*, Tübingen 1994, 275-282.

5   See also E.J. Epp, as in note 4, here 52-56.

6   Librarian's Report 1901, Archives of Magdalen College Oxford.

7   K. and B. Aland, *Der Text des Neuen Testaments*, Stuttgart 1981 (^{2}1989), 85, 111, *et al.*

8   Since J. O'Callaghan's identification in 1972 ('Papiros neotestamentarios en la cueva 7 de Qumrân?', *Biblica* 53/1972,91-100, there have been many negative comments; but since 1984, an increasing number of papyrologists, historians and classical philologists have argued in favour of 7Q5 = Mk 6:52-53. For a survey, see B. Mayer, ed., *Christen und Christliches in Qumran?*, Regensburg, 1992, and C.P. Thiede, *The Earliest Gospel Manuscript? The Qumran Fragment 7Q5 and its Significance for New Testament Studies*, Exeter/Carlisle 1992. Most recently, O. Montevecchi, honorary president of the International Papyrologists' Association, has stated that the Markan identification is certain ('Ricerchiamo senza pregiudizi', interview with S. Paci, *30 Giorni* XII/7-8 [1994] 75-76). In the case of 7Q5, the *latest* possible date is known: AD 68, but the identification is under discussion. With p^{64} and p^{67}, the Matthew papyri, no-one doubts the identification, but we are debating the date.

9   The *Oxyrhynchus Papyri Part I*, London 1898, 59-60, here 59.

10 Martial, *Epigrams I*, 2, commonly dated to AD 84-86.

11 Cf Ph.W. Comfort, *The Quest for the Original Text of the New Testament*, Grand Rapids 1992, 46.

12 C.H. Roberts/T.C.Skeat, *The Birth of the Christian Codex*, London 1983, 21-23, here 22.

13 As in note 11.

14 As in note 11, 49.

15 F.G. Kenyon, *Books and Readers in Ancient Greece and Rome*, Oxford ^{2}1951, 110.

16 See note 35.

17 See Josephus, *Antiquities of the Jews*, XX, 200-201. I am grateful to Benedikt Schwank, Beuron/Eichstätt, for reminding me of the importance of this event. One might also consider AD 64/65, the fire of Rome and the ensuing persecution of the Christians, when Jews and Christians were clearly distinguished: Jews were spared, Christians were executed. Indeed, Italo Gallo, one of the papyrologists who wrote introductions into our discipline, is convinced that the change from scroll to codex must have happened 'not later than 70 A.D.': I. Gallo, *Greek and Latin Papyrology, Classical Handbook I*, London 1986, 14.

18 C.H. Roberts, 'An Early Papyrus of the First Gospel', *Harvard Theological Review* 46, 1953, 233-7, here 237.

19   As in note 18, 237.

20   Minuscule 461, written in 835.

21   Attributed to Peter Parsons, *The Times*, December 24, 1994, front page.

22   O. Murray, P. Parsons, T.W. Potter, P. Roberts, 'A "stork-vase" from the Mola di Monte Gelato'. *Papers of the British School of Rome*, vol. ixx, 1991, 177-195, here 195. This article was brought to my attention by T.W. Potter.

23   As in note 22, 193.

24   See H. Cotton/J. Geiger, *Masada II. The Latin and Greek Documents*, Jerusalem 1989.

25   R. Roca-Puig, *Un papiro griego del Evangelico de San Mateo*, Barcelona ^{2}1962. M. Baillet/J.T. Milik/R. de Vaux, *Les 'Petites Grottes' de Qumran*, DJD III, Oxford 1962, 142-146.

26   P.W. Skehan/E. Ulrich/J.E. Sanderson, eds., *Qumran Cave 4*, IV, DJDIX, Oxford 1972.

27   E. Tov, ed., *The Greek Minor Prophets Scroll 8 Hev XII gr*, Oxford 1990.

28   See E. Würthwein, *Der Text des Alten Testaments*, Stuttgart, ^{5}1989, 194.

29   P.J. Parsons, 'The Scripts and Their Date', in E. Tov, as in note 27, 19-26, here 24 and 26.

30   J. O'Callaghan, 'Paleografia Herculanense en algunos papiros griegos de Qumrân', in *Homenaje a Juan Prado*, Madrid 1975, 529-532.

31   H. Hunger 'Zur Datierung des Bodmer II', *Anzeiger der phil.-hist. Klasse der österr. Akad. d. Wissenschaften*, 4, 1960, 12-23, criticized by E.G. Turner, as in note 40, 108.

32   Y.K. Kim, 'Palaeographical Dating of p^{46} to the Later First Century', *Biblica*, 69, 1988, 248-257.

33   For arguments against Kim's case see B.M. Metzger, *The Text of the New Testament, Its Transmission, Corruption and Restoration*, 3rd enl. ed. Oxford 1992, 265-6, and my critique of Metzger's position in my re-edition of the Magdalen Papyrus, as in note 35, 17-18 and note 32.

34   See C.H. Roberts, *An Unpublished Fragment of the Fourth Gospel in the John Rylands Library*, Manchester 1935.

35   C.P. Thiede, 'Papyrus Magdalen Greek 17 (Gregory-Aland p^{64}), A Reappraisal', *Zeitschrift für Papyrologie und Epigraphik* 105 (1995),13-20, with plate. Reprint in this volume.

36   Pap4QLXXLeviticus[b], see note 26.

37   4QLXXLev[a], see note 26.

38   See note 26, 7-13, here 8.

39   C.P. Thiede, 'Papyrus Bodmer L. Das neutestamentliche
      Papyrusfragment p^{73} = Mt 25, 43/26 2-3', *Museum Helveticum* 47/1
      (1990), 35-40, with plate.

40   Summary with photograph in E.G. Turner, *Greek Manuscripts of the
      Ancient World,* 2nd ed., rev. and enl., ed by P.J. Parsons, London
      1987, 72.

41   In LXX manuscripts of Jewish origin up until and including the 1st
      century AD, there is a variety of usage: JHWH can be found
      inserted in Hebrew of palaeo-Hebrew characters; there is the Greek
      vocalized (!) abbreviation *Iota/Alpha/Omega* (a good example:
      4QLXXLev[b], from Qumran Cave 4, see note 26); in extant
      manuscripts which have *kyrios* for JHWH, the Greek word is never
      abbreviated. Thus, the early Christian introduction of *KC* for *kyrios*
      combines the newness of the Christian message (*KC* had not been
      used before) with a purposeful allusion to an accepted and
      well-known system, namely that of abbreviating the Lord's, i.e.
      God's, name. See also A. Pietersma, 'Kyrios or Tetragram: A
      Renewed Quest for the Original LXX', in A. Pietersma/C. Cox
      (eds.), *De Septuaginta, Studies in Honour of John William Wevers*,
      Mississauga 1984, 85-101.

42   C.H. Roberts, *Manuscript, Society and Belief in Early Christian Egypt,*
      London 1979, 46.

43   For names and references see D. Guthrie, *New Testament Introduction,*
      4th ed, rev., Leicester 1990, 53-56.

44   G.N. Stanton, 'Presuppositions in New Testament Criticism', in I.H.
      Marshall, ed., *New Testament Interpretation,* Exeter 1977, 60-71,
      here 68.

45   J.A.T. Robinson, *Redating the New Testament*, London 1976, 357-358.

2

The Papyrus Magdalen Greek 17 (Gregory- Aland p^{64}): A Reappraisal

It would be a very brave man who would
deny that such a text, or any text, might
be susceptible to further improvement.

H.C. Youtie[1]

The oldest extant papyrus fragment of the Gospel according to St Matthew consists of five small scraps, three of which are kept at Magdalen College, Oxford, the other two at the Fundación San Llucas Evangelista, Barcelona. It was dated, by Colin Roberts, to the later second century.[2] Roberts himself was the first scholar to recognize the relationship between the three Magdalen scraps and the two remnants in Barcelona (P.Barc.inv.1, p^{67}) as parts of one and the same original codex.[3] Further attempts to link this codex to fragments of Luke's gospel preserved at the Bibliothèque Nationale, Paris (Suppl. Gr. 1120 = Gregory-Aland p^{4}), had to be abandoned;[4] although the fragmentary codex at the Bibilothèque Nationale had, at one stage, contained Matthew - as seems to be obvious from a scrap with the title Εὐαγγέλιον κατὰ Μαθθαῖον - the Paris codex is written on much darker, brownish papyrus and is considerably later (by up to one hundred years). As yet, there is no candidate among extant papyri to supplement p^{64} and p^{67}. However, after more than forty years since Roberts first published the

Magdalen fragment, some additions and corrections appear to be called for.

1. The Catalogue Number

Whereas the earliest publications of and about the fragments do not give them a college library number, van Haelst's *Catalogue*,[5] faithfully copied by all later publications including the latest, 27th edition of Nestle-Aland, *Novum Testamentum Graece*, calls them 'Gr.18'. There are, however, no such fragments at Magdalen College Oxford. The College handlist had indeed numbered the papyrus 'Magdalen Greek 18', but this was an obvious mistake due to a tiny scrap found in an envelope among the correspondence relating to the Matthean fragment,[6] a mere 1.8 x 1.9 cm, with two fragmentary lines containing just two complete letters (*Iota/Nu*) and five incomplete ones on one side (the other side is blank), in a later, larger script unrelated to the three fragments of Matthew. The College Library now correctly numbers the three Matthean fragments 'Gr.17', and this should therefore be the number used in all lists and catalogues of New Testament papyri.

2. Contents

There are some discrepancies between the editions of and references to Magdalen Gr.17:[7] in his first edition of 1953, Roberts had transcribed the contents as Mt 26:7, 10, 14-15, 22-23, 31, 32-33.[8] On two pages preceding his supplement to Roca-Puig's second edition of the Barcelona fragments, he offered a new 'Transcripción del P. Magd. de Oxford', translated into Spanish by Roca-Puig.[9]

Dated '9.6.60', this new transcription offers several alterations: Col II, recto (a), line 1 (Mt 26, 31) now recognizes the *nomen sacrum* for Jesus as IC rather than IH; in line 2, the visible part of the line is now extended to σκανδαλισθη... rather than σκανδα...; and in Col II, *recto* (b), he tentatively adds a new first line for verse 32, προαξ[ω and changes, in line 2, γαλεγλαιαν to γαλιγλαιαν. Furthermore, he now corrects the contents; Mt 26:7-8, 10, 14-15, 22-23, 31, 32-33.[10] There is a very good reason for Robert's insistence on the separation of v. 31

from vv. 32-33: v. 31 is on a separate scrap of papyrus. The three scraps of Magdalen Gr. 17, all of them with text on *recto* and *verso*, offer six 'units', Mt 26: 7-8 (fr.1, *verso*), 10 (fr.2, *verso*). 14-15 (fr.3, *verso*), 22-23 (fr.3, *recto*), 31 (fr.1, *recto*), 32-33 (fr.2, *recto*). Thus Roberts' system with a separate v. 31 is to be preferred for reasons of clarity and should be copied by Nestle-Aland *et al.*

3. A Scribal Error and Three Variants

The peculiar variants of Gr.17 were duly noted by Roberts; in three instances, however, he himself seemed uncertain and mistaken, and one further variant has so far remained unnoticed.

i) fr.3, *verso*, line 2 (26:14): Roberts had seen that δώδεκα is written in the numerical symbol ιβ - the lower half of the *Beta* is clearly visible. It is, however, equally obvious that there is no space for an *Omicron* between *Beta* and the *Lambda* of λεγόμενος. Thus we have a rare example of λεγόμενος without the article, a construction paralleled by e.g. Matthew 2:23 (εἰς πόλιν λεγομένην Ναζαρέτ, John 4:5 (εἰς πόλιν τῆς Σαμαρείας λεγομένην Συχάρ). In Magdalen Gr.17 p^{64}, the omission may of course merely be a scribal error.

ii) fr.3, *recto*, line 1 (26:22): Roberts had stated, in his 1953 edition,[11] that 'the papyrus must have read λεγειν εις εκαστος αυτω, an order which is unique...' However, this unique variant is far from evident. The three severely damaged letters in line 1 which Roberts had identified as *Tau/Omega/Mu* are in fact *Tau/Omega/Nu*. The *Nu* is the final letter of αυτων, and thus our papyrus would have read ...ἔκαστος αὐτῶν μήτι ἐγώ εἰμι..., the text of p^{45}, p^{37}, Bezae Cantab. (D) *et mult.al.* There is only one standard edition of the Greek New Testament which has this as the best reading;[12] p^{64} now confirms the papyrological evidence for it as against the text preferred by other editions.[13]

iii) fr.1, *recto*, line 2 (Mt 26:31): For reasons of stichometry, the ὑμεῖς after πάντες should be omitted. With it, line 1 would have 20 rather than the average 16 letters. This omission, in the oldest ms of Matthew's gospel, confirms, once again, the tendency of all early papyri to keep the Greek simple, to pare it to the bones, free from rhetorical embellishments.[14]

iv) fr.2, *recto*, line 2 (26:32): One has to read γαλεγλαιαν α..., as Roberts had transcribed it in his 1953 edition, not γαλιγλαιαν α..., as in the printing error of the second transcription dated 1960. This variation of the common Γαλιλαίαν for Galilee is of course odd, and Roberts adds a note to his 1960 edition which reads 'V. 33, vel γαλειλαιαν'.[15] But apart from the fact that it is v.32, not 33, the *Gamma* is as unmistakable as the *Epsilon* which precedes it. *Epsilon* + *Iota* for *Iota* is common enough to be unremarkable; as for *Gamma* instead of *Iota*, this is nothing but a scribal error not quite inexplicable in view of the identity of the vertical strokes of *Iota* and *Gamma* in this papyrus. The scribe of Magdalen Gr.17 was not averse to original decisions; even this mistake is, in a way, original.

4. The Date

The date commonly given to Magdalen Gr.17 (and P.Barc.1), c. 200,[16] may look like a safe 'dumping ground', but this might be too late. One has to keep in mind, of course, that Roberts revolutionized the dating of the papyrus in his first edition of 1953, when he suggested 'a date in the later second century'.[17] At the time, he was confronted with the estimate provided by the Rev. Charles B. Huleatt, a former demy (foundation scholar) of Magdalen College, who had acquired the fragments at Luxor in 1901 and had given them to his old college in the same year.[18] Huleatt had suggested a date in the third century, and a note in the display cabinet with Gr.17 in the Old Library of Magdalen College still reads: '2nd half of 3rd century (probable date)'. In the librarian's report of 1901, H.A. Wilson quoted an oral assessment from no less an authority than A.S. Hunt who even thought that 'they may be assigned with more probability to the fourth century'. As Roberts pointed out in his commentary,[19] Hunt and his colleague B.P. Grenfell had assumed, on principle, that manuscripts written in a codex could not be earlier than the third, preferably the fourth century. He quotes the amusing example of P.Oxy.I,35, a Latin codex fragment of an otherwise unknown *History of the Macedonian*

Wars now at the British Library,[20] which they analyzed as belonging to the second century, perhaps even before AD 79 - for palaeographical reasons - but which they nonetheless assigned to the late third or fourth century *because it is a vellum codex*.[21] As mentioned above, Roberts then proceeded to argue, comparatively, for a late second century date of Magdalen Gr.17, backed in this by Bell, Skeat and Turner. One of the decisive arguments he adduced is the fact that 'in the Magdalen fragments the minute omicron and the flat omega, common in third century hands, are absent'.[22]

Since the publication of Roberts' paper, new papyri have become available, and they appear to favour an even earlier date. This may not come as a surprise, since one tendency of the re-evaluation of New Testament papyri at least since the 60s has been a redating with, occasionally, somewhat drastic and not undisputed consequences.[23] It may be argued that the result of this continuing process is a mounting degree of uncertainty, rather than certainty, as to the reliability of palaeographical datings of literary hands; but even so, one should not eschew the challenge. For Magdalen Gr.17/P.Barc.1., one such unexpected example is a leather scroll discovered in the Nahal Hever, near the Dead Sea, the so-called Greek Minor Prophets Scroll 8HEVXIIgr.[24] With minor variations, D. Barthélemy (who first published parts of the scroll in 1963), C.H. Roberts, W. Schubart, E. Würthwein and R. Hanhart all opt for c. AD 50/mid-first century AD.[25] Tov, in his new and complete edition, leaves the task of dating the scroll to P.J. Parsons who does not rule out a mid- to late first century date by referring to P.Oxy.2555, but prefers a date in the later first century BC 'as possible, though not of course necessary'.[26]

Obviously, then, there seems to be scope for differing assessments, between the late first century BC and the middle, or, at the latest, the second half, of the first century AD, with a clear preference for the mid-first century AD. Without entering the debate about the date of Matthew's gospel,[27] we may note that the historical *terminus post quem* for any of the gospels is the year of the last events reported about the crucified and risen Jesus, AD 30, and we may note that this would give us enough space to accommodate a comparison between the Nahal Hever scroll and Magdalen Gr.17.

Even at first glance and using , as a point of reference, the plate in Schmidt/Thiel/Hanhart, the identity and near-identity of several letters is striking: *Alpha, Epsilon* (a letter fluctuating in both scripts), *Iota, Omicron, Rho* and *Nu* are particularly close. An equally obvious difference, on the other hand, may be seen in the *Etas* and *Mus*; but the second scribe of the Nahal Hever scroll provides the comparable *Eta* and *Mu* more than once.[28] The Nahal Hever Scroll of the Minor Prophets may be at the extreme end of the spectrum, but it is not the only first century analogy. Further material is provided by papyri in the script of Herculaneum, for which AD 79 is the natural focal point.[29] Interestingly, there is a small, unidentified Greek fragment from Qumran Cave 7, 7Q61, for which the archaeological *terminus ante quem* is AD 68, which has the characteristic *Eta* with the horizontal stroke above the median, evident in Magdalen Gr.17.[30] There is also a Greek papyrus from Qumran Cave 4 which shows several letters resembling Papyrus Magdalen Gr.17, such as the *Alpha,* the *Beta,* etc.: pap4QLXXLeviticus[b]. As Parsons points out, the script is far from uniform, but this papyrus from Cave 4 could be dated to the mid-first century AD.[31]

Unwittingly, he then proceeds to offer an interesting case study: in his drawings of letters of the preceding fragment 4QLXXLev[a] (parts of a leather scroll which he dates to the first century *BC*), the *Alpha, Beta, Delta, Epsilon, Eta, Iota, Kappa, Eta* etc. are identical or near-identical to what we find in Magdalen Gr.17. In fact, the letters he draws could have been taken straight out of Gr.17. Looking at the fragments themselves, there would seem to be at least two differences, however: the Qumran Leviticus[2] is sloping slightly to the right, and the letters are very close to each other, occasionally even connected (ligatures). Even so, archaeology alone cannot have influenced Parson's very early dates - there is scope until AD 68, after all, when the caves were abandoned, and one might well prefer mid-first century dates AD for both 4QLXXLev[a] and pap4QLXXLev[b]. But, and this is the point, the prevailing tendency to date material of a nature comparable to Magdalen Gr.17 to a period even preceding the earliest possible date of Matthew's gospel suggests, with all due caution, the possibility of redating the fragments from Oxford and Barcelona - which are, after all, definitely Matthean - to a period somewhat earlier than the late second century previously assigned to them. Certainty will remain elusive, of course.

To sum up, even though Herculaneum and Qumran (with its Greek fragments in two caves, 4 and 7) are still under survey, they both have their archaeological termini: all comparative material taken directly from their finds suggests dates prior to AD 79 and 68 respectively. It goes without saying that scribal characteristics found in those places may well have continued to be in use afterwards, towards the end of the first century, and occasionally even later. For our present purposes, we may proffer a tentative suggestion: the material from Nahal Hever, Herculaneum and Qumran could point towards a first century date for Magdalen Gr.17/P.Barc.1.

At this stage, we must turn to the *nomina sacra* and their influence on the date: Magdalen Gr.17 has two, probably three abbreviations of holy names and words: ιϲ for Ἰησοῦς (fr.2, *verso*, 1.1, probable because of the stichometry of the line; fr.1, *recto*, 1.2, definitely) and κε for κύριε (fr.3, *recto*, 1.2). For historical reasons, Roberts had suggested that the use of these and other *nomina sacra* had become established practice among Christians in Jerusalem *even before the year AD 70.*[32] He did lack the palaeographical evidence, though, and even for John Rylands Gr.457 (p^{52}), which he himself had edited,[33] he did not suggest *nomina sacra* in the reconstructed, missing parts of the extant lines, although this would have been possible within the given stichometry.[34] Magdalen Gr.17 might offer the missing link: a Christian codex fragment of the first century, perhaps (though not necessarily) predating AD 70, with the *nomina sacra* postulated by Roberts.[35]

Some time ago, such a date would have been ruled out for the simple reason that a copy of a codex of Matthew - and there is no dispute whatsoever about the identification of the Oxford and Barcelona papyri - cannot have reached Egypt at such an early stage of the gospel's germination and transmission. But we have learned from the methodological error of Grenfell and Hunt, described above, and we possess that famous fragment of a *codex* of John's gospel kept at the John Rylands University library Manchester, p^{52} (J. Rylands Libr. Gr.P.457). Within the range of dated and datable papyri Colin Roberts compared to

p^{52} for his first edition in 1935, he finally decided in favour of what is arguably the latest possible date, c. AD 125. He could, however, have been less cautious by preferring the other end of the spectrum, documented by P. Fayyum 110 of AD 94 or P.Lond.2078, a private letter from the time of Domitian, AD 81-96. There is also a good resemblance to p^{52} in P.Gr.Berol. 19c, part of a scroll with *Iliad X*, from the end of the first century.[36]

In their monograph, *The Birth of the Codex*, C.H. Roberts and T.C. Skeat argue that the Christians had chosen the codex form for copies of Old Testament texts and their own writings *before AD 100*.[37] Near the end of the first century, the Roman poet Martial praises his and his publisher friend Secundus' marketing enterprise, the introduction of a library of classical works in the codex format; the Latin codex fragment of a *History of the Macedonian Wars* mentioned above may be the only surviving example of this possibly short-lived venture.[38] Under the influence of Roberts' cautious dating and five years before Kim's paper,[39] Roberts and Skeat do not name any first century Christian codex to corroborate their theory with some practical evidence. The present state of affairs, however, suggests that the Oxford fragments Magdalen Gr.17, with their Spanish counterparts, would be among the prime examples of the birth of the Christian codex prior to the turn of the century.

5. Conclusion

The fragments of Matthew's gospel in the Old Library of Magdalen College Oxford, henceforth to be listed as Magdalen Greek 17 rather than 18, remain the oldest extant papyrus of that gospel; but it may be argued that it could be redated from the late second to the late first century, some time after the destruction of the Temple in Jerusalem. It appears to be the oldest known codex with *nomina sacra*. Lists of New Testament papyri should reflect the fact that the three fragments of Magdalen Gr.17=p^{64} preserve texts on all six sides, not just on five, as is the impression conveyed at present.

p^{46} is a 'new', additional witness to a construction of Mt 26:22 preferred by the papyri p^{37} and p^{45} and several later manuscripts, but ruled out by most widely used editions of the Greek New

Testament, Nestle-Aland²⁷ (1993) and The Greek New Testament UBS⁴(1993). The accumulated evidence now clearly suggests ...ἔκαστος αὐτῶν μήτι...as the better text, and this should be acknowledged by future editions of the Greek New Testament, in concurrence with Bover-O'Callaghan³1994. This improved reading and two further variants, λεγόμενος without the article in 26:14 and, in particular the likely omission of ὑμεῖς after πάντες in 26:31, appear to confirm the impression that the very earliest papyri tend to preserve a simple but clear and effective Greek untouched by the literary ambitions of later scribes.

P. Magdalen Greek 17, Transcription

Fr.1, *verso* (Mt 26:7-8)cf Table IX

[κατεχεενεπ]ι̣[της]κε̣	16
[φαλης]αυτουανακει	16
[μενουι]δοντεσδεοι	16
[μαθηται]η̣γανακτη	15

Fr.2, *verso* (Mt 26:10)

[οισειπεναυ]τ̣[ο]ι̣[cτι]	16
[κοπουσπαρ]εχετε[τη]	16
[γυ]ναικιεργονγα[ρ]	15

1.1 *nomen sacrum* ι̅ς̅ for Ἰησοῦς stichometrically plausible, cf fr. 1.1, *recto* 1.1.

Fr.3, *verso* (Mt 26:14-15)

[τοτ]επορε̣[υθεισεις]	16
[τωνι]βλεγομ[ενοσιου]	17
[δασι]σκαριω]τησπρος]	17
[του] ς̣αρχιερ[εισειπεν]	18
[τιθε]λ̣ετεμο̣[ιδουναι]	17

1.2: Numerical symbol ιβ for δώδεκα. The article ὁ before λεγόμενος is omitted; cf Matthew 2:23; John 4:5.

Fr.3, *recto* (Mt 26:22-23)

[τοσαυ]τω̣ν[μητιεγω]	15
[ειμι]κ̣εοδ̣[εαποκρι]	15

[θεις]ε̣ιπενοε̣[μβαψας]   17
[με]τ̣ε̣μουτ̣[ηνχειρα]   15
[εντ]ω̣τ̣ρ̣υ̣[βλιωουτος]   16

1.1: Text as in p45, p37(vid), D, et al.: ἕκαστος αὐτῶν.

1.2: Nomen sacrum κ̅ε̅ for κύριε.

Fr.1, recto (Mt 26:31)

α   υτοιςοις̣π̣α̣ν̣τ̣[ες]   15
    ςκανδαλισθη[ςεςθε]   17
    ενεμοιεν̣τ̣[ηνυκτι]   15
    τ̣αυτηγεγ̣[ραπταιγαρ]   17

1:1: The initial α of αὐτοῖς is projected into the left margin; as in p^{67}, 5.21 (τι) and 5:527 (ς̣ατε), this signifies the first complete line of a new section which began in the preceding line.

Nomen sacrum ις for Ἰησοῦς. ὑ̣μεῖς is omitted at the end of the line (stichometry!)

Fr.2, recto (Mt 26:32-33)

π̣ρ̣ο̣αξ[ωυμαςειςτην]   16
γαλεγλαιανα[ποκρι]   16
θειςδεο̣πετρ̣ος̣ε̣[ι]   15

1.2: γαλεγλ̣α̣ιαν: scribal error for γαλειλαιαν.

NOTES

1.   H.C. Youtie, The Textual Criticism of Documentary Papyri, Prolegomena, London 21974, 66.

2.   C. Roberts, 'An Early Papyrus of the First Gospel', Harvard Theological Review 46 (1953), 233-7, here 237, referring to the corroborative verdicts of H. Bell, T.C. Skeat and E.G. Turner.

3.   C. Roberts, 'Complementary Note' in R. Roca-Puig, Un papiro Griego del Evangelio de San Mateo, Barcelona 21962, 59-60.

4.   K. Aland's suggestion, based on an observation by P. Weigand, in his 'Neue Neutestamentliche Papyri II', New Testament Studies 12, 1965-66, here 193-5; repeated, as probable ('probablement') by J. van Haelst, Catalogue des Papyrus littéraires juifs et chrétiens, Paris 1976, 146 (no. 403), and by C.H. Roberts/T.C. Skeat, The Birth of the Codex, London 1983, 40-41, 65-66, but discontinued by Aland himself in his and his wife's Der Text des Neuen Testaments, Stuttgart 21989 105, where p^4 is categorized as 'Normaltext', but

$p^{64/67}$ as 'fester Text' and 106/110, where the dates are given as 'III' and 'um 200' respectively.

5. J. van Haelst, *Catalogue des Papyrus littéraires juifs et chrétiens,* Paris 1976, 125 (no.336).

6. I owe this information to K.S. Speirs, Assistant Librarian, Magdalen College Oxford, in a letter dated 23rd February 1994.

7. Conversely, they all agree as to P.Barc.1 (p^{67}), Mt 3:9,15; 5:20-22, 25-28

8. See note 2, here 236.

9. See note 3, here 57-59.

10. The 'standard' Greek New Testament, Nestle-Aland271993, has 26:7-6, 10, 14-15, 22-23, 31-33.

11. See note 2, here 236.

12. Bover-O'Callaghan, *Nuevo Testamento Trilingüe,* Madrid31994, 152. αυτων before μητι is also favoured, albeit in brackets, by Merk, *Novum Testamentum Graece et Latine,* Rome111992, 94.

13. E.g. Nestle-Aland 27, 1993, λέγειν αὐτῷ εῷς ἕκαστος μήτι ἐλώ   εἰμι.

14. Cf for John Rylands Gr.P.457 (p^{52}, John 18:31-33,.37-38): see C.P. Thiede, as in note 34, 13-19.

15. See note 3, here 58.

16. Latest example: Nestle-Aland *Novum Testamentum Graece*[27] 1993, 687.

17. See note 2.

18. Letter to the college librarian, H.A. Wilson, dated Messina, Dec.5, 1901.

19. See note 2, here 234-5.

20. Brit.Lib.P.745.

21. *The Oxyrhynchus Papyrus Part I,* London 1898, 59-60, here 59.

22. See note 2, here 237.

23. E.g. Herbert Hunger, 'Zur Datierung des Bodmer II', *Anzeiger der phil-hist. Klasse der Österr. Akad. der Wissenschaften,* 4, 1960, 12-23, arguing for a date in the first quarter of the second century, against the traditional consensus which dates Bodmer II (p^{66}) to 'c.200'; or Y.K. Kim 'Palaeographical Dating of p^{46} to the Later First Century', *Biblica* 69, 1988, 248-57, taking away some one hundred years from the usual dating of P. Chester Beatty

II/University of Michigan Inv. 6238, 'c. 200'. See also note 32
below.

24. E. Tov, (ed.), *The Greek Minor Prophets Scroll 8HevXIIgr,* Oxford
1990.

25. For Barthélemy, Roberts, Schubart and Würthwein see the summary in
E. Würthwein, *Der Text des Alten Testaments,* Stuttgart [5]1988, 194,
with plate; for Hanhart, see W.H. Schmidt/W.Thiel/R.Hanhart,
Altes Testament, Stuttgart et al. 1989, 194-5, with plate.

26. P.J. Parsons, 'The Scripts and Their Date', in E. Tov, as in note 15,
here 24 and 26.

27. For a survey, see D. Guthrie, New Testament Introduction, Leicester
[4]1990, 43-57.

28. For a single plate, see E. Würthwein, as in note 16; for the two scribes,
see P.J. Parsons, as in note 24, here 20.

29. See W. Schubart, *Griechische Paläographie,* Munich21966, 111; J.
O'Callaghan, 'Paleografia Herculanense en algunos papiros griegos
de Qumrân', in *Homenaje a Juan Prado,* Madrid 1975, 529-32.

30. M. Baillet/J.T. Milik/R. de Vaux,(eds., *Les 'Petites Grottes' de
Qumrân, DJD III,* Oxford 1962, companion vol. *Planches,* p.XXX.

31. P.J. Parsons, 'The Palaeography and Date of the Greek Manuscripts',
in P.W. Skehan/E.Ulrich/J.E.Sanderson, eds., 'Qumran Cave 4', IV,
DJD IX, Oxford 1992, 7-13, here 8. Such references to Greek
manuscripts from Qumran are all the more legitimate as they did
not originate at Qumran and could represent a wide variety of
Jewish diaspora hands. Cf. E. Tov, 'Hebrew Biblical Manuscripts
from the Judaean Desert: Their Contribution to Textual Criticism',
Journal of Jewish Studies 39/1, 1988, 5-37, here 19; *et al.*

32. C.H. Roberts, 'Nomina sacra: Origins and Significance' in *id.,
Manuscript, Society and Belief in Early Christian Egypt,* London
1969, 26-48, here 46. Cf also J. O'Callaghan, *'Nomina sacra' in
papyris graecis saeculi III neotestamentariis,* Rome 1970, for an
analysis of *nomina sacra* in p^{46} which may, according to Kim, be
late first century. B.M. Metzger, *The Text of the New Testament, Its
Transmission, Corruption and Restoration* 3rd enlarged ed. Oxford
1992, 265-6, thinks that it is precisely the occurrence of *nomina
sacra* in p^{46} which counts against Kim's advocacy of such an early
date. But whatever the quality of Kim's arguments as such, this
could well be a circular argument on Metzger's side. If, for other
palaeographical reasons, certain papyri with *nomina sacra* turn out
to be first century, then this would favour Roberts' theory of the
early origins of *nomina sacra* rather than Metzger's preference for
later dates..

33. See C.H. Roberts, 'An Unpublished Fragment of the Fourth Gospel in the John Rylands Library, Manchester', 1935; enlarged and amended in *Bulletin of the John Rylands Library* 20, 1936, 45-45.

34. See C.P. Thiede, 'The Textual Peculiarities of p^{52}',in *id., The Earliest Gospel Manuscript?* Exeter 1992, 13-19, here no. 9, 17-18.

35. It seems to me that the 'watershed' is the Christian change from scroll to codex, most likely some time after the destruction of the temple in the year AD 70 which contributed to the end of Jewish-Christian activity among their fellow Jews and terminated the strategical reasons for using the scroll format and for resisting the temptation to put Jesus on a par with God (Jahwe) palaeographically by means of *nomina sacra* which had, until then, been the privilege of Jewish scribes using the tetragrammaton for the name of God.

36. See W. Schubart, as in note 29, 117-8.

37. The Birth of the Codex, London 1983, 61.63. Cf, more recently, T.C. Skeat, 'The Origin of the Christian Codex', *ZPE* 102, 1994, 263-268.

38. See note 20 and Martial, Epigrams, I.2; see also Roberts/Skeat, as in note 24, 24-29, E.G. Turner, *The Typology of the Early Codex,* Pennsylvania 1977, and J. van Haelst, 'Les Origines du Codex', in A. Blanchard, ed. *Les Débuts du Codex,* Turnhout 1989, 13-35.

39. See note 23.

3

Radiocarbon Dating and Papyrus p^{64} at Oxford

Given the considerable popular interest in the origins of Christianity and the techniques used to interpret the documentary evidence from its earliest years, it makes sense from time to time to look at the way in which changing techniques have affected individual source materials.

The redating of Papyrus p^{64} of the Gospel according to Saint Matthew, from the second to the first century, was achieved only through the use of comparative palaeography. Dated or datable manuscripts provided the basis for comparison.[1] The number of comparable manuscripts is much greater than was quoted in the context of the re-edition of p^{64} and there are several points of reference among the Oxyrynchus papyri.[2] Yet despite its increasing use comparative palaeography is still an evolving science. In 1903, it was thought that a fragment of a codex like that of p^{64} belonged, by definition, to the beginning of the fourth century, or perhaps to the end of the third century.[3] Today our system of co-ordinates is much more exact, and we have arrived at a date which is considerably earlier.

One can ask oneself the question as to whether or not there is an objective, precise, independent method which is capable of confirming (or refuting) the results of palaeography. Were such a method available it would certainly mean that we could proceed more confidently, as we would be provided with benchmarks against which to compare our own best efforts.

Now the routine answer to anyone searching for such an independent verification is that radiocarbon dating[4] has successfully shown itself capable of performing such a task.

Can we then 'radiocarbonize' the three small fragments of the Oxford papyrus and/or the two fragments of p^{64} in Barcelona which form part of it? The papyrus is made from material which is of vegetable origin and therefore should lend itself just as well to this method (in principle at least) as do parchment or leather of animal origin.[5] In 1991, the 'Institut für Mittelenergiephysik' in Zurich dated eight scrolls which came from three caves at Qumran and confirmed exactly the generally accepted dating of comparative palaeography.[6]

For the analysis at Zurich quite large scrolls were chosen with letter free margins so as not to damage or destroy any trace of ink or writing. Even the present day generation of radiocarbon apparatus, which allows for the application of the 'Accelerator Mass Spectrometry' (A.N.S.) method, requires a minimum of 20 to 25 milligrams of material to be consumed during the analysis. So it is easy to see that the small fragments from Qumran will not be analyzed in such a manner. In other words, the Greek fragments, those from cave 4 and cave 7, among them the papyrus of the Gospel according to Saint Mark, Q5,[7] are excluded.

As far as the three fragments of papyrus p^{64} at Magdalen College, Oxford are concerned, we can now be even more precise: in spite of the uncontested fact that there is ink and letters or traces of letters everywhere right up to the damaged edges, we took the decision to present the fragments to the Carbon Dating Laboratory at the University of Oxford for a feasibility study. The result was clear and definite: not to mention the problem of destroying the writing, all three are much too light. In figures: fragment 1 = 45 milligrams; fragment 2 = 25 milligrams; fragment 3 = 21 milligrams.[8] That means - as the experts at Oxford told us - that fragments 2 and 3 would disappear completely and fragment 1 would be halved.

It goes without saying that the two fragments from Barcelona, even though slightly larger, are equally excluded for the same reason.

One final remark: the exactitude of radiocarbon dating depends on the material being authentic in the sense of having a reliable 'track record' of careful neutral conditions of preservation and conservation. If the object to be analyzed is of unknown origin, or seriously influenced by preceding events, the variability of the result can be enormous.

The controversy surrounding the Turin Shroud gives us a good example of the problems that can arise in this regard. Among the criticisms levelled against the result (between 1260 and 1390) we always find a reference to several fires in Turin Cathedral in the Middle Ages, which would have caused the shroud to be damaged by fire and water. Further reference is often made to the pieces of linen used to repair that damage, as well as to other factors affecting its condition. These problems are just the kind of exterior influence which one must always take into consideration. The medieval date emerging from an experiment with radiocarbon dating could well be no more than the date of the last fire, or of the last repair, rather than the date of the material's true origin.

As far as the Egyptian papyri are concerned, a considerable number of them are of unknown origin - they were bought in the market at Luxor, like the p^{64}, or elsewhere, and their conservation was often negligent, or was handicapped by accidents (a 'good' example from outside Egypt being the damage caused by water to some papyri from Khirbet Mird, conserved in the library of the Catholic University, Louvain).

To summarize, even the most cursory examination of the history of radiocarbon dating techniques makes it clear that even when it is possible to provide a sample of suitable size and weight for the requirements of radiocarbon dating, there is no guarantee that equal or more precise results than those of the 'traditional' dating of comparative palaeography will be forthcoming. There are no easy solutions to the problems of dating manuscripts, just as there are no easy solutions to the problems of interpreting what they mean.

NOTES

1   Cf in this volume 'Papyrus Magdalene Greek 17 (Gregory-Aland p^{64}). A re-evaluation.'

2   The oldest fragment of Aristophanes, P. Oxy XXXI 2545, dated towards the end of the first century BC or the beginning of the first century AD is just one obvious example.

3   Cf note 1.

4   A resumé of the method and its future evolution is given by S.G.E. (Sheridan) Bowman, *Radiocarbon Dating,* London, Second Edition

1995. There is also a specialist journal, *Radiocarbon*, founded in 1958.

5   A first attempt was made as early as 1950, when W.F. Libby dated the cloth used for wrapping some of the scrolls from Qumran (his result: around the year 0 including a ten percent possibility of error or two hundred years more or less in either chronological direction). Later, Libby received the Nobel prize for his method: cf W.F. Libby, *Radiocarbon Dating,* Chicago 1952 72.

6   Cf G.A. Rodley, 'An Assessment of the Radiocarbon Dating of the Dead Sea Scrolls', *Radiocarbon* 35 (1993) 335- 338; and the Report of the Analysis by G. Bonani/M. Broshi/I. Carmi/S. Ivy/J. Strugnell/W. Wallfli 'Radiocarbon Dating of the Dead Sea Scrolls', Atiqot 30 (1991), 27- 32. The scrolls in Hebrew and Aramaic date from before Jesus Christ, the oldest of them belonged to the second century BC. There is a single one which probably belongs to the beginning of the first century AD.

7   See chapter 1.

8   I am grateful to C.Y. Ferdinand, the Librarian of Magdalen College, Oxford, for communicating the results.

4

The Origin and Tradition of Mark's Gospel in the Light of Recent Investigations

There appears to be a consensus in recent research; the Gospel of Mark was written just prior to the destruction of Jerusalem and the Temple, that cataclysmic event which took place in AD 70. It is believed that we can be fairly confident in asserting this because Mark's way of dealing with the prophecy of the destruction does not appear to presuppose the actual destruction. Even so, there is - strictly speaking - a period of about forty years during which this gospel could have been written. For if we argue as historians, a date any time between the crucifixion and resurrection of Jesus in AD 30 and the eve of the destruction of Jerusalem in AD 70 remains possible - these are the earliest and the latest conceivable dates for the Gospel of Mark.

One might well ask: 'Does it matter?' For those of us who find the argument about dating or redating the New Testament somewhat boring, and for those who do not regard the gospels as primary sources of authentic information anyway, it is a subject of at best secondary importance. But as historians - and every New Testament critic should be a historian, too - we must try to get as close as possible to the primary evidence, to the eyewitness material, to reliable oral and literary tradition. In other words, the New Testament documents deserve the same unbiased and sober, scholarly treatment that is normal and everyday practice in dealing with secular sources of antiquity.

After all, it is one of the long-lived myths perpetuated by some New Testament critics that the gospels are theological rather than historical documents. Yet no-one who has ever read the prologues to Tacitus' *Agricola*, to Livy's Roman history *Ab urbe condita*, Thucydides on his approach to reporting speeches, or closer still to the world of the New Testament, the liberal, cavalier attitude to research exemplified by Josephus Flavius, will seriously dare to accuse Mark, Luke or any of the others of tendentious writing beneath the standards of ancient historiography.

In this context, the search for the date of composition gains additional weight. And here, Marks's gospel has profited by the results of recent research, covering a wide range of subjects from the Dead Sea Scrolls of Qumran to Irenaeus of Lyon. In this chapter I shall try to highlight some of these results and their consequences for taking an overall view of the origin of Mark's gospel.

The question of early papyri

Mark's gospel has not been well served by papyri in that there are comparatively few manuscripts that have survived from the early period of the textual tradition. To be precise, there is no individual papyrus of Mark's gospel on its own prior to the important codex p^{45} (= Dublin, Trinity College, Chester Beatty I/Vienna, Austrian National Library Pap.G 31974, with large parts of all four gospels and Acts), which is commonly dated to the early third century, but may well be up to one hundred years older. Important as this codex is, it could not contribute to the debate about the origin of Mark, for it is too late. Thus it was indeed a sensational surprise when, back in 1972, the leading Spanish papyrologist José O'Callaghan claimed that there was a tiny fragment of Mark's gospel among the Dead Sea Scrolls.[1] Quite apart from the question as to how it could have reached the caves of the Essene settlement, the latest possible date of this Greek papyrus fragment, 7Q5, was striking. Since the settlement and the caves had been left in AD 68, when the 10th Roman Legion *Fretensis* marched on Qumran, and since a neutral, palaeographical dating of the fragment had suggested the year AD 50 at the latest (a dating confirmed by later analysis),[2] there suddenly appeared to be papyrological evidence for the existence of this gospel in AD 50, and of a copy in the vicinity of Jerusalem prior to AD 68. Admittedly, a majority of New Testament critics approached the fragment with gritted teeth, refusing to accept it or even ignoring it altogether, but even when there seemed to be a consensus *against* O'Callaghan's identification of 7Q5 as Mark 6:52-53, the question did not go away. At long last, in October 1991, an international symposium was held at the Catholic University of Eichstätt, Germany, and the participants - including opponents - agreed that a considerable number of arguments could be mustered in favour of the identification. A well-established papyrologist, Herbert Hunger of the University of Vienna, analysed the most controversial of the twenty visible and partly damaged letters by comparing them with contemporary Greek papyri, and concluded that *none* of the solutions suggested by O'Callaghan, myself and others contradict the available evidence from first century papyri. Since the papers of this symposium have in the meantime been published,[3] Hunger's material is now available to anyone with an interest in this fragment.

Literary papyri are hardly ever complete. Some of them are so small and damaged that it needs the ingenuity of expert scholars with elaborate equipment to make sense of them. 7Q5 is no exception. It is definitely not the smallest Greek fragment from antiquity, but - with twenty letters on five lines - it is certainly small enough to warrant very careful analysis. Even Herbert Hunger pointed out that one particular letter in line 2 of 7Q5 remained problematical: Was it a *Nu* or a *Iota*? He managed to show that it *could* be a *Nu* (as is obligatory if the text is Mark 6:52-53), but it certainly seemed elusive. This did not deter Hunger from supporting the Markan identification. All that had to be shown, after all, was the *possibility* of a *Nu*; and Hunger knew something that many critics appear to have forgotten: suggested identifications of individual letters must remain hypothetical as long as they cannot be connected with a readable text *that makes sense*. When José O'Callaghan tackled the fragment and matched it with Mark 6:52-53, he arrived at this identification on the basis of other parts of the fragment: letters in line 3 and line 4. Having reached the stage of a preliminary identification, he then had to make sure that no other letter or letters in that fragment contradicted it. In other words, all he had to show in the case of that extremely damaged letter in line 2 was that it *could* have been a *Nu*. This he did, quite successfully - as was confirmed by Herbert Hunger and his comparative analysis.

Fortunately, further progress has been made since that International Qumran Symposium at Eichstätt. Fragment 7Q5 was analysed by the Forensic Laboratory at the Department of Investigations of the Israel National Police in Jerusalem, and a clear remnant (about one-third) of a straight diagonal stroke, going from top left to bottom right, became visible. This, then was conclusive evidence for *Nu* against *Iota*.[4]

Learning from Details

Can the identification of the gospel of Mark, and, indirectly, the gospel's date, really depend on one single letter? Could a whole edifice of consequences be made to rest on a possible *Nu*? This is a fair question, certainly, and yet papyrologists must not be distracted by possible theological, exegetical or text-critical consequences of their work. If they are, it would be like an acrobat allowing himself to become more and more nervous the further he or she is from the ground. It is when the stakes are higher that we must cling to our belief in the validity of our techniques. O'Callaghan certainly never speculated about what the effects on New Testament scholarship would have been of Mark written prior to AD 68 and deposited at Qumran, and he was right to do so.

Interestingly, we have a recent example of the problems caused by a single letter in a small papyrus. It is an example so apposite that I feel justified in quoting it even though it also appears in this volume elsewhere. In 1989, Hannah M. Cotton and Joseph Geiger of the Hebrew University Jerusalem published a papyrus found at Masada, the Jewish fortress overlooking the Dead Sea. It was a scrap measuring 16 x 8 cm, with one incomplete line in Latin on each side.[5] The text on the *recto*, fifteen visible letters, two of them severely damaged, could be identified as Virgil, *Aeneid* 4:9. The text on the *verso* also consists of fifteen letters, three of them damaged. One long and rare Latin word is clearly legible: 'tibutantia', which means wavering or stammering. And yet the line could not be identified, not even with the help of the *Ibykus* computer programme of extant Latin literature. Things might be different if the beginning of the incomplete line could be read differently. Cotton and Geiger had suggested a *D* followed by an *E* and an *S*. The *D* is only partly visible, the *E* and the *S* are unambiguous. How tempting it would be to suppose that the *D* was in fact an *L* and the *E* an *I*: with *LIS* instead of *DES*, the line could be identified as Calpurnius, *Eclogae* 5:4 - *Talia verba refert tremulis titubantia labris.*

However, the *D* is likely and the *E* is evident; thus, we have to admit that the *verso* of the Latin Masada fragment cannot be identified as part of extant Latin literature.

But it is this 'negative' result which helps us; as a matter of fact, we can draw at least two helpful conclusions from the Masada Fragment 721 for our present purposes.

First, an old myth, perpetrated by, among others, Kurt Aland, must finally be laid to rest. The myth can be summed up in Aland's own words, first uttered in 1974 and reprinted, curiously enough without any correction, in 1990.[6] Aland describes his method of identifying small papyrus fragments and concludes:

> Fragmente von Rollen kommen (...) für das hier beschriebene Verfahren nicht in Betracht, denn hier fehlt die Kontrollmöglichkeit durch den Text auf der Rückseite.

The Masada fragment 721 warns us against relying on the *verso* of fragments for identification. Even though both lines were written by the same scribe and on the same height of the papyrus, they obviously do not belong to the same text. An attempt to identify the *recto* with the help of the *verso* would have failed dismally. The text on the *recto* had to stand alone, and it would have done so successfully even if not a single trace of ink could be found on the other side. This conclusion is all the more important as Aland linked his erroneous theory with an attempt to dispute O'Callaghan's 7Q identifications. For Aland, these tiny scraps from Cave 7 remained unidentifiable not least because of the missing text for checking purposes on the *verso*. He then qualifies his view by adding:

Bei ihnen (d.h. bei Rollenfragmenten) bedarf es für eine Identifizierung entweder der von vornherein feststehenden Zugehörigkeit zu anderen Fragmenten (...) oder eines ausführlichen Textbestandes, der ein sicheres Urteil erlaubt.

Neither of these criteria is met by the *recto* of the Masada fragment. Fifteen letters, two of them severely damaged, on one line can hardly be described as 'ausführlicher Textbestand', and a 'Zugehörigkeit zu anderen Fragmenten' does not apply either. What is more, no-one in their right mind would ever have thought it possible to find a fragment from Virgil on Masada; it was at least as unexpected as a New Testament fragment at Qumran. Thus, it did not even belong to an expected topographical content - no 'Zugehörigkeit' here - unless, of course, one began to think about it, as one had to do in the context of Qumran, as well. In short Cotton and Geiger reconstructed a Virgilian hexameter of thirty-nine letters from fifteen fragmentary ones. To put it differently, they had to work with a mere 38.5% of the line which they then managed to identify. They had neither a *verso* nor a socio-topographical context to help them, but they succeeded.

This leads us to the second helpful pointer to be gained from Masada fragment 721. We have bid farewell to the myth of foreknowledge; the idea that one just knows what can be found or what cannot be found. To quote Aland again, he knows that

'es einen Papyrus mit dem Text des Markusevangeliums (vi.52-53 z.B. gehört zur markinischen Redaktion, setzt also das fertige Evangelium, nicht eine von Markus benutzte Vorstufe voraus) aus der Zeit um 50 n. Chr. in Qumran nicht gegeben haben kann, es sei denn, man setzte die Niederschrift des Evangeliums etwa um 40 n. Chr. an. Denn gleich wo das Markusevangelium verfaßt wurde, in Palästina ist es mit Sicherheit nicht entstanden, es muß also ein gewisser Zeitraum - der mit 10 Jahren noch sehr niedrig angesetzt ist - für die Verbreitung vom Abfassungsort bis nach Palästina angenommen werden. Wenn 7Q7 mit Mark xii.17 von O'Callaghan noch vor 50 n. Chr. angesetzt wird, rückt die zeitliche Ansetzung des Markusevangeliums in eine noch frühere Zeit. Ein solches Datum will schlechterdings nicht zu den Resultaten der neutestamentlichen Einleitungswissenschaft passen...'

It might seem unfair to highlight the naivety of an otherwise highly respected New Testament scholar by quoting from an article first published eighteen years ago, but Aland and his disciples seem to be convinced that this is still the correct approach to 7Q and New Testament criticism. They included this very article, without the slightest alteration, in the *Supplementa* published in 1990.

Let us look at the unscientific presuppositions heaped upon one another in these few lines:

- he knows that there cannot have been a papyrus of Mark from about AD 50 at Qumran (unless the gospel was written in the 40s);

- he knows, even with certainty, that Mark was not written in Palestine;

- he knows that therefore (!) there must have been at least ten years to make it possible for the gospel to reach Palestine from its place of origin;

- he insinuates that O' Callaghan regarded fragment 7Q7 as a certain fragment from chapter 12 of Mark's gospel - which O' Callaghan never did - and then proceeds to infer from his own incorrect statement that O'Callaghan and his followers would argue for an even earlier date of the gospel;

- and finally, he tops it all by knowing what fits and what does not fit the 'Resultate der neutestamentlichen Einleitungswissenschaft'.

None of these self-confident positions is fully accurate, and some even fly in the face of international research to such an extent that one wonders how this paper could ever have been reprinted in 1990. The real problem, however, is the damage such presuppositions have done and still do to the progress of an informed debate on the textual tradition of literary documents from antiquity. In such a context, the Virgil fragment from Masada helps us to correct the myth perpetrated by Kurt Aland and to concentrate on the facts.

Before fragment 721 was found and identified as from Virgil *Aeneid* 4:9, it would have been laughable to suggest finding

Virgil on Masada, the Jewish nationalistic stronghold, where Zealots and Essenes met in a final stand against the occupiers of their country. In fact, had Hannah Cotton and Joseph Geiger been of Kurt Aland's ilk, they would have ruled out the mere idea as preposterous even before it might have occurred to them. They acted, however, as scholars and papyrologists and let the facts speak for themselves. Once the tiny fragment *was* identified as Virgil they then proceeded to analyse the follow-up question: How and when could it have got there? In other words, they did not try to argue it away; rather they tried to find convincing answers to given data. In the end the answers they give take account of the literary and socio-topographical world as far as it can be reconstructed. They established that the Latin fragments found at Masada - all of them in one place, the so-called *locus 1039* - must have come from the Roman camps around Masada; that the 'collection' (with papyrus 721 as the only literary text) was created shortly after the fall of the fortress in Spring 73 or 74; that they were written *in situ*, i.e. in the camps, just before that fall; and that this is corroborated by the palaeographical comparison. Furthermore, they ventured to suggest that it cannot have been a writing exercise since that line from the *Aeneid* does not contain the characteristics usually chosen for such exercises, but rather that it probably was a line addressed to someone called Anna - in which case 'soror' would have erotic undertones not unknown in Latin literature - or that verse 4:9 reflects the writer's feelings of horror at what he had witnessed at Masada.

Anna soror quae me suspensam insomnia terrent

Anna, my sister, what nightmares terrify me in my anxiety - the first line from Dido's first speech, found at Masada, in what is now the oldest Virgil papyrus, takes on a whole range of meanings which do justice to the context of the discovery, and, as Cotton and Geiger helpfully add, they also contribute to our understanding of the transmission of literature in the Roman army, perhaps even of the literacy and education of Roman soldiers.

The date given to the Masada Virgil, 73/74, is a mere five to six years later than the *terminus ante quem* for any text found at

Qumran (over against later texts found in the Wadi Murabba'at, the Nahal Hever, and so forth). And Masada is within easy walking distance of Qumran. The same world, it seems, and yet the classical philologists dealing with the Latin and Greek finds at Masada appear to be capable of a balanced, fact-orientated approach to their material that has not yet permeated a surprising number of New Testament critics.

On sober reflection, the identification of a fragment from the gospel of Mark at Qumran could be interpreted along the same lines which helped us to understand the Masada Virgil: texts could reach destinations across the Mediterranean within weeks. There was of course the imperial post which carried mail for civil servants and the military. And there were *tabellarii*, letter-carrying messengers, as well as individuals who acted as voluntary couriers. They could reach the Italian harbour of Puteoli from Corinth in five days, or as Cato once did, Africa from Rome in under three days.[7] A place like Masada was not cut off from the outside world, and the writer of fragment 721 could have *sent* those lines to his 'Anna', had he intended to do so, as much as the officer Iulius Lupus could *receive* a letter sent there and documented in Masada papyrus no. 724.

Distances - in place, in time, and in spirit?

One wonders why and how that old legend is still being kept alive by Aland and others, the legend that one has to allow at least ten years for a gospel to be spread from its place of origin to a place in Palestine. Let us assume for a moment that Mark's gospel was written in Rome. I, in common with the majority of scholars, think that it was indeed written in Rome (although the American scholar E. Earle Ellis has just rescuscitated and corroborated arguments in favour of an origin in Caesaria Maritima, thereby demonstrating, at least, how shaky Aland's certainty about ruling out Palestine really is).[8] We may rest assured that it could have reached a Palestinian harbour within a fortnight. The Christian community in Rome would of course have done everything in its power to see it distributed to the communities in the Holy Land as soon as possible. It was, after all, no 'secret gospel'. Needless to say, it would have taken care to send more than one scroll - after all, there was more than one community to supply. Aland claims elsewhere[9] that the possibility of four different fragments from Mark, by four different scribes and therefore from four different scrolls - a theory, incidentally, that is not shared by any other papyrologist who has analysed those fragments - that such a possibility 'would go beyond the scope of phantasy and turns O'Callaghan's hypothesis into a chimera'. Does it really? Should the 'chimera', the illusion, not much rather be seen in his own unlikely idea that a church interested in the distribution of its documents sends only one copy to one of its central communication places, and that it takes ten years to do so? The historical facts tell a different story. If the Christians in Rome (or Alexandria, or wherever) had intended to spread the news, the gospel, to their home communities, the whole process of getting it there and passing it on to, say, a target group like the inhabitants of Qumran, was indeed a question of a few weeks. That concept of at least ten years is so preposterous it should be relegated to the scrap heap of critical legend as soon as possible.

If we continue with the next obvious question: 'How and why Qumran, of all places?' we encounter answers that are at least as plausible as those offered by Cotton and Geiger for the existence of a Latin literary text on Masada.

There is one characteristic of the early Christian communities which has never been doubted by historians; that is, their immediate concern to pass on the message about Jesus as the suffering and risen Messiah. But not every day was Pentecost, when thousands of pilgrims came to Jerusalem and could be used as easy target groups. One had to think strategically, one had to begin where success was at least conceivable. In other words, a group like the Sadducees did not even expect a Messiah - any Messiah that is - regardless of who the claimant might be. They rejected the mere possibility of a bodily resurrection.[10] On the other hand, there was one fellow Jewish community which was approachable on these and other counts, the Essenes. Our knowledge of their thinking and their theology is increasing rapidly thanks to the general availability of *all* Qumran texts. The recent dispute about the tiny fragment 4Q285 (= BM 5) which, according to Robert Eisenman, tells the story of a suffering Messiah[11] is a case in point. However, we still do not know what the Essenes called themselves. The name we and first century authors like Pliny the Elder and Josephus Flavius give them is not documented in their own writings. Thus, we should not be surprised if they are not mentioned by name in the New Testament. But there can hardly be any doubt by now that they are referred to more than once. Most importantly they appear as converts to Christianity, as found in Acts 6:7:

> So the word of God spread. The number of disciples in Jerusalem increased rapidly, and a large number of priests became obedient to the faithful.

Given the fact that the Pharisees had no class of priests, and that the Sadducees, with their priests, theologically refused all basic presuppositions of a messianic message, only one group remains - the Essenes. Luke's statement in Acts appears increasingly trustworthy thanks to the latest analyses of Qumran texts and of archaeological investigations into the living quarters of the Essenes in Jerusalem.[12]

In brief, not only can it be shown that the first Christians and the Jerusalem Essenes were next-door neighbours on the south-western hill of Jerusalem (today's Mount Zion), but also (and this has been shown by Pixner, Betz and Riesner, cf note 12), that they had a common gate on that hill, the so-called 'Gate of the Essenes' mentioned by Josephus and recently rediscovered, the very gate through which Jesus in all probability entered Jerusalem on his way from Bethlehem to the Last Supper - a Last Supper, incidentally, which may well have taken place in an Essenian guest-house.

If we consider these two elements - the evidence for the conversion of a number of leading Essenes, and the archaeological evidence for their location in Jerusalem, with a gate that connected Jerusalem with Bethany, but also with Bethlehem and, of course, with Qumran itself - we arrive at a scenario which makes the existence of New Testament documents among the Dead Sea Scrolls from Qumran not only likely but almost mandatory.

After the Resurrection and Ascension the first Christians would have continued the contacts they had with the Essenes during the lifetime of Jesus, taking the earliest opportunity to give them their first documents, including early collections of sayings. They would have done so in **AD 66** *at the latest* - in that year the Jerusalem Christians fled the city during the initial stages of the uprising against the Romans and went to Pella in Transjordan.[13]

Since Cave 7 is obviously a collection or library in its own right - with exclusively Greek texts exclusively on papyrus - it is not unlikely that the fragments found in that cave represent the remnants of a Christian collection handed over to the Essenes for perusal and safekeeping. In fact, we may assume that the carriers of the collection were to be found among the priests who had converted to the Christian faith according to Acts 6:7.

The earliest gospel document: how do we know?

We have drawn a wide circle with Masada fragment 721 as our starting point to arrive back at Qumran Cave 7 and the actual papyri found there. We have seen to what extent the conclusions to be drawn from the Masada Virgil can be applied to the Qumran Mark. Having established, to put it bluntly, that a copy (or several copies) of Mark, and possibly of other New Testament writings at Qumran, is not only to be expected, but highly probable in the first place, we now have to resume the question which I presupposed at the outset: how do we apply the tools of our trade to an analysis of the text in question, and how can we improve upon Aland's errors of method?

Since 1955, a handful of scholars have had access to the original papyrus; among them José O'Callaghan, his severest critics Boismard and Benoît, and myself. Others have worked on the basis of photographs, a method which is of course much less reliable than the study of the original. A German scholar, Hans-Udo Rosenbaum, managed to distort the evidence of the papyrus by misinterpreting a poor quality photograph of 7Q5,[14] and a computer reconstruction of 7Q5 by the Australian Stuart Pickering arrived at impossible results, because it relied - admittedly - on unreliable photographs. In fact, even one of the greatest papyrologists, Sir Frederick Kenyon, committed a similar mistake in his edition of the Chester Beatty codex p^{46}. Editing the codex on the basis of photographs, he read an 'X' on plate 74 v, where there clearly is none on the original papyrus folio.[15] I would myself have fallen into that trap if I had relied on photographs alone when I edited the first edition of the New Testament papyrus p^{73}, the so-called Bodmer L (*L* for *fifty*). On the photograph with which I had been supplied by the Bibliotheca Bodmeriana, there is a clearly visible horizontal 'stroke' underneath line 2 of the *recto*. What a wealth of speculations could have been based on that trace! However, when I went to Cologny-Geneva to work with the original papyrus, I quickly established that there is no such line on the *recto* (nor on the *verso*, for that matter).[16] It was merely a technical error on the photographic plate - not the first and probably not the last to be encountered by papyrologists.

What about the reliability of working with the original papyrus, then? I have been able to work with the original 7Q fragments on five separate occasions, and the results of these visits to the John Rockefeller Museum in Jerusalem have helped me to clarify and improve my own publications. But perhaps even here, truth - like beauty - lies in the eye of the beholder. In the debate on line 2 of 7Q5, Benoît, who saw the original, insisted on his *Alpha*, and Baillet, who also claimed to have seen the original, called the possibility of a *Nu* absurd and impossible.[17] In fact, they continued to insist on a *Iota adscriptum* followed by what they thought could be an *Alpha*. Only the forensic analysis of the decisive letter in line 2, mentioned above, finally settled the matter.

Needless to say, the success of that forensic analysis has encouraged people at the John Rockefeller Museum and at the Department of Investigations of the Israel National Police to carry on along those lines. A computer print-out of the magnified detail has already been published as an appendix to the documents of the Eichstätt Symposium.[18] We shall continue to scrutinize the whole fragment, carrying on where we left it in April 1992. At that stage the last comparison we just managed to make was that between the different *Etas* in 7Q5 - a comparison which led to the conclusion that the remnants of ink partly destroyed in the gap in line 2, on the right hand side, must belong to an *Eta*, too; yet another corroboration of the Markan identification.

Even so, one has to realize that strokes of ink which must once have been there cannot be made visible again - at least not with existing technical equipment. For example, the left vertical stroke of the *Kappa* in line 3 is no longer complete, but it must once have been, and the same is true of the link between *Alpha* and *Iota* in the word *kai* in line 3, or of the right horizontal stroke of the *Nu* in line 2. It may well be, of course, that the reappearance, under the electronic stereo microscope, of the diagonal stroke of our decisive *Nu* in line 2 is due to a comparatively rare occurrence: to the scribe almost 'incising' the papyrus with his nib in the process of beginning that stroke on the top left. In fact, his stylus may even have caused what looks like a 'warping' of the papyrus material just at the very top of the stroke.

A further follow-up step will then be the analysis of the other seventeen fragments from cave 7, and of the one reversed, 'mirror-image' imprint on clay. 7Q4 is already continuing to gain acceptance as 1 Timothy 3:16 to 4:3.[19] But there are others, smaller and extremely small ones, and in their case, a close examination under laboratory conditions may well yield further letters or clarify doubts about damaged ones.

Philology and historical criticism

In spite of some recent claims to the contrary, there is sufficient evidence for the archaeological date commonly given to the closure of the Qumran caves, AD 68.[20] This is the latest possible date for the depositing of texts - needless to say, the date of their copying and the date of their composition must therefore each have been earlier still. Since palaeographical comparison has shown that fragment 7Q5 was written in about AD 50 (at one stage C.H. Roberts had even stated that AD 50 was the latest possible date)[21] a surprisingly early date for the origin of the complete gospel of Mark was brought into focus from a different perspective. I say *from a different perspective* because there had always been serious New Testament scholars and historians who had dated Mark to the 40s of the first century - for different reasons, but with weighty arguments.

The most influential of these may have been John A.T. Robinson, with his *Redating the New Testament*, first published in 1976. John Wenham, in his *Redating the Synoptic Gospels*, continued this line of thought in 1991.[22] Most of the reasoning for such a date can be and was based on a re-evaluation of evidence from church history. An important ingredient is to be seen in the reliability of the tradition of a first visit of St Peter to Rome in AD 42, i.e. in the second year of the reign of Claudius, a visit which lasted for only about two years, until the apostle was free to return to Jerusalem after the death of Herod Agrippa in AD 44. After several stopovers, he was certainly back in Jerusalem in time for the so-called Apostolic Council in AD 48.

It had always been clear to me that another ingredient in this line of reasoning is the famous statement by Irenaeus, in his *Adversus Haereses* 3:1,1, where he says that Mark's gospel was written (and passed on) *meta de ten touton éxodon*, i.e. after the *exodos* of the apostles Peter and Paul. For philological reasons alone, one had to doubt that this statement was meant to imply a composition after the *deaths* of Peter and Paul. In Greek literature, *exodos* usually means 'departure', 'going away'. A very obvious example of this usage is known to every reader of the Bible: the Greek title of the second book of the Torah, of the Pentateuch, is *Exodos* - and no-one would ever have theorized that it is about the death of the people of Israel rather than about their going away, their departure from Egypt.

In the New Testament *exodos* occurs three times (Luke 9:31, 2 Peter 2:15, Hebrews 11:22). In Hebrews, it alludes to the Israelites' flight from Egypt; in the other two passages, it alludes to the deaths of Jesus and Peter respectively. But here, a vital condition is met: the context establishes the meaning. No such certainty is provided by the passage in Irenaeus. 'Death' or 'departure'? That is precisely the question. One could have argued, as I did elsewhere,[23] that a lack of context substantiating the rarer meaning of 'death' should be used as an argument in favour of 'departure'. One could also have argued, as John Chapman did back in 1905,[24] that the grammatical tense employed by Irenaeus for the verb *paradidomi*, i.e. *paradedoken*, obviously implies that the message of Peter was passed on after his death by having been written down before his death - otherwise Irenaeus would have used the *aorist* instead of the perfect tense or he would have said something else altogether. Furthermore, Irenaeus uses the present participle *kerysómenos* to tell us that Luke wrote while Paul was still preaching. And if

Paul was still active while Luke wrote, this implies, at least according to a philologically correct understanding of Irenaeus, that Peter was still alive while Mark's gospel was being composed. This leads us to a date of AD 67 at the very latest. And this date was arrived at on philological grounds, by a mere, strict analysis of the passage concerned.

And yet, since J.D. Michaelis' *Introduction to the New Testament* of 1973, most commentators have insisted on the death of Peter as the prerequisite for the composition of Mark's gospel. *Exodos* means 'death' - this equation has remained stronger than all other arguments.

The breakthrough in this matter came in the autumn of 1991, when the American scholar E. Earle Ellis delivered a paper at the Qumran symposium held at the University of Eichstätt.[25] Again, it was a matter of taking a detail seriously, of asking a sensible question which should have and could have been asked long ago. Ellis perused the works of Irenaeus to find out if and when this author unmistakably uses *exodos* to signify 'death'. The result was as clear-cut as it is surprising to many: Irenaeus *never* uses *exodos* when he wants to say 'death'. For 'death' he always uses *thanatos*. In the same Book III of *Adversus Haereses* he does so no less than thirty-eight times.

Thus, Irenaeus can no longer be quoted as someone who argues against the apparent convictions of Papias and Clement of Alexandria, who are witnesses to an early date for Mark's gospel. Quite the contrary, he now joins and even corroborates them by stating quite clearly that this gospel was composed during Peter's lifetime. Furthermore, it must remain an open question if the so-called 'Anti-Marcionite' prologue was written just before or just after *Adversus Haereses*. Thus, we cannot use the anonymous Latin author to verify or falsify the results of this analysis. However, since the prologue's expression, 'post excessionem', is at least as ambiguous as 'exodos', without a proper context, it does not contribute to a solution. On the other hand, it will be much more interesting to try and determine what Irenaeus (and possibly the prologue) mean by 'departure'. Whose, and when, after all? Paul and Peter at the same time, or at different stages?

The Anti-Marcionite Prologue, interestingly enough, mentions only Peter - no trace here of Paul. In fact, none of the other fathers links Peter with Paul in the context of gospel origins. Could it be that Irenaeus just carried both names over from his general statement that Peter and Paul both founded the Roman church? I think so. The construction of these two sentences immediately following each other strongly suggests that 'meta de ten touton exodon' is linked with the statement about the establishment of the church in Rome - and, as Irenaeus himself must have known, they did not found that church simultaneously and together, but strengthened and structured it in successive visits. Even if one does not accept a first visit of Peter to Rome in AD 42, there can be no doubt about a chronological precedence of Peter's arrival in the city to that of Paul.[26] Thus, Irenaeus condenses his information, in a conscious effort to highlight the equality of rank and importance of both apostles.

The Anti-Marcionite Prologue, as well as Clement and Papias, who have no such strategical aims, concentrates on Peter and Mark alone. The Prologue's sentence puts it in sober terms: 'Post excessionem ipsius Petri descripsit idem hoc in partibus Italiae evangelium.'

The peculiarities of Irenaeus and the Prologue's terminology narrow down the date of the gospel to the period between AD 44 - the earliest possible moment for a departure of Peter from Rome and his return to the city in c. AD 58, after the despatch of Paul's letter to the Romans, where he is not mentioned in the list of greetings. Since there is no trace in any earlier literature of any departures of Peter from Rome after his second arrival, we therefore can also take both Irenaeus and the Prologue to imply that Peter did indeed spend some time in Rome on a *first* visit.

It might be possible to narrow down the date of Mark even further. For example, one could argue that Luke betrays knowledge of Mark's authorship of a book about Jesus as early as Acts 13:5, where he calls him 'ten hyperéten', literally 'the servant'. It is certainly noteworthy that he does not call him the 'hyperétes' of Barnabas and Paul, but uses the word like an attribute: Mark *the* 'hyperétes'. And this may of course be an allusion to Luke's usage of the term in his prologue to the gospel, where the 'hyperétai' are described as 'hyperetai tou logou' and are defined as those who collected and compiled information about Jesus in writing (Luke 1:2).

Soon after this description in Acts 13:5, Mark suddenly leaves his companions in Perge and returns to Jerusalem. Why? No reason is given (Acts 13:13). There could be a rather compelling one, however: Mark could have heard of Peter's return to Jerusalem. For him then, to meet the very source of his gospel and to show him the result of his work, would have been considerably more important than playing third fiddle to Barnabas and Paul. Peter must have been back in Jerusalem by AD 48, in time for the Apostolic Council; Perge can be dated to c. AD 46. In this scenario, Mark's gospel was indeed written in the comparably short span of time between AD 44 and AD 46. And perhaps two statements by Clement of Alexandria elucidate the matter further: first, apparently, Peter reacted in a neutral, non-committal way (in Eusebius, *Church History* 6,14:7), but then, on a separate occasion, he endorsed and ratified it for study in the churches (in Eusebius, *CH* 2, 15:2). Could it be that this faithfully reflects the process after Peter's departure from Rome? Mark and the apostle met in Jerusalem, in c. AD 46; Peter was not quite satisfied with the text he saw, and Mark composed his own 'redaction', the second version, which was finally approved by Peter.

None of the known facts contradict such a reconstruction, but it must of course remain hypothetical. What concerns us in our present context, is something else - it is the conclusion that the re-evaluation of Irenaeus and its consequences, however far one would want to take them, fit the evidence from Qumran Cave 7. In fact, the earlier the gospel must be dated, the easier it becomes to understand two textual peculiarities of Qumran fragment 7Q5: the omission of 'epi ten gen' (to the land) makes sense prior to AD 70 when the 'ge', the habitation also called 'Gennesaret', was still there, for everyone to see, until the Romans destroyed it in AD 70; *before* that date, 'epi ten gen' would have been sheer pleonasm. And then there is the spelling variation of *Tau* for *Delta* at the beginning of 'tiaperásantes', not unknown in quite a few other contemporary texts.[27] It makes even *more* sense before the Temple was destroyed in AD 70 - for until then, everybody could see the barrier stone prohibiting non-Jews from entering the holy precinct: a stone on which the very word for barrier, *dryphakton*, was spelled with *Tau* instead of *Delta*.[28]

Philology, papyrology, archaeology; all the disciplines will continue to help us in our quest for an accurate reconstruction of the earliest textual tradition. We are working at a mosaic, with stones still missing, but with a recognizable picture appearing before our eyes. This process should encourage all scholars to try and contribute to an even better understanding of Mark's gospel, and, by implication, the literary tradition of the New Testament.

NOTES

1   First publication: J. O'Callaghan, 'Papiros neotestamentarios en la cueva 7 de Qumrân?', *Biblica*, 1972, 91-100; cf C.P. Thiede, *The Earliest Gospel Manuscript? Qumran Fragment 7Q5 and its Significance for New Testament Studies*, Exeter 1992.

2   See now H. Hunger, '7Q5: Markus 6.52-53 - oder? Die Meinung des Papyrologen', in B. Mayer, ed. *Christen und Christliches in Qumran?*, Regensburg 1972, 33-56.

3   B. Mayer, ed., as in note 2.

4   Report with photographs: C.P. Thiede, 'Bericht über die kriminaltechnische Untersuchung des Fragments 7Q5 in Jerusalem', in B. Mayer, ed., as in note 2, 239-245.

5   H.M. Cotton, J. Geiger, eds., *Masada II: The Latin and Greek Documents*, Jerusalem 1989, 31-35 and plate 1, 721 a/b.

6   K. Aland, 'Über die Möglichkeit der Identifikation kleiner Fragmente neutestamentlicher Handschriften mit Hilfe des Computers' in J.K. Elliott, ed., *Studies in New Testament Language and Text*, Leiden 1976, 14-38, here 21-22 and 32-33; K. Aland, *Supplementa zu den neutestamentlichen und den kirchengeschichtlichen Entwürfen*, ed. by B. Köster et. al., Berlin/New York 1990, 117-141.

7   See C.P. Thiede, *Jesus - Life or Legend?*, Oxford 1990, 121-123; Italian edition, *Gesù, storia o leggenda?*, Bologna 1992, 118-120.

8   E.E. Ellis, 'Entstehungszeit und Herkunft des Markus-Evangeliums', in B. Mayer, ed., as in note 2.

9   K. Aland, 'Neue neutestamentliche Papyri III' *NTS* 20, 1974, 357-381, here 362-363, uncorrected (!) reprint in K. Aland, *Supplementa*, as in note 5, 142-157.

10   See e.g. Matthew 22:23-33.

11   First public announcement in *The New York Times International*, 8
      November 1991, and in the London *Times*, 9 November 1991. The
      debate about this fragment and its correct interpretation (not the
      Messiah will be 'pierced', *he* will 'pierce' *his* opponents) is
      summed up in O. Betz, R. Riesner, *Jesus, Qumran und der Vatikan.
      Klarstellungen*, Freiburg/Giessen, 1993, 103-110.

12   Latest summary, confirming the results of B. Pixner, the leading
      archaeologist on this subject: O. Betz. R. Riesner, as in note 11,
      176-184.

13   Eusebius, *CH* 5.3,3; see C. Koester, 'The Origin and significance of the
      Flight to Pella Tradition', *CBQ* 51, 1989, 90-106.

14   H.-U. Rosenbaum, 'Cave 7Q5! Gegen die erneute Inanspruchnahme des
      Qumran-Fragments 7Q5 als Bruchstück der ältesten
      Evangelien-Handschrift', *BZ* 31, 1987, 189-205.

15   See C.P. Thiede, *The Earliest Gospel Manuscript? The Qumran
      Fragment 7Q5 and its Significance for New Testament Studies*,
      Exeter, 1992, 36-37.

16   C.P. Thiede, 'Papyrus Bodmer L, Das neutestamentliche
      Papyrusfragment p 73 = Mt 25.4,3/262-3', Museum Helveticum
      47/1, 1990, 35-40, with plates.

17   M. Baillet, 'Les manuscrits de la grotte 7 de Qumrân et le Nouveau
      Testament', *Bib* 53, 1972, 508-516, here 510; cf P Benoit, 'Notes
      sur les fragments grecs de la grotte 7 de Qumran', *RB* 79, 1972,
      321-324, here 323.

18   B. Mayer, ed., as in note 2, 243.

19   C.P. Thiede, 'Papyrologische Anfragen an 7Q5 im Umfeld antiker
      Handschriften', in B. Mayer, ed., as in note 2, 57-72, here 59-64.

20   See, with literature, C.P. Thiede, as in note 15, 22.

21   C.H. Roberts, in M. Baillet, J.T. Milik, R. de Vaux, 'Les "Petites
      Grottes" de Qumran', *DJD* III, Oxford 1962, 144; cf C.P. Thiede,
      as in note 15, 24-25.

22   See also G. Zuntz, 'Wann wurde das Evangelium Marci geschrieben?'
      in H. Cancik, ed., *Markus-Philologie*, Tübingen 1984, 47-71; F.
      Camacho Acosta, 'La datación del evangelio de Marcos:
      Replanteamiento de la cuestion' *Isodorianum* 1, 1992, 59-84: and,
      of course, E.E. Ellis, as mentioned above, as in note 8.

23   C.P. Thiede, *Simon Peter - From Galilee to Rome*, Exeter 1986, [2]Grand
      Rapids 1988, 157-158.

24   J. Chapman, 'St Irenaeus in the Dates of the Gospels', *JTS* 6, 1905,
      563-569, here 567.

25   See E.E. Ellis, as in note 8.

26   See S. Dockx, 'Chronologie zum Leben des heiligen Petrus', in C.P. Thiede, *Das Petrusbild in der neueren Forschung*, Wuppertal 1987, 85-108.

27   E.g. S.B. 1 5110, dated AD 42 (!), with *t*ikes instead of *d*ikes.

28   See C.P. Thiede, as in note 19, 70-72.

5

Notes on a Papyrus of Luke's Gospel in Paris

One of the oldest papyri of St Luke's Gospel is kept at the Bibliothèque Nationale in Paris: Supplementum Graecum 1120 = Gregory-Aland p^4. It contains parts of chapters 1 to 6,[1] is commonly dated to the third century and has been thought to belong to the same codex which once also included the papyri of St Matthew's Gospel at Magdalen College Oxford (p^{64} = P. Magdalen Greek 17) and at the Fundación San Llucas Evangelista in Barcelona (p^{67} = P.Barc.Inv.1). The redating of the Oxford and Barcelona fragments to the latter part of the first century suggested in my re-edition of the Oxford papyrus[2] poses the obvious question: Is the Paris papyrus of St Luke's Gospel really a third remnant of one and the same codex, and therefore also of a first century date, and thus, by definition, the oldest surviving manuscript of this gospel?

In my re-edition of p^{64}, I gave the history of the theory of identicality which was first suggested by P. Weigandt, and which having been propagated by K. Aland is now popular as ever, having been accepted by papyrologists such as J. van Haelst and C.H. Roberts.[3] Among more recent contributors to the debate, Ph.W. Comfort had shown himself convinced that p^4, p^{64} and p^{67} belong to the same original codex.[4] The arguments adduced in favour of the identity may, at first sight, look impressive, but they have always been counterbalanced by an obvious material fact, namely that while on the one hand there is a similarity in the general appearance and in several individual letters, in the area of writing on the leaves, in the page size, in the double column format of each page, but less so in the number of lines per column, and the number of letters per line; Furthermore, even Aland had already noticed that p^{64}/p^{67} are written on light brown papyrus, whereas the colour of p^4 is an organic dark brown. Thus, Aland himself finally abandoned the theory of identicality, even though he did not do so in straightforward terms. His differentiation is hidden in the way in which he describes the papyri in his more recent publications. In his *Der Text des Neuen Testaments* he categorizes p^4 as 'Normaltext', whereas p^{64}/p^{67} are described as 'fester Text': p^4 is dated 'III' i.e. somewhere in the third century; p^{64}/p^{67}, however, as 'um 200'.[5] This indirect discontinuation remained largely unnoticed, until Ph. W. Comfort took the matter up, on the basis of my re-edition of p^{64}, and concluded that the three papyri do not in fact belong to the same codex after all.[6]

In the meantime, I have had the opportunity to analyze the original papyrus fragments in the manuscript room of the Bibliothèque Nationale on February 22 and 23, 1995. The following is a brief summary of the most important and distinctive aspects to be gathered from p^4 = Supplementum Graecum 1120.

First, it should be noted that the fragments from Luke's gospel are not kept in box 2 of Suppl.Gr.1120, as is the impression given by most references to it ever since J. Merell's publication,[7] but in box 5. Scholars going to Paris to work with the fragments will gain valuable time by applying for the right box straight away.

Secondly, the fragment of a title page preserved with the other papyri in Suppl.Gr.112, 'Ευαγγελιον κατα Ματθθαιον' which encouraged some scholars to believe that the Oxford/Barcelona Matthew may at one stage have belonged to the same codex, is written in a hand distinctly different from all three papyri; it is broader and wider, with a flat *Mu* and markedly elongated upper horizontal strokes in the two *Gammas*.

Thirdly, there can be no doubt that the material of the papyrus in p^4 and in p^{64}/p^{67} respectively is different. The dark brown of the Paris fragments, over against the light hue of the Oxford/Barcelona scraps, is organic and cannot be ascribed to different means of preservation and conservation. This observation alone seems to exclude the possibility of the Paris fragment originally belonging to one and the same codex as the other two.

Fourthly, one of the striking features linking p^{64} with p^{67}, the projection of a letter into the left margin in order to signify the first complete line of a new section which began in the preceding line,[8] is markedly different in p^4. The Paris scribe always used two letters, rather than one, for this purpose. The photographs supplied in the first edition of p^4 are unfortunately pretty useless for any serious analysis,[9] but even from these the unambiguous examples of $\alpha\rho/\chi o\mu\varepsilon\nu o\varsigma$ in fragment B, *verso*, Ire colonne, Lc III,23 (planche IV) and of $\varepsilon\lambda/\varepsilon\gamma\varepsilon\nu$ in fragment D, *verso*, Ire colonne, Lc V,36 (planche VI) can be made out, *pars pro toto*. While this would not necessarily rule out the identicality of the scribes - any scribe might change his 'idiosyncrasies' from time to time, perhaps even on behalf of a specific patron or customer - it would not happen within one and the same book. Thus, it would appear to rule out identical origin for the codices.[10]

Fifthly, the differences between the letters of p^{64}/p^{67} and p^4 are less apparent and may be less significant than the similarities listed by Comfort and others. But they are remarkable. For example, the scribe of p^4 has a tendency to raise *Omega* and *Omicron* above the bottom line, but to keep his *Rho* right on the line, much in fact like his *Tau*, which in p^4 and p^{67} extends underneath the bottom line in the same way as the *Upsilon*, and which always has a straight top bar in p^4, but not always as on p^{64}. Fragment A, *recto*, of p^4 offers the clearest examples. In any case, the similarities might justify a closer analysis of the possibility that all three papyri were in fact written by the same person or at the same copying centre, using different styli, at different periods, and for different customers.

Finally, in my re-edition of p^{64}, I was satisfied with the *status quo* as to the date of p^4, since the question of its date was, at the time, of no significance in the context of my paper. However, my work with the original fragments in Paris and the corroborative arguments provided by Comfort in his latest article appear to me to point towards a date not much later than that of p^{64}/p^{67}, 'at least the second century'.[11] If that is the case, then indeed the papyrus kept at the Bibliothèque Nationale in Paris is our oldest extant manuscript of St Luke's Gospel, superseding the third century papyri p^{69} (Oxford, Ashmolean Museum, P.Oxy.2383), p^{75} (Luke and John, Cologny, Bibliotheca Bodmeriana, P.Bodmer XIV-XV) and p^{45} (four gospels + Acts, Dublin, P. Chester Beatty I/Vienna, Österr. National-Bibliothek P.Gr.31974). In order to move this debate on two further steps need to be taken. First, we need a new critical edition of the text of the Paris papyrus p^4. Nothing serious has been done since M.-J. Lagrange[12] and J. Merell.[13] Secondly, in more general terms, we need a thorough reappraisal of the date given to all early Christian papyri. The so-called Biblical Uncial style has been taken for granted to such an extent that no space has been left for the acceptance of internal and external arguments pointing towards earlier origins. The present debate may be the beginning of a critical and self-critical process which will help us to understand the textual tradition of the New Testament, its origins as much as its development in the first century.

NOTES

1.   1:58-59; 1:62-2,1.6-7; 3:8-4:2.29-32. 34-35; 5:3-8; 5:30-6:16.

2.   C.P. Thiede, 'Papyrus Magdalen Greek 17 (Gregory-Aland p^{64}). A Reappraisal', *ZPE* 105, 1995, 13-20, with plate, cf chapter 2.

3.   See note 2.

4.   Ph.W. Comfort, *The Quest for the Original Text of the New Testament*, Grand Rapids 1992, 81-83.

5.   K. and B. Aland, *Der Text des Neuen Testaments*, Stuttgart[2]1989, 105, 106, 110. See also the dates given in the list 'codices Graeci et Latini in hac editione adhibiti', Nestle-Aland, *Novum Testamentum Graece*[27].

6.   Ph. W. Comfort, 'Exploring the Common Identification of the Three New Testament Manuscripts: p^4, p^{64}, and p^{67}', *Tyndale Bulletin* 46.1, 1995, 43-54.

7.   J. Merell 'Nouveaux fragments du papyrus 4', *Revue Biblique* 47, 1938, 5-22, planches I-Vii between 16 and 17, here 5: 'Il se trouve aujourd'hui à la Bibliothèque Nationale, sous le n° Gr. 1120, suppl. 2.'

8.   See note 2.

9.   See note 7.

10.   I am grateful to Philip Comfort for already referring to my observations on the paragraph in in his paper. See above, note 6.

11.   See Comfort, as in note 6.

12.   M.-J. Lagrange, *Critique Textuelle, vol. 2, La critiques rationelle,* Paris 1935, 118-124.

13.   See note 7.

6
St. Peter: A New Approach to a Biography

1. Origin

Of all the disciples it is probably Peter who most engages our attention when we read the New Testament for the first time as children. Whether this is because of his obvious humanity, or the bravery he showed in standing up to the high priest's guards, is difficult to say. What is clear is that along with Paul he played a vital role in the spread of Christianity, and thus the traditional image we have of him as a strong, but otherwise unremarkable fisherman cannot be adequate.

In the following article, originally written for a German biblical encyclopaedia, I have essayed some new biographical approaches towards Peter, with the intention of seeing whether or not it is possible to paint a fuller picture of him.

The name given to Peter at birth was in Hebrew Simeon and in Greek Simon. This name, in both Greek and Aramaic, was used by the Greek writer Aristophanes in his play *The Clouds* 423 BC, and, just like the entirely Greek name of his brother Andrew, it is indicative of the Hellenized environment in which Peter was born and grew up. According to John 1:44 he came from Bethsaida by the Sea of Galilee, which also was the home town of Greek-named Philip. Bethsaida had been given the epithet Julias after the daughter of Augustus and was granted the status of a city by the Tetrarch Philip who was a great patron of Greek culture. Considering this background we can fairly assume that Peter would have grown up knowing Aramaic and Hebrew and would also have had a good grounding in Greek, even if he was not perfectly trilingual. As the owner of a medium sized fisheries firm on one of the greatest international trade routes of the Middle East, the *Via Maris,* he would have had to constantly practise and improve his language skills. We know that his father's name was Jona from both Matt. 16:17 and John 1:42. Peter was married (Mk l:39; Matt. 8:14; Lk 4:38) and took his wife with him on his journeys at least from Pentecost onwards (1 Cor. 9:5). His house, which was re-discovered in Capernaum (see Mt.9:27-31; Mk. 1:29; 2:1; 3:20; 9:33), is situated near the synagogue (see Mk. 1:21-29) and has a forecourt (see Mk. 1:33). The references to his unmistakable Galilean accent (Mk. 14:70; Matt. 26:73) and the description of John and Peter as unskilled simple people (Acts 4:13: *agrammatoi kai idiotai*) must not lead us to assume that Peter was an ignorant, provincial backwoodsman. Peter had also benefited from Jewish elementary education, which gave a better than average understanding for that time, especially in the use of languages, texts and mnemonics (see Marou, Riesner). The deprecating comments of the Sanhedrin in Jerusalem can only be read as indicating that Peter did not have the higher education of the scribes. Peter and Andrew spent at least some time in the milieu of John the Baptist (see John 1:40-41) before they met Jesus. It is questionable whether they were disciples of John the Baptist; more likely they, like Jesus, were 'passing through', possibly returning from the Passover celebration in Jerusalem accompanied by Philip and Nathanael. The presence of people who were later to become disciples of Jesus in the circle around the Baptist at the time of Jesus' baptism was still cited as a criterion at the by-election of the twelfth apostle (Acts 1:21f).

2. Discipleship

According to John 1.40-42, after Jesus' baptism Peter already receives a hint of what his future tasks would be: 'You shall be called Cephas'. Cephas (*Kepa* in Aramaic) means 'rock', as John adds by way of explanation, which is identical with the Greek epithet *Petros.* Other than this passage in John only Paul continues to use the Aramaic form: 1 Cor. 1:12; 3:22; 9:5; 15:5; Gal. 1:18; 2:9,11,14. This naming (which in Jn 1:42 can also be read in the future tense as 'you will be called Cephas') is not directly connected with Peter's confession in Matt. 16:15-18.

John himself already includes a passage foreshadowing the confession established much later in chapter 6 verse 69. When considering the question of Peter's naming it is also worth re-examining the passage Matthew 16.15-18 and comparing it chronologically with 10:2, and Mk. 3:16. After all, others had recognized the Messiah before Peter (Jn 1:34; Jn 1:41). The importance of the Peter confession is that unlike the others Peter's reaction came at a point decided and engineered by Jesus himself. By replying as he did he continued on the path which had already lead to his calling at the Sea of Galilee: Lk 5:1-11 (especially vv 5, 8, 10 ff). Right from the start Peter held a prominent position among the disciples. All four Gospels refer to Peter (with or without Andrew) as the one called first: Mk 1:16-17, Mt 4:18-20, Lk 5:4-10, Jn:40-42. Each time the disciples are listed he is shown in the first place (Mk 3:13-19, Mt. 10:1-4, Lk 6:12-16, see also Acts 1:13). Again and again he is shown as representing or deputizing for the disciples before Jesus (see amongst other passages Mt 8:29, Mt 14:27-28, 15:15, 18:21, Mk 9:5, Lk 12:41). When Jesus chooses a smaller group from among the twelve for a particular purpose Peter is always named first here too: in the group of three with Zebedee's sons John and James (Mk 5:37, 9:2-5, 14:33 par); when the group is enlarged to four by Peter's brother Andrew: Mk 13:3. Again Peter is sent with them to prepare the room for the Last Supper (Lk 22:8-13). The emphasis on Peter shows most clearly in Mk 16:7 ('But go and say to his disciples and Peter : 'He is going ahead of you into Galilee') and in Mk 1:36 ('But Simon and his companions', see also Lk 9:32).

When Jesus himself calls Peter the 'rock' upon which he will build his church (*ekklesia*) he utters that special word which was to prove most momentous in terms of church history. Yet whilst Jesus' naming of Simon as Peter is unique, it only truly makes sense against a background of 'rock words' in the Old Testament (Isa 51:l f, 28:16) and may be compared with the Essene texts of Qumran (lQS 8.6-8: in the last days the council of the community will stand fast like a stone, like foundations that will not waver). Unlike the Qumran text Jesus does not talk about the community, but about the one man Peter. It is revealing that Peter himself in his first epistle (2:4-6) takes us further by referring the quotation in Isaiah 28:16 not to himself but to Jesus and through him to every Christian living the faith. The special promise heard by Peter in Mt 16:19 ('I will give you the keys of the Kingdom of Heaven; what you forbid on earth shall be forbidden in heaven, and what you allow on earth shall be allowed in heaven'), consists of two clearly distinguishable parts. The first sentence gives all that Jesus has to Peter in a future sense (see also Rev 3:7b, 1:18), however, only for the duration of this world ('what you forbid on earth'). Whilst the tasks of the second part of Mt 16:19 are also carried out by other disciples (see 18:18, and also Jn 20:23 and 2 Cor 2:15), Peter remains as Christ's trustee the foundation of the whole community/church, which is built upon him and over whom the gates of hell (see Isa 38:10) shall not prevail (see the writings of Maier, Burgess). Peter therefore is deliberately contrasted with the 'scribes' and 'Pharisees'. They shut the doors of the Kingdom of Heaven in people's faces (Mt 23:13), whereas Peter is able to unlock the Kingdom of Heaven with the keys entrusted to him by Jesus (see also Isa 22:22). Thus on one hand he is the foundation of the *ekklesia* and on the other hand he is also the one who will lead the people of God into the realm of the resurrection (see Oscar Cullmann on this subject). Where the Pharisees have failed (within the Jewish people, of whom Jesus and Peter were naturally a part), Jesus now appoints Peter in their place. It becomes transparent that Peter did not receive his special place(s) on the basis of his own strength and importance: all references from the almost parallel accounts of his human weaknesses and failings show this clearly. Prior to the Peter-confession at Caesarea Philippi this is made most apparent in the Matthean account of Peter's unsuccessful attempt to walk to Jesus across the water (Mt 14:28-33). The spontaneous readiness to do as Jesus did foundered just before reaching the destination (he managed some steps), because of his inadequate pre-Easter faith. Still Peter is shown as willing to take on too much, even though clearly his existing faith is too 'little' (Mt 14:31). On the other hand, here Peter's unreserved trust in Jesus is justified. It is Jesus who has the power to save the one who cries for help and who is sinking. Of greater consequence is Peter's failure to keep his promise to be the only one not to leave Jesus, if necessary. (Mk 14:29, Mt 26:33, Lk 22:33, Jn 13:37). This promise is destined not to be kept, and

Jesus follows Peter's statement with the announcement that he would be betrayed by Peter. This inconsistency, this uncertainty in Peter's pre-Easter behaviour is also apparent in the act of courage immediately preceding the betrayal: Peter cuts off the ear of the High Priest's servant (Jn 8:10 par), without fleeing himself. (Jn 18:14, Lk 22:54, Mt26:58, Mk 14:54, comp 4:51 f). He follows Jesus to the next place of greatest danger, the court of the High Priest. Peter's path after the betrayal, starting with "weeping bitterly", (Lk 22:62 par., see Ps 51:19) is connected with the promise of Jesus in Lk 22:32: 'but I have prayed for you, Simon, that your faith may not fail; and when you are restored, give strength to your brothers'. After Easter, the pre-Easter promise is confirmed and intensified on the shore of the Sea of Galilee: Jn 21:15-17.

The early Christians documented the importance of a turning point in their portrayal of Peter: in the early period he is never pictured with keys, but with a cock at his feet and his index finger pointing at his chin. According to Lk 23:49 it seems that Peter watched Jesus' crucifixion from near-by, from the so-called Second Wall (see also Riesner). Acts 5:29-32, 10:39, and 1 Pet 5:1 also confirm that Peter was an eye-witness of the crucifixion. Paul places Peter first among the witnesses of the resurrection (1 Cor 15:5), because in the document 1 Cor 15:1-9, which must be understood as tenable in law, women could not be cited as witnesses according to the understanding of the law at that time. But even the gospels reporting without this consideration stress Peter's special position at the empty grave: the angel says to the women 'But go and say to his disciples and to Peter...' (Mk 16:7, see also Lk 24:10-12, Jn 20:1-2). Peter is the first disciple to enter the empty tomb (Jn 20:4-8, Lk 24:12) and leaves 'amazed' - not in the sense of the ignorant 'being surprised'. In distinction to John, who according to Jn 20:4-8 also has a special faith experience at the empty tomb, Peter experiences individual appearances of the Risen One without any witnesses: Lk 24:34, 1 Cor 15:5. Whilst it is John who by the Sea of Galilee recognizes the Risen One by the boat (Jn 21:7), it is Peter who does something definite by jumping into the water to get to Jesus as soon as possible. After confirmation of his appointment (Jn 21:15-17) Peter receives a prophesy of his death from Jesus. (21:18-23). It does not follow from the text, however, that this section could have been written down after Peter's actual crucifixion in Rome and we therefore are dealing with a *vaticinium ex eventu:* the definitive interpretation of the 'hands stretched out' on the cross (not only the preparation for being tied up at his arrest) was not made until Tertullian c. 213 AD (Scorpiace 15). As 'rock' and now also 'shepherd' (see Jn 21:15-17 with Jn 10:11, 1 Pt 5:1-4) Peter presided over the community at the end of the gospel accounts.

3. The Apostle

After the Ascension of Jesus, Peter emerges as the responsible organizer (Acts 1:13-21). It is Peter who is the leading speaker and preacher (Acts 2:14-41, 3:12-26), the miracle worker (Acts 3:1-11, 5:14f, 11:36-42), the representative of the first congregation before the Rulers (Acts 4:8-22, 5:27-33), the protector of discipline in the congregation (Acts 5:1-11, see also Acts 8:14-24), the 'overseer' of the first missionary journeys (Acts 8:14-25). He it was who carried the mission to the heathen (after the precedent set by Philip, Acts 8:26-39) into the very heart of the Roman Empire, defending it theologically against the orthodox Jewish Christians and affirming it in the story of Cornelius (Acts 10:1-48, 11:1-18). Peter was also Paul's teacher, informed about the life and work of Jesus (Gal 1:18), and was a prudent delegate at the time of the departure from Jerusalem after the release from Herod Agrippa's prison (Acts 12:17, see chapter 12).

In all the roles shown here Peter appeared as a signpost, setting a standard for the actions of early Christians. This applies in particular to the mission to the heathen even if this was only systematized by Paul. The undisputed recognition of Peter's authority at that time is confirmed not in the least by Paul himself (Gal 1:18). The first big break comes with the departure from Jerusalem 'to another place' (Acts 12:17) probably in the spring of AD 41 (Dockx; Eusebius, *Chronicon,* ed. Schoene, 152-57; *C.H.* 2,14,6; 15:2). Hieronymus (*De vir. ill.* 8) and Papias (in Eusebius, ref. above) assume the arrival of Peter in Rome in AD 42. He may have arrived there after possible breaks in his journey (see Eus. *C.H.* 3:2, and also Dockx, *Antioch, Asia Minor, Corinth?*) in autumn AD 42 or earlier, at least in the second year of Claudius. Luke's knowledge that Rome was the destination is shown in the way he formulates Acts 12:17: *eis héteron tópon* refers to the identical formulation of the much used LXX version of the book of Ezekiel (see12:3). The key to the 'other place' comes in Ez 12:13; eis Babylóna - to Babylon - in Luke's and Peter's time generally meaning 'Rome' (see Seydl, Belser, Lyonnet, Thiede). Luke using a code, which can only be understood by those with knowledge of LXX, makes sense in view of the dedication of his twin work to the high-ranking Roman civil servant Theophilus; thus Peter's escape from prison is reported but the challenging flight into the capital of the empire is in code. In the same way Luke is restrained when reporting other actions against the state. Compare how he forgoes to identify Peter as the man who cut off the High Priest's servant's ear. As according to the custom of antiquity Theophilus would have taken responsibility for the copying and distribution of the work at his expense, (Haenchen, Hengel), these precautions were well founded. Eusebius and Hieronymus report that Peter was· *episkopos,* 'overseer', 'bishop' (see Phil 1:1) of the Roman congregation, but did not, however, reside continually there.

The Roman Church still recognizes an office connected with a title, a Titular Bishop, who exercises his authority mainly outside Rome; and Hieronymus and Eusebius would have been informed (like everyone else who knew e.g. Acts 15) that Peter could not have operated in Rome continuously for twenty-five years. Admittedly Peter would not have been the first missionary in Rome (see Acts 2:10); however, Paul indirectly assumes that the actual foundation of the congregation or its consolidation goes back to Peter (Rom 15:20, 23f, see K. Lake). Actually Rome was a natural destination for Peter: on the one hand he had advance information through Cornelius, the Roman officer, and on the other his main involvement had been with Jews and Godfearers, and thus the c. 50,000 Jews in Rome and their environment made an ideal target. The assumption that Peter and Mark jointly stayed in Rome on this first occasion (Edmundson, Wenham and Robinson) needs to be seen in the context of the first version of Mark's gospel having been completed around AD 44/45 (Robinson). After Peter's departure from Rome (made possible by the death of Herod

Agrippa in AD 44 and the resulting end to the persecution edict), but prior to the arrival of Mark in Jerusalem at the beginning of the first mission journey in AD 46/47 (Acts 12:25), Peter himself was back in Jerusalem at a time no later than AD 48 for the so-called Council of Jerusalem (Acts 15:2-29, comp Gal 2:1-10) possibly again after stopping on the way (Antioch?). Here he takes on the decisive role as conciliator: his speech (Acts 15:7-12) breaks the ice and makes it possible for Paul and Barnabas to report convincingly on the tactics and successes of their form of mission to the Gentiles, so that James accepts their strategy, and a joint letter of commendation can be written for both missionaries.

However, not long after the 'Council of Jerusalem', perhaps in April 49 (Dockx), there is a dispute between Paul and Peter in Antioch (Gal 2:11 to 14:21). Although the 'Council of Jerusalem' had made a decision on common table and communion between Jews and Gentiles, there was obviously not yet such a common table arrangement at Antioch (Gal 2:12), but separate house churches, as we can also assume was the case in Rome given the grouping of names in Romans 16:3-15. The different situation required flexibility in the application of the Jerusalem decision. Peter at first sided with the gentile Christians, eating with them as a Jew and thus making the decision of the 'Council of Jerusalem' real and at the same time showing it in practice to the Jewish Christians. Yet he then gave in to those who 'came from James' (Gal 2:12), showing the diplomatic skills expected from a 'rock' and 'shepherd' by turning to the Jews - probably for the duration of the stay of James' people - who were his 'responsibility' anyway. In this way he managed to please both parties and avert the threat of a possible split. Barnabas, the old expert on Antioch (Acts 11:22-24) who had proved his diplomatic skills earlier (in favour of Paul, Acts 9:27) sides with Peter (Gal 2:13). Whilst this can be re-constructed in Peter's favour from Paul's sharp attack, Paul's behaviour can also be understood. In his view Peter's action was a betrayal of the Gentile Christians for whom he himself had taken special responsibility. He even feared that Peter's example might force them now to join Jewish Christians with all the consequences (Gal 2:14). There is also the question in the background as to whether, when dealing with 'the truth of the Gospel', one has to walk an unalterable path (Paul), or whether one may show some flexibility in the context of the situation (Peter and Barnabas). It was thus that Peter's understanding of his office was tested in the most decisive manner. The people of Antioch obviously decided in favour of Peter. Soon thereafter Paul leaves the city and returns only once, on his way to Galatia (Acts18:22). Peter stays, possibly for another seven years (Dockx). Paul suffered a defeat here (Dunn), which he realized later and in 1 Cor 9:20-22 works into his teaching (Tertullian, *Adv. Marc.* 1.20). Thus this episode and its consequences would be a sign of the stature of both apostles in terms of their ability to learn and grow.

4. The Final Years

Peter arrived back in Rome for the second time around AD 57. This second journey to Rome is not dealt with in Acts and has to be reconstructed from both Epistles of Peter, and from sources of early church history. In these he is mentioned by name with persons from the New Testament (Pudens, Linus). Claudius is no longer Emperor, and Nero has taken over the imperial reins (for the effect on Petrine writing see Neugebauer). Under Nero the Fire of Rome starts in the early hours of l9th July 64, and this is followed by the first large scale, systematic persecution of Christians, which seems to have continued with varying intensity and extent until the death of Nero. The First Epistle of Clement, commonly dated to AD 96, but probably written around 69/70 (Robinson), connects Peter's death with this persecution situation (1 Clem 5:1-4). The persecution under Nero was fresh in Clement's mind, and he calls the martyrs 'fighters of the recent past' (5:1). However, it is not Nero who is mainly blamed for the martyrs' deaths, but rather jealousy and envy inside the community itself. This could be an allusion to the 'zealot' Jewish Christians, who had already made difficulties for Paul (Acts 21:20-30, Rom 2:17-29, 13:1 to 7:13, Phil 3: 2,5,19 f.), and Peter possibly returned to Rome in 57 to face them (Thiede). Unlike Paul, who was in prison when he wrote his Epistle to the Philippians, (see esp. Phil 1:15-17), Peter was able to act unimpeded. Any actions against the state had to be channelled sensibly, be they of a zealot or social reforming nature, to ensure steady development of the congregation without dangerous arguments with the civic authorities (see also 1 Pet 2:11-17, 3:1317, 2 Pet 3:14-16, Rom 12:14-21, 13:1-14, 16:17-20, Phil 1:15-17, 3:2-20). The information in 1 Clem 5:1-4 is confirmed by the Roman historian Tacitus (ann. 15.3844). In 15.44 he reports, that during the persecution after the fire, at first only those who confessed were arrested, but then later also those who were denounced. Furthermore the description of the acts of persecution are similar in Tacitus (15.44,4) and Clement (1 Clem 6:1-2).

It is conceivable that Peter's (and Paul's) opponents within the various factions of the Roman congregation used the opportunity offered by the persecution to rid themselves of the insufficiently 'progressive', 'anti-Roman' apostles. 1 Clem 5.1-4 certainly suggests this expressly and Tacitus (ann. 15.44) indirectly. Here Peter himself may have remembered the prophecy of Jesus which he witnessed on the Mount of Olives. (Mk 13:12): 'And brother will deliver up brother to death, and the father his child, and children will rise up against parents and have them put to death'. The date of Peter's death can only be ascertained approximately; according to Eusebius' *Chronicon* Peter died in the fourteenth year of Nero, that is between 13th October 67 and 9th June 68. (compare with Hieronymus, *De vir. ill.* 5). A date for his death towards the end of AD 67 would coincide with the twenty-five year period which according to Eusebius and others should be estimated for the whole phase of Peter's Titular-Episkopos-Office from the point of his first arrival. The earliest sources report unanimously that Peter was crucified (Lactantius, *De mortuis persecutorum* 2.6) and on his own request head down (Origen, Genesis commentary 3, in Eus. *C.H.* 3,1,2). All this can also be found in *Acta Petri* 37 (8) - 39 (10) with legendary embellishments, which also give us the 'Quo Vadis' story.

Peter was buried on the Vatican hill, the area where St. Peter's Basilica is now. That it was possible for relatives or followers to bury those executed during the persecution or after sentencing without then being subject to a penalty under Roman law is already shown in John 19:38. It is unlikely that a grand monument was erected, rather a simple, tiled flat tomb 'alla cappucina', as are still to be seen in the necropolis of *Ostia*

Antica. In about AD 200, however, the Roman Gaius reports an obviously significant memorial (*tropaion,* ref. Eus. *C.H.* 2. 25-7, comp. Mohrmann). Such tropaion, like the traces of tombs from the Neronian period, are established by archaeological evidence (see Guarducci). The complicated measures taken for the construction of Constantine's first St. Peter's Church about AD 315 had to take account of the awkward location of the *tropaion,* confirming the faithfulness and strength of local tradition preserved here (see also Lampe). The discovery of the inscription *Petros eni* ('Peter is in here') on the so-called Red Wall (Ferrua) emphasizes this tradition. Important Peter relics are in St John Lateran (relic of head above altar) and under St. Peter's in the *tropaion,* now accessible again. The result of an examination of the Vatican bones appears to point to the period of Peter (Walsh). It needs to be recorded that archaeological and church historical evidence reliably prove the tomb's location on the southern slope of the Vatican hill.

BIBLIOGRAPHY

E. Bammel, 'Petrus, der 'Stellvertreter' Christi', in E. Bammel, *Jesu Nachfolger. Nachfolgeüberlieferungen in der Zeit des frühen Christentums,* 1988, 52-60.

J.E. Belser, *Einleitung in das Neue Testament,*1901, 197-198.

J.A. Burgess, *History of the Interpretation of Matthew 16, 17-19 from 1781 to 1965,* 1976.

O. Cullmann, *Petrus. Jünger, Apostle, Märtyrer,* [3]1985.

S. Dockx, 'Chronologie zum Leben des heiligen Petrus', in C.P. Thiede (ed.), *Das Petrusbild in der neueren Forschung,* 1987, 85-108.

J.D.G. Dunn, *Unity and Diversity in the New Testament,* 1977, 254.

G. Edmundson, *The Church in Rome in the First Century,* 1913.

A. Ferrua, 'La Storia del sepulcro di San Pietro', *La Civiltà Cattolica* 103, 1952, 25/Plate 3.

A. Fridrichsen, 'Propter invidiam'. Note sur 1 Clem V', *Eranos* 44, 1946, 161-174.

M. Guarducci, 'Die Ausgrabungen unter Sankt Peter' in R. Klein, *Das frühe Christentum im römischen Staat,* [2]1982, 364-414.

E. Haenchen, *Die Apostelgeschichte,* [16]1977, 143.

M. Hengel, *Die Evangelienüberschriften*, 1984, 31-32.

E. Kirschbaum, *Die Gräber der Apostelfürsten St. Peter und St. Paul in Rom*, ³1974.

K. Lake, *The Earlier Epistles of St Paul*, 1911, 378-379.

P. Lampe, *Die stadtrömischen Christenin den ersten beiden Jahrhunderten*, ²1989.

S. Lyonnet, 'De Ministerio romano S. Petri ante adventum S. Pauli', *Verbum Domini*33, 1955, 143-154.

G. Maier, 'Die Kirche im Matthäusevangelium: Hermeneutische Analyse der gegenwärtigen Debatte über das Petrus-Wort Mt 16, 17-19', in C.P. Thiede (ed.), *Das Petrusbild in der neueren Forschung*, 1987, 171-191.

H.I. Marrou, *Geschichte der Erziehung im klassischen Altertum*, 1957.

Ch. Mohrmann, 'A propos de deux mots controversés de la Latinité chrétienne: tropaeum - nomen', *Vigilae Christianae* 7, 1954,154-173.

F. Neugebauer, 'Zur Deutung und Bedeutung des 1. Petrusbriefes', in C.P. Thiede (ed.), *Das Petrusbild in der neueren Forschung,* 1987, 109-144.

R. Riesner, 'Golgota und die Archäologie', *BiKi* 1/40, 1985, 21-26.

R. Riesner, *Jesus als Lehrer,* ³1988.

J.A.T. Robinson, *Wann enstand das neue Testament?*, 1986.

W. Rordorf, 'Die neronische Christenverfolgung im Spiegel der apocryphen Paulusakten', *NTS* 28, 1981, 365-374.

E. Seydl, 'Alttestamentarische Parallele zu Apg 12,17', *Der Katholik* 79, 1899.

M.R. Strom, 'An Old Testament Background to Acts 12:20-23', *NTS* 32, 1986, 289-292.

C.P. Thiede, *Simon Peter - From Galilee to Rome,* ²1988.

C.P. Thiede, 'Babylon, der andere Ort: Anmerkungen zu 1. Petr. 5,13 und Apg 12,17', in *Das Petrusbild in der neueren Forschung*, 1987, 221-229.

J.E. Walsh, *The Bones of St Peter*, 1983.

J. Wenham, 'Did Peter go to Rome in AD 42?' *TynB* 23, 1972, 94-102.

7

Archaeological Rome in New Testament Times

It is not easy to determine precisely when Christians first appeared in Rome. Some of those who listened to Peter's sermon at Pentecost and who had come from Rome themselves (Acts 2:10) might have taken the news of their newly found faith back with them to the capital of the empire soon after AD 30. In AD 42 Peter arrived in Rome for a stay of some three years, and this was followed by a second stay in around AD 57. Whilst this information has to be derived from sparse and partially coded details in Acts, the existence of a Christian community before Paul is clearly assumed by the Epistle to the Romans and Acts 28:15ff. It is also clear from Acts 18:2 that it was unable to grow steadily between these basic dates. Like Aquila and Priscilla, other Roman Christians would have been expelled from the city; no later than the death of Claudius in AD 54 the expulsion edict ended automatically and the rebuilding of the community became possible. The Greek formulation *tina Ioudaïon onomáti Akúlan,* 'a Jew named Aquila', suggests that those expelled would have been mainly Jewish Christians. That Aquila and Priscilla had been baptized prior to their meeting Paul, can be deduced from the omission of their names from the Pauline baptism list 1 Cor. 1:14-16. That the term *ioudaioi* may include Jewish Christians can be gleaned from the passages; see also Acts 16:20 f, 39; Gal. 2:13. At that time the number of Jews in Rome had reached around 50,000 (Juster; see also Leipoldt/Grundmann) and the comparatively small number of Jewish Christians was not always clearly distinguished from this larger group. In his account of Claudius' edict (*Historia* 60,6,6), Cassius Dio, who reports that Jews were not expelled, but were prohibited from assembling, was in all probability thinking of another, earlier occurrence in AD 41 (Bruce). The Roman historian Suetonius (Claudius 25.4) connects the expulsion (called thus by him) with unrest incited by one Crestus (*impulsore Cresto*), The same sound of - e and - i - (see Tac. ann. 15:4 'Crestianos' for Christians; ref. also the pun 'Cristianus'/'Crestianus' in Tertullian, *Apologeticum* 3.5), would tend to indicate it is doubtful whether there was a real life Jew of that name resident in Rome: a Roman would have understood 'Cristus' as the common proper name of Crestus, which is evidenced by many inscriptions, on the *Via Appia Antica* near the *Casal Rotondo* and on the tomb of *Caecilia Metella*. Suetonius also wants to say that the Christ-centred preaching of the Roman Jewish Christians had caused 'tumult' (*Ioudaeos ... assidue tumultantes*) among the Jews of the city. From Acts 6:9 to 7:60 we know that something similar had occurred in Jerusalem, and from Acts 13.50 and Acts 18.12-17 that there had been similar events in Pisidian Antioch and Corinth. The proximity to the Court and the fact that disturbances probably occurred on a larger scale might explain the measures taken by Claudius (the third expulsion of Jews after 139 BC and AD 19). Towards the end of the period covered by the Epistle to the Romans the proportion of Gentile Christians became important in the re-establishment of the community: Romans 11:17-24 is addressed especially to Gentile Christians, and the list of greetings, Romans 16:3-15, probably contains Gentile Christian names (Lightfoot). The second decisive event in the life of the Christians in Rome came as a result of Nero's persecution following the fire in Rome in AD 64. Both events occurred after the period covered by the New Testament writings, with the exception of Revelations, which does reflect upon the aftermath of the Neronian persecution rather than the anti-Christian procedures at the court of Domitian which were not really a persecution at all.

Archaeological traces of the early Roman Christians in the New Testament period are rare and in part disputed. Early church sources have preserved local traditions, which have not yet been fully researched. The location of Peter's tomb is established, and its topographical environment points to it being of the same period as Peter. Paul's tomb under St Paul's outside the walls at Via Ostiense and his place of execution (as a Roman citizen) at Tre Fontane (*Aquae Salviae*) are also historically established. The actual existence of house churches during the Petrine/Pauline period (Rom 16:5: *kai tën katoikon autón ekklesiam,* also the probability of a division of the list of names in Romans 6:3-1:5 according to leaders of the house churches: ref. Judge/Thomas) has led people to search for traces of them, particularly since later texts like the *Liber Pontificalis,* the *Acta of Praxedis* and *Pudentiana* and the *Notitia Ecclesiarum Urbis Romae* (among others), provide useful information and the Roman church has maintained the tradition of the *tituli* in its titular churches. The names of at least two of them can be traced back directly or indirectly to New Testament times. These are *Santa Pudenziana* (*Titulus Pudentis/Pudentianae*) and *Santa Prisca* (*Titulus Priscae*). If with Origen one assumes (see also the Commentary on John 6.54 in Eus. *C.H.* 4,23,11), that the Clemens of Phil. 4:3 is identical with the 'third Bishop of Rome' and could possibly be identical with the author of the First Epistle of Clement, one might suggest that *San Clemente (Titulus Clementis)* was a candidate for the third titular church. *Santa Pudenziana* is in a valley near the *Via Urbana,* the ancient *Vicus Patricius.*

Beneath today's church a private house was discovered which had still been standing in republican days, or at least in the first half of the second century AD (see Vanmaele). Although Christian inscriptions from that time are missing from this site, one can recognize the background from local tradition, which visualizes the house of (the Senator) Pudens, the man mentioned in 2 Timothy 4:21, who together with his daughters Praxedis and Pudentiana accommodated Peter (and possibly also Paul). Next door are baths named after Timotheus and Novatus; parts are still visible from the outside in the *Via Balbo.* Today's church dates back to the fourth century, no later than the time of Pope Damasus (366-384).The mosaic in the apse dating from the end of the fourth century is the most significant early Christian mosaic still in existence (it depicts Christ, surrounded by Peter and Paul as well as other apostles, two women who represent Praxedis and Pudentiana or possibly 'Ekklesia' and 'Synagogue', against a background of fourth century Jerusalem), and it stresses the importance the Roman church of the post Constantine period attached to this building

and the local traditions associated with it. *Santa Prisca*, on the
Aventine Hill, could preserve the remains of the the house
church of Aquila and Priscilla, mentioned in Romans 16:3-5.
Under today's church a private Roman house of the first century
and a Mithraeum of the second/third century were found. As
with the house under *Santa Pudenziana*, this house was also laid
out spaciously. According to von Harnack this could have been
the third century administrative centre of the Roman church.
The church visible today was built during the fifth century and
underwent considerable change in subsequent centuries. There
is documentary evidence for the existence of a church building
in the late third century. *San Clemente* is situated at the foot of
Mount Caelius, not far from the Colosseum. Excavations have
revealed a spacious residence dating back to the second half of
the first century. Nearby, connected by an alley of the same
period, is a Mithraeum, part of a brick built *insula* (multi-storey
apartment building for several tenants). The exact date of both
areas is difficult to establish and not undisputed, yet there is
proof that some remains predate the Fire of Rome in AD 64
(Nolan; see also Guidobaldi, and the sceptical Nestori). The
predecessor of today's church originated in the fourth century.
The crypt is still visible in the form of a pillared basilica with
three aisles. Although there is no titular New Testament
connection, not even indirectly, the *Titulus Sancti Laurentii* in
Lucina should be mentioned here. Today's church of *San
Lorenzo in Lucina* is near the Mars Field and immediately
beside Augustus' Horologium (sun dial). The latest excavations
have revealed a house and an *insula* of the second half of the
first century, some with *opus reticulatum mixtum* frescos and
mosaic floors (Bertoldi). Whilst today's name goes back to
Laurentius, the third century martyr, there is separate evidence
for the local name 'in Lucinis': *In Lucinis* Pope Damasus was
elected in 366; the earliest traces of a hall, however, point to the
period of Trajan (after AD 98). It is not yet settled whether
Lucina is a Roman matron or an epithet for the Roman goddess
Juno (here the 'goddess of birth'), with whom a 'pozzo' (well),
recently discovered, may be connected. It could also have been
a water distribution basin for the *insula* or a baptistery. The
latter attribution would be affirmed by the chronology of the
excavations under *Santa Pudenziana*, *Santa Prisca* and *San*

Clemente. With the help of local tradition, traces were found in all these places which can be interpreted as first century early Christian. In each case this was accomplished by traces of the building having been used as heathen centres of worship or for secular use dating back mainly to times of persecution in the second century. Finally in the post Constantine period the first proper church building was erected on the site. We must wait and see if *San Lorenzo in Lucina* can definitely be categorized in this titulus tradition of the New Testament period. Against the attempts to date the building to the second half of the first century there are other attempts to assume a date in the second half of the second century (Rakob, Guidobaldi). A basic problem in securing traces of early Christian heritage of the first (and second) centuries may be the fact that early meeting places were placed in attics of *insulae,* which have not been preserved (see Tertullian, *adv. Val.* 7; comp. Acts 1:13; 20:8f). Christian use of catacombs only dates back to the second century and later - for the earlier dating in the first century (De Rossi and his school) there are hardly any convincing arguments left - and we do not have space to describe them here. The results available so far from investigations of the Christian heritage for the New Testament period is sparse, but definitely sufficient to regard details of the New Testament and early Christian tradition, within present possibilities, as not unlikely, if not even as plausible.

8
Shorthand Writing and the New Testament

The study of the of the ancient world contains within it many specialist sub-disciplines, more indeed than can be found in most other forms of academic research. One such discipline is the study of Tachygraphy (from the Greek *tàchys* meaning fast), which is in fact a form of shorthand.

Speedwriting using symbols may have been available even in Old Testament times - Psalm 45:2 (LXX) mentions a 'fast writer' (*Oxygráphos,* from the Greek *oxỹs* meaning fast), which can be understood as a synonym for the technical term *tachygráphos,* the shorthand writer.

The first precise mention of a tachygrapher/stenographer appears in Plutarch (Cat. min 23) in his report on the meeting of the Roman Senate on the 5th of December 63 BC. Cato's speech was preserved because it was recorded by Cicero's speedwriters who were sitting in various places in the senate Chamber using symbols (*typois*). This shorthand had in fact been developed in the first century BC by Tiro, a freedman of Cicero, and called 'Tironian notes' after him. As recorded by Suetonius (*De Vita Caesarum,* 8,3,2), the Emperor Titus (AD 39-81) was also a significant master of the art.

There is still some controversy regarding the historical roots of Tachygraphy - mainly due to the difficulty of separating the earliest references clearly into Brachygraphy (from the Greek *brachys* meaning short) - that is longhand with some characters which were the forerunners of systematic symbols - and genuine shorthand, that is to say Tachygraphy. There is evidence for brachygraphic forerunners as far back as the fourth century BC. The Greek translator of Psalm 45 in the LXX text definitely knew what he was talking about, when in around 200 BC he put *oxygráphos* as a translation for the Hebrew term *sofer macher*, rather than using *grammateús tachÿs* as in Ezra 7:6 . Psalm 45:2 refers deliberately - and would have been so understood by Greek language readers of the third century BC - to a shorthand writer. The reference to an oxy- (tachy)grapher cannot simply be intended to indicate a 'fast writer'. Whilst it must be assumed that it was known in Greek-speaking Palestine even in the third century BC, the New Testament does not refer to the use of shorthand. However, interestingly enough there was a notable find of a leather manuscript in Greek tachygraphy (still not deciphered) at Wadi Murabba'at by the Dead Sea. This may be dated to the beginning of the second century AD (see P. Benoit, J.T. Milik, R. de Vaux, ed., *Les Grottes de Muraba'at. Discoveries in the Judaean Desert II*, 1961, 275-277; plate 164). For the New Testament context see also page 156 of B. Gerhardson's *Memory and Manuscript* (1961), and pages 191-98 of R. Riesner's *Jesus als Lehrer* (3rd ed., enl., 1993).

The question of the use of forms in tachygraphy in New Testament times becomes significant because of the thesis that is sometimes advanced, that Matthew/Levy the customs official - an educated man who would have needed to have been versed in practical forms of writing in order to carry out his professional activities - may have been able to use tachygraphy, and thus may have taken down in shorthand words spoken by Jesus. This has been suggested as an explanation for the presence in his gospel, and nowhere else, of such long, complex and continuous speeches as those found in the Sermon on the Mount.

The most prominent exponents of this approach are E.J. Goodspeed in his *Matthew, Apostle and Evangelist* (1959, see page 16), R.H. Gundry, *The Use of the Old Testament in St Matthew's Gospel* (1967, see pp. 182-184), and most recently B. Orchard and H. Riley in *The Order of the Synoptics*, (1987, see pp. 269-73). The latter authors also advanced a similar argument for Mark, referring to the public speeches made by Peter in Rome, which according to Papias (Eusebius *C.H.* 3.39, 15-16 and 6,14,6) are the basis for the Marcan Gospel, and which may have been recorded by two tachygraphers (see also E.G. Turner, *Greek Papyri*, plate VI, 1980). G. Kennedy ('Classical and Christian Source Criticism', in W.O. Walker, ed., 1978, *The Relationship among the Gospels*, 125-192) makes a similar argument in which he sees immediate note-taking as a preparatory stage in the drawing up of the literary text.

Whether or not such theories are accurate is almost impossible to determine absolutely on the basis of the evidence. What can be said however is that such techniques were current during the period, that at least in the case of Matthew there is circumstantial evidence that given his profession he may have been acquainted with such techniques, and that it makes practical sense that at least some of those who heard Jesus - or for that matter Peter - would have wished to have made a contemporaneous account of his words if they were able. Beyond this we cannot go, except of course for drawing attention to Tertius, Paul's secretary in Romans 16:22, who may have been used for this long and complicated letter precisely because he was (according to E.R. Richards, *The Secretary in the Letters of Paul*, 1991, 169-172) a trained shorthand writer.

BIBLIOGRAPHY

H. Boge, *Untersuchungen zur altgriechischen Tachygraphie und zur Frage der Priorität ihrer Erfindung*, dissertation, 1962.

H. Boge, *Griechische Tachygraphie und Tironische Noten. Ein Handbuch der antiken und mittelalterlichen Schnellschrift*, 1973.

H. Boge, 'Die Entzifferung griechischer Tachygraphie auf Papyri und Wachstafeln, mit Bemerkungen zu den Gießener tachygraphischen Fragmenten sowie zur Geschichte der Tachygraphie und zur Frage der Priorität ihrer Erfindung', *Kurzberichte aus den Gießener Papyrussammlungen* 36, 1976.

G. Costamagna, M.F. Baroni, L. Zagni, *Notae Tironianae quae in Lexicis et in chartis reperiuntur novo discrimine ordinatae*, 1983.

V. Gardthausen, *Das Buchwesen im Altertum und im byzantinischen Mittelalter*, [2] 1911, 272-298.

Ch. Johnen, *Allgemeine Geschichte der Kurzschrift*, 1940.

U. Fr. Kopp, *Lexicon Tironianum*, 1965.

A. Mentz, 'Geschichte und Systeme der griechischen Tachygraphie', in *Archiv für Stenographie* 58/III (1907), 97-107, 129-145, 161-171, 204-206, 225-239.

A. Mentz, *Die Tironischen Noten. Eine Geschichte der römischen Kurzschrift*, 1944.

A. Mentz, F. Haeger, *Geschichte der Kurzschrift*, [2] 1974.

E.R. Richards, *The Secretary in the Letters of Paul,* 1991, 26-47.

A. Wikenhauser, 'Der heilige Hieronymus über Psalm 45 (44)', 2, in *Archiv für Stenographie* 59/III, 1908, 187 ff.

9

On the Development of Scroll and Codex in the Early Church

For a long time, it has been taken for granted that the Christian textual tradition began with the use of the codex, rather than the scroll.[1] The basic premise behind this assumption was the fact that there were no extant early Christian papyrus fragments from scrolls.[2] But even before the scroll fragment 7Q5 from Mark's gospel turned up,[3] it should have been obvious that there must have been Christian scrolls initially, and that the most plausible explanation for their non-existence among the papyri is the very introduction of the codex. As soon as the new format became the norm, scrolls fell out of use, at a speed and extent which differed from region to region. Existing copies were put aside, new texts were written on codices straight away, no effort was made to preserve, collect, let alone venerate the old scrolls of the first generation. If it were not for the 'Christian Library' in Qumran Cave 7, with its latest possible date of AD 68, the evidence for the early Christian scroll, conclusive as it is, would be literary and art-historical rather than papyrological.

The New Testament itself clearly presupposes the scroll, not only in Jewish usage, at the synagogue (Luke 4:17: *biblion* is used for 'scroll', and the verb to describe the action of Jesus, *anaptusso*, means 'unroll'), but also in an entirely Christian context, as in 2 Timothy 4:13, where the scrolls are contrasted with the *membranas*, the (parchment) notebooks, or in Revelations 6:14, where the sky is compared to a scroll which will be rolled up (*helissomenon*). In Northern Africa, a collection of Paul's letters on scrolls survived until AD 180. *The*

Passion of the Scillitan Martyrs (Passio Martyrum Scillitanorum), written immediately after the trial and execution of the martyrs in AD 180, refers to the scrolls of Paul's letters in a *capsa*, the technical term for the cylindrical container of scrolls.[4] In the Roman Domatilla Catacombs, a late second century mural shows Paul with two such *capsae* (the one to his right is badly damaged), each containing five scrolls: the five scrolls of the Torah or Pentateuch, and the five scrolls of the historical Christian base texts (the gospels and Acts); in other words, the five introductory texts of the Jewish and Christian literary traditions juxtaposed and placed on a par. Nearby in the same catacombs, the martyr Petronilla is shown with a *capsa* and, above it, an open codex. This combination documents the historical awareness of the Christian community of Rome. Paul is shown with scrolls only, but Petronilla, who died (according to tradition) in AD 98, is already portrayed with a codex in addition to the *capsa*. Some two hundred years later, no artist would have invented such scenarios; there had been good, historical reasons for them.

Thus, Bruce M. Metzger was of course right when he suggested that Luke's gospel, and its sequel, the book of Acts (and, by inference, the other gospels), were originally written on scrolls, with each of these two texts long enough to fill one scroll: 'Doubtless this is one of the reasons why Luke-Acts was issued in two volumes instead of one'.[5] If we accept, as we must, with or without the tangible evidence of the scroll fragment 7Q5 = Mk 6:52-53, that the very first stages of the literary tradition of the New Testament were committed to the scroll, and that we may witness, *within* the New Testament, the first steps towards a transition from the scroll to the codex *via* the notebook (2 Timothy 4:13), two questions will have to be answered: Why did the changeover occur and when did it occur? There is of course an almost inexhaustible amount of literature on the first question,[6] but it seems to me that the most satisfying answer can be attained by trying to tackle the second question first.

The decision to begin with the scroll was a natural one. It did not even need a formal decision, since the very first Christians and the first Christian writers were Jews. (Among the authors of our canonical New Testament, only Luke may have been a non-Jew, although this is far from certain.)[7] In other words, they would have continued to use their traditional format as a matter of course, and should they have reflected on its usefulness, strategical considerations would have been paramount. As long as Christian missionary activities could still be presented as a particular form of inner-Jewish dialogue about the Messiah and about Jesus as the God-sent incarnation of Isaiah's and Daniel's prophecies (and so forth), the accepted quasi-sacred format of the scrolls of the prophets, of the Torah, etc., had to be emulated in order to underline an uninterrupted tradition from prophecy to fulfilment. This is what is depicted in visual form in the mural showing St Paul and his *capsae*, and we find references to this practice in Rabbinical writings.

The Babylonian Talmud mentions the existence of Christian scrolls in Jewish possession which shall not be saved in case of fire, even though God's name is contained in them.[8] And on the basis of such an allusion, it is even less surprising than it would otherwise have been that fragments of such Christian papyrus scrolls were found in a Qumran cave. The Babylonian Talmud, in its present form, is not contemporary to the split between Jews and (Jewish)-Christians. It is all the more noteworthy that it preserves information on the Christian scroll which could not have been invented at a later stage.

In the history of early Jewish-Christian relations, there are four first-century dates which demonstrate the growing, and eventually unbridgeable, rift between the two communities: the stoning of James, the 'brother of the Lord' (Gal 1:19) on the instigation of the high priest Ananus in AD 62; the persecution of the Christians (but not the Jews) by Nero after the fire of Rome in AD 64/65; the destruction of the Temple (which had remained a meeting place of orthodox Jewish Christians and Jews even after AD 62) by the Romans under Titus in AD 70, and the so-called 'Birkat ham-mînîm', the curse on Christians from the 'Eighteen Benedictions', the formal acceptance of which must be dated, on the basis of the unequivocal reference in the Talmudic treatise *Berakot 28 b* which is attributed to Rabbi Gamaliel and the Academy at Jamnia (originally Jabneel or Jabneh), to AD 80 at the latest.[9]

The result of the anti-Christian benediction was the expulsion of the Jewish-Christians from the synagogue, so that the last remaining natural places of contact, after the destruction of the Temple, had disappeared. At about the same time, Jewish Christians built their first separate church on Jerusalem's south-western hill (today called Mount Zion); its remnants can still be seen in the so-called 'Tomb of David' - which of course never was David's tomb, since the king was buried on the eastern Ofel hill; the tell-tale indication of a synagogal building, the niche for the Torah scrolls, usually directed towards the Temple Mount (and, in synagogues outside Jerusalem, towards the city) is clearly pointing towards the site of Golgotha and the Empty Tomb, as anyone with a compass can check; the builders were Jewish-Christians who continued to honour a traditional Jewish feature of architecture.[10]

This Jewish-Christian synagogue on Mount Zion underlines the last stage of the separation, which was, on the Jewish-Christian side, not a separation by choice, but of necessity. Since the scrolls of the Torah and generally of what would later be known as the Old Testament remained an integral part of worship, the continued use of the niche made sense; however, it was certainly too small to contain, say, five Christian scrolls in addition to those of the Torah. Thus, even here, at this first century Christian church in Jerusalem, the Christian texts had to be stored elsewhere. And by then, the strategical reasons for the continuation of the scroll format for indigenous Christian writings had disappeared; the benediction against the *minim* had merely formalized a process for which the three preceding events would have been sufficiently provocative on their own.

In this context, the Neronian persecution and the destruction of the Temple may be seen as less important than the stoning of James, since both the former were external actions outside Jewish (or Christian) influence or responsibility, whereas the illegal execution of James was a deliberate act of Jewish aggression which could even be termed internecine. Even though he was, in the absence of Peter, the leader of the (Jewish-)Christian church of Jerusalem, James was known and revered as a devout Jew who continued to pray in the Temple every day so fervently that he earned the nickname 'camel knees'.[11] The information regarding the blatantly illegal action by Ananus and the Sanhedrin is precise and historically reliable, and comes from a Jewish source without any vested interest in Christian apologetics: Josephus' *Antiquities of the Jews* XX, 197-203.[12] The fact that the Sanhedrin's move was so obviously against Roman law and led to foreseeable consequences[13] shows how desperate the High Priest and his henchmen must have been to provoke and seal the break between the official Jewish authorities and the Christian community.

As Josephus tells us, not all Jerusalem Jews were on the side of Ananus and the Sanhedrin; some of them, perhaps those of a pharisaic persuasion, informed the Romans whose new procurator had been absent from the city when the execution took place.[14] This means that by AD 62, there was as yet no monolithic Jewish separation (whether aggressive or not) from the Christians; some, at any rate, seem to have preferred debate within the framework of the law. Thus, the original reasons for the Christian use of the scroll - continuation of a common Jewish tradition and visible identity of format in a strategical, evangelistic situation operating with the Torah and the prophets - were beginning to be eroded but did not have to be abandoned completely.

It may have been at precisely this juncture that Christian scrolls reached one of the non-violent groups, the Essenes, and were deposited in one of the Qumran caves when the Christians left the Jerusalem area for Pella in AD 66 (or perhaps immediately after AD 62[15]).[16] The Neronian persecution which would have lasted, in Rome and its vicinity at any rate, until the death of Nero in AD 68, marked the end of an active Jewish mission in that part of the Roman Empire. Here, as elsewhere, missionary activity among non-Jews, initiated by Peter and systematically pursued by Paul and his helpers, became increasingly important. With the death of the first generation of (Jewish) disciples and apostles by AD 68 (only John seems to have survived beyond that date and until the end of the century), the decrease of an 'inner Jewish' mission was merely hastened by external and internal events which widened the gulf.

When the Jewish Christians were allowed to return to Jerusalem after the destruction of the city in AD 70, they found a wasteland without Jews and built their synagogal church on the rubble of their former living quarters. The Essenes had been dispersed, never to return; Qumran had become a Roman fortress, access to the caves was barred; much later, when the Romans left, the Christians would not know where to look for the scrolls - as it had not been they who had hidden the documents, and nothing happened until the Bedouins rediscovered the caves in 1947. The anti-Christian 'benediction' from Jamnia, c. AD 80, confirmed a status quo for which AD 68/70, from AD 62 *via* AD 64/65 are the historical stations.

To put it differently, separation was marked by a series of trenchant actions or events, the cumulative effect of which resulted in a complete break which even the (Jewish-)Christians could no longer mend. By 68/70 at the latest, they were free to abandon the scroll and to convert to the codex which they themselves helped to develop out of the *membranae*, the note book already used by Paul. The practical, economical, tactical reasons for this change have been enlisted and explained elsewhere.[17] In view of the shift of missionary emphasis from Jews to Gentiles, it was certainly more than helpful that the Romans, familiar with the notebook even at a pre-newtestamental stage (*membranae* is a *Latin* technical term for which 2 Timothy 4:13 is our first Greek reference)[18] were not averse to using and advertizing the codex, even though they continued to prefer the scroll for a couple of centuries.[19] Given the popularity of the Latin codex at the end of the first century and into the early second century, during Martial's lifetime, one may even ask why it did not catch on during the second and third centuries, and why it was only in the mid- to late fourth century that the codex became the majority format for non-Christian literature. The answer probably lies in the very fact that the codex was being used by the Christians to such an extent that it became identified with them: the codex was the Christian format. 'Decent' Roman litterati would not want to be seen copying the scribal habits of an illicit religion. Only with Constantine and the Christianization of the Roman Empire would the codex begin to enjoy an accepted and acceptable position.[20]

It is one of those ironies of textual tradition that we have only one scroll fragment from a gospel and only one codex fragment from Graeco-Roman literature to show for what must have been a much more widespread phenomenon in the first century. But whatever future developments of method and analysis may yield, a papyrus *scroll* fragment from Mark's gospel (7Q5) fits the circumstantial evidence for mid-first century developments as convincingly as a papyrus *codex* fragment from Matthew (p^{64}).

NOTES

1   See, among others, K. & B. Aland, *Der Text des Neuen Testaments*, Stuttgart ²1989, 85, 111: 'Christian literature was apparently committed to the codex format from the very beginning. It took surprisingly long for this realization to win through.' (111) Cf M. Hengel, *Studies in the Gospel of Mark*, London 1985, 78: 'From the beginning - in contrast to contemporary book production elsewhere - these scribes write on codices'. Other scholars, like C.H. Roberts, T.C. Skeat and B.M. Metzger, were more circumspect in their assessment; see below.

2.   K. & B. Aland discuss potential exceptions, which they dismiss for technical reasons: see note 1, 111.

3   See Chapter 1 in this book, 'The Origin of the Gospels and the Magdalen Papyrus'.

4   J. Armitage Robinson, *Texts and Studies*, vol. 1 No. 2

5   B.M. Metzger, *The Text of the New Testament, Its Transmission, Corruption, and Restoration*, 3rd enlarged ed. Oxford 1992, 6.

6   See, for example (with further references) C.H. Roberts/T.C. Skeat, *The Birth of the Codex*, London 1983; J. van Haelst, 'Les Origines du Codex', in A. Blanchard, ed., *Les Débuts du Codex*, Tournhout 1989, 13-135; G. Cavallo, 'Codice e storia dei testi greci antichi. Qualche riflessione sulla fase primitiva del fenomeno', *Bibiliologia* 9 1989, 13-135, 169-180; T.C. Skeat, 'The Origin of the Christian Codex', *ZPE* 102 1994, 263-268; I. Andorlini, 'Precisazioni sulla data di alcuni testi di medicina in forma di codice', in A. Bülow-Jacobsen, ed. *Proceedings of the 20th International Congress of Papyrologists*, Copenhagen, 1994, 410-413. See also S.R. Llewellyn/R.A. Kearsley, *New Documents Illustrating Early Christianity*, Sydney 1994, Vol. 7, 250-256.

7   Colossians 4:14, usually interpreted as including Luke in a list of non-Jews, says in fact nothing of the kind; he probably was a 'hellenist', but so were many devout Jews - see, for example, Acts 6:1-7. The only indirect evidence for his non-Jewish roots is a remark by Jerome to the effect that Luke was a 'proselyte' from paganism to Judaism before he converted to Christianity (*Quaest. hebr. in Gen.*) Against an over-interpretation of Col 4:14, see

already A. Deissmann, *Licht vom Osten. Das Neue Testament und die neuentdeckten Texte der hellenistisch-römischen Welt.* Tübingen [4]1923, 376-377.

8   See J. Genot-Bismuth, *Un Homme Nommé Salut. Genèse d'une 'hérésie' à Jérusalem*, Paris, [2]1989, 205-207, here 205, with particular reference to Sabbat 16,1 and Sabbat 116a.

9   For the best summary of the case, see F. Manns, *John and Jamnia: How the Break Occurred Between Jews and Christians*, Jerusalem 1988, 15-30. Recent attempts at post-dating the anti-Christian 'Benediction' to the Bar Kochba period fail to convince; for this position, cf recently B. Wander, *Trennungsprozesse zwischen Frühem Christentum und Judentum im 1. Jahrhundert n.Chr.*, Tübingen, Basel 1994, 272-275.

10   For the archaeological evidence and date, see É. Puech, 'La synagogue judéo-chrétienne du Mont Sion', *Le Monde de la Bible* 57, 1989, 18-19, and above all, B. Pixner, 'Wege des Messias und Stätten der Urkirche.' *Jesus und das Juden-Christentum im Licht neuer archäologischer Erkenntnisse*, ed. by R. Riesner, Giessen, [2]1994, 287-326. In his book, Pixner also discusses J.E. Taylor's controversial and archaeologically unreliable attempt at negating an early Jewish-Christian presence in first century Jerusalem (J.E. Taylor, *Christians and Holy Places. The Myth of Jewish-Christian Origins*, Oxford 1993): See his chapter 32, 'Bemerkungen zum Weiterbestehen judenchristlicher Gruppen in Jerusalem', 402-411.

11   See Eusebius, *Church History* II, 23, 3-18, quoting Hegesippus.

12   For a recent survey of the event and its context, see B. Wander, as in note 9, 263-267, 288-289.

13   Other Jewish citizens lodged a complaint with King Agrippa II and the Roman procurator Albinus with the result that Ananus was deposed after a mere three months in office; Josephus, *Antiquities*, XX, 203.

14   Porcius Festus (see Acts 24:27) had died; his successor Albinus 'was still on his way' to Judaea (Josephus, *Antiquities* XX 200); see also note 13.

15   For conclusive arguments in favour of the historicity of the Pella episode, and for the debate about its date and duration, see B. Wander, as in note 9, 267-270.

16   For different scenarios explaining the reasons why and how Christian scrolls reached Qumran, see E. Ruckstuhl, 'Zur Frage einer Essenergemeinde in Jerusalem und zum Fundort von 7Q5.' in B. Mayer, ed., *Christen und Christliches in Qumran?*, Regensburg 1992, 131-137; B. Pixner, 'Archäologische Beobachtungen zum Jerusalemer Essener-Viertel und zur Urgemeinde' in B. Mayer (as above), 89-113, here 112; H. Burgmann, 'Die Höhle 7 war kein

Einzelfall', in B. Mayer (as above), 227-236; C.P. Thiede, *The Earliest Gospel Manuscript? The Qumran Fragment.7Q5 and its Significance for New Testament Studies*, Exeter/Carlisle 1992, 54-63.

17   See above, note 6.

18   Cicero, *Epistulae ad Fam.* 9,26,1 indicates that copies of letters were preserved in such notebooks. Cf E.R. Richards, *The Secretary in the Letters of Paul*, Tübingen 1991, 3-4, 65, 164.

19   Our only literary source for the codex in first century Graeco-Roman literature is Martial, who refers to codices, sold by his friend, the publisher Publius Secundus, as convenient 'pocket-book' editions for journeys (*Epigrams* 1,2, to be dated to Ad 84-86), and who lists several such editions by name: Homer (*Epigrams* 14,184), Virgil (14,186), Cicero (14,188), Livy (14,190) and Ovid (14,192). So far, only one fragment has come to light: a damaged page from a parchment codex of an otherwise unknown *History of the Macedonian Wars* (P.Oxy. I 35 = British Library Papyrus 745), datable to the late first century, but perhaps even before AD 79; see B. Grenfell/A. Hunt ed. *The Oxyrhynchus Papyri Part 1*, London 1898, 59-60, here 59, and C.P. Thiede, 'Papyrus Magdalen Greek 17 (Gregory-Aland p^{64}). A Reappraisal' *ZPE* 105 (1995) 13-20, here 15-16, and in chapter 2 of this book.

20   A similar phenomenon occurred at the same time, the late first, early second century, when the Jews discontinued the use of their own Greek translation of the Old Testament, the 'Septuagint' of the third century BC. The Christians had been using it to such an extent that it had become 'Christian property' in Jewish eyes. Alternative Jewish translations were produced so that the 'soiled' Septuagint could be avoided.

10

A Pagan Reader of
2 St Peter: Cosmic
Conflagration in 2 Peter 3
and the *Octavius* of
Minucius Felix

Post haec laeti hilaresque discessimus

Thereupon we went our way cheerful and lighthearted.
(*Octavius* 40.4)

In a recent paper on the second letter of Peter,[1] R. Riesner
offered an analysis of the importance of its eschatology and
argued for a date of the letter which may possibly fall within
Peter's lifetime. He also includes a paragraph on early Christian
attitudes toward the Stoic concept of ἐκπύρωσις, and he refers
to the usual source, Plato's *Timaeus* 22c, where, however, the
term as such does not occur, and notes that such 'pagan
parallels' and the popularity of the *topos* among Gnostic groups
like the Valentinians cause Irenaeus (*Adversus haereses* 1.7.1)
and Origen (*Contra Celsum* 4.11.79) to refute the idea, as Philo
had already done before them.[2] Riesner alludes to the
comparable frequency in Essene writings and to several Old
Testament 'starting points',[3] and goes on to say that no matter
how one might evaluate the hellenistic influence on the
acceptance of the ἐκπύρωσις–concept into 2 Peter, there is a
vital contrast to the teaching of the Stoa: the Stoics expected a
restituted world, i.e. a νεὸς κόσμος, whereas 2 Peter is looking

forward to a completely new creation, a καινὸς οὐρανὸς καὶ γῆ καινή (3.13) - something, Riesner says, that would appear to make it topical today.

Riesner's is the latest and most stimulating approach to eschatological concepts in 2 Peter. It is also the first serious attempt by a German scholar to take up and evaluate the work of E.M.B. Green.[4] Not least among the points raised by his paper is the observation that Fathers like Irenaeus and Origen hesitated to get involved in the prophecy of a cosmic conflagration, for fear of its Gnostic undertones and its pagan parallels. In this chapter I venture to introduce another author into the debate, the first *Latin* writer not only to discuss the conflagration as a Christian, but to do so positively and with a strong emphasis on its biblical basis: M. Minucius Felix with his scenic dialogue *Octavius*. Furthermore, I want to argue that Minucius not only knew the Stoa, via Cicero's *De natura deorum*, but also the only New Testament document unequivocally to refer to a cosmic conflagration, 2 Peter. In developing this argument, the *Apologies* of Justin Martyr will play an important role, and I want to point out unmistakable allusions to 2 Peter both in Justin and, contrary to popular opinion, in Minucius, who may well prove to be the first Roman after Clement (1 Clem. 9:2 = 2 Peter 1:17, etc.) to use 2 Peter directly.

II

The perennial question of the date of the *Octavius* and its chronological relationship with Tertullian's *Apologeticum* will concern us later. Irrespective of the answer, the *Octavius* remains the first Latin Christian text to *discuss* the cosmic conflagration.[5] Before we return to this issue, let us first briefly sketch the development of the conflagration idea from the Old Testament via 2 Peter to the Greek Fathers.

The earliest Old Testament reference to a cosmic conflagration occurs in Deut. 32:22, in the so-called 'Song of Moses'. If we look at the standard text of the LXX and assume for a moment that γῆ in Deut. 32:22 means the same as γῆ in 2 Pet. 3:7 + 10, the parallel is close indeed. Later in the Old Testament, the example of Isa. 34:4 has been adduced often enough, and 66:15-16 might also refer to a judgment of cosmic destruction by fire. Other passages pointing clearly in the same direction are Zeph. 1:18 + 3:8 and Mal. 4:1, all of them implying a cosmic, not just a localized, conflagration, with Zeph. 3:8-13 and Mal. 4:2-3 going one step further to forebode 2 Pet. 3:13.[6] In other words, the idea of a cosmic conflagration is well documented throughout the Old Testament, and we may assume that a passage from the Torah, such as Deut. 32:22, would have been a particularly important precedent for the author of 2 Peter.

Outside the Old Testament, Jewish apocalyptic writings were equally eloquent: 1QH3:29-36 +6:18-19; 1 En 1:5-8 + 102:1 and Jubilees 9:15 are only three of many examples.[7] As for the New Testament, the oft-repeated statement, 'the idea that the world will be finally annihilated by fire appears only in 2 Peter in the New Testament',[8] is slightly misleading: M. Green[9] lists Mt. 3:11, 1 Cor. 3:13, 2 Thess. 1:8, Heb. 12:29, 1 Pet. 1:7 and Rev. *passim* as being passages where judgment by fire is exemplified. Two of these, 1 Cor. 3:13-15 and 2 Thess. 1:7-10, especially the latter, are close to both Old Testament prophecy and 2 Peter, all the more so if we remember that 2 Pet. 3:10-13 is not simply about annihilation, but also about a just reward to the faithful, a promise to be kept by God, in heaven, and here on earth: καὶ γῆ καινή, visible through Rev. 21:1f.

Another New Testament passage that has never been taken seriously in the debate about the ἐκπύρωσις is Heb. 6:8. It is a metaphorical passage, beginning with v. 7, and it goes without saying that the agricultural image of the land that produces thorns and thistles and is in danger of being cursed, alludes to the earth *and* men and the forthcoming judgment upon them. In the end, the earth, (γῆ, v.7) will be burnt: ἧς τὸ τέλος εἰς καῦσιν. The apparent parallel to 2 Pet. 3:17 = 10:12 is all the more striking as the key-word here, καῦσις, appears in the conflagration text 1 En. 102:1, and lies behind the verb used twice in 2 Pet. 3:10+ 12 (στοιχεῖα δὲ καυσούμενα λυθήσεται; καὶ στοιχεῖα καυσούμενα τήκεται).[10]

In view of this use of terminology and the undeniable, well-established fact that the stoic ἐκπύρωσις has nothing whatsoever in common with the biblical concept of a cosmic conflagration, καῦσις might well prove to be a more precise term in the context of the New Testament and could therefore help us to distinguish between the stoic and the biblical phenomenon.

Having reached 2 Pet. 3:7+10-12, we can establish that it is based on Old Testament precedents and has parallels in early first-century Jewish apocalyptic texts and in at least one new Testament writing.[11]

III

Notwithstanding its place among other Old Testament and New Testament passages, 2 Pet. 3:7 + 10-12 is the culmination of biblical conflagration prophecy. Anyone wanting to link the idea of a cosmic conflagration with *Christians* and *Christian theology* would have had to know - or to know of - 2 Peter. 2 Peter begins with a reference to the previous destruction of the world by the Deluge (v.6) which will be followed by a destruction through fire (v.7). It is obvious from v.7 that Peter is speaking of the destruction of *ungodly men* ($τὴν ἀσεβῶν ἀνθρώπων$), not of all mankind. Verse 10 states that the final conflagration is part of the *parousia* that could take place at any time - taking up Mt. 24:42-44, interpreting Mt. 24-29 + 35, and echoing 1 Thess. 5:1-2.

Two problems arise in the Greek text of vv.10-12. The first occurs in 2 Pet. 3:10 and is of a textual nature. It concerns the question of whether $εὑρεθήσεται$ ('will be found', given by א, B, K, P, 424^C 1175, syr^{ph}, *et al.*) should be substituted by $κατακαήσεται$ ('will be burnt up'), given by A, 048, 049, syr^{h,} cop^{bo}, *et al.*), or by some other emendation, as the $λυόμενα$ added in p^{72}, the oldest extant witness. Although the reading of p^{72}, less clumsy than commonly thought, should be taken more seriously, the tendency of recent scholarship seems to be in favour of an unsupplemented $εὑρεθήσεται$ which would indeed appear to make exegetical sense if seen through the eyes of W.E. Wilson[12] and R. Bauckham.[13] The solution, however, is of secondary importance to the concept of a cosmic conflagration as such.

The second problem concerns the exact meaning of $στοιχεῖα$ which appears in vv. 10 and 12. Different explanations are possible. It could refer to the cosmic elements, earth, air, fire and water. This is the usage of the late-first-century *Shepherd of Hermas* (Vis. III, 13.3, adding, however, the numeral: καὶ γὰρ ὁ κόσμος διὰ τεσσάρων στοιχείων κρατεῖται), and the mid-second-century Aristides, *Apologia* 3-7. However, this explanation, based on Greek philosophy, is not borne out by occurrences in the LXX, nor by the majority of the Fathers. The *Wisdom of Solomon*, written in the mid-second century BC and known to the author of 2 Peter (cf also 2 Pet. 2:2 = Wis. 5:6; 2 Pet. 2:7 = Wis. 10:6), points towards an all-encompassing meaning of 'element', including the four, but going beyond them to the stars, the great lights in heaven: στοιχεῖα occurs in 7.17 and 19.18, and its wider meaning is indicated in 13.2:... Ἀλλ' ἢ πῦρ, ἢ πνεῦμα, ἢ ταχινὸν ἀέρα ἢ κύκλον ἄστρων, ἢ βίαιον ὕδωρ, ἢ φωστῆρας οὐρανοῦ, πρυτάνεις κόσμον θεοὺς ἐνόμισαν.

This is echoed by *Oracula Sybillina* 2.206-207, alluding to 2 Pet. 3:10:

καὶ τότε χηρεύσει στοιχεῖα πρόπαντα τὰ κόσμον,
Ἀὴρ, γαῖα, θάλασσα, φάος, πόλος, ἤματα, νύκτες.

The next step is an interpretative narrowing-down to the heavenly bodies, based on the second occurrence of στοιχεῖα in 2 Pet. 3:12, and its obvious allusion to Isa. 34:4, where 'powers of the heavens' will melt (τακήσονται), τήκω here being the key word, appearing in 2 Pet. 3:12 (τήκεται), and taken up in the context of a cosmic catastrophe by 2 Clem. 16:3 and *Apoc. Pet.* 5 (Ethiopic), both clearly using 2 Peter. Not much later, Justin (*Apol.* 2.5.2, etc.) and Theophilus (*Ad Autolicum* 2.15; etc.), seem to be the first Greek Christian authors to equate στοιχεῖα directly with 'stars'. Some decades later, or possibly, contemporary with 2 Clement, *Apoc. Pet.*, Justin and Theophilus (see below, VI), M. Minucius Felix is much less restrictive than these four appear to be: his non-Christian interlocutor, Quintus Caecilius Natalis, begins his attack on the Christian view of a cosmic conflagration with the following words:

Quid quod toto orbi et ipsi mundo cum sideribus suis minantur incendium, ruinam moliuntur, quasi aut naturae divinis legibus constitutus aeternus ordo turbetur, aut rupto elementorum omnium foedere et caelisti conpage divisa moles ista, qua continemur et cingimur, subruatur? (11.1).

Further, they threaten the whole world and the universe and its stars with destruction by fire, as though the eternal order of nature established by laws divine could be put to confusion, or as though the bonds of all the elements could be broken, the framework of heaven be split in twain, and the containing and surrounding mass be brought down in ruin.

Here we have the στοιχεῖα as used in *Wisdom* and 2 Pet. 3:10-12 itself: the idea is certainly meant to be inclusive, not exclusive. Minucius Felix, ascribing these words to Q. Caecilius Natalis, thus appears to be alluding to 2 Peter, not to one of its later exponents. (Cf VI below and note 22.)

IV

Having established the evidence for cosmic conflagration in biblical terminology, we must now ask why Irenaeus and Origen appear to dislike it, before moving on to Minucius Felix who does not have any problems with it. However, it was Justin Martyr who first defended the Christian concept against the Stoic one.[14] He was of course familiar with the Greek Stoa, and would have known its Roman adaptation by Seneca, particularly *Ad Marciam de consolatione*, 26.6, perhaps the most unequivocal Latin reference to a final cosmic conflagration, and the *Quaestiones naturales* 3.29.1, Seneca's account of the teaching of the Babylonian astrologer-philosopher Berossus.

In the famous passage in his *Apologia I*, 20, however, he refers to only one aspect of stoic thinking, the doctrine that the Universe was dissolved and renewed periodically, through an ἐκπύρωσις, which made everything return to the primeval element fire, before it could be reconstituted. His source for this information in Rome could have been, among others, Cicero's *De natura deorum* 2.118.[15] His reaction is interesting in that he does not quote or allude to a single Old Testament or New Testament text to refute the stoics. He merely says that already the Sybilla and Hystaspes had spoken of a destruction of transitory matter through fire. This is an allusion to *Oracula Sybillina* 4.172-77 (and possibly also to 2.196-213, part of the later Christian Sybillines), and the *Oracle of Hystaspes*, a Jewish-Hellenistic text later adapted, like the *Orac. Syb.*, for Christian purposes, mentioned by Clement (*Stromateis* 6.5.43)

and Lactantius (*Divinae institutiones* 7.15.19; 7.18.2-3).[16] We do
not know if the emperor Antoninus Pius, the addressee of
Justin's first Apology, was familiar with the two texts; if the
evidence of *Apol. I*, 44.12, is anything to go by, there must have
been a pre-Antoninan edict placing the possession and reading
of works like the Hystaspes Oracle, the Sybillines and the Old
Testament prophets under pain of death. They must therefore
have been popular in and influential on religious life, and we
can safely assume that the Christians among Justin's readers
knew them. Justin, however, does not take the matter further;
neither does he *identify* the Sybil or Hystaspes as individual
Christian or non-Christian voices, nor are his statements a
straightforward denunciation of Greek philosophy: having
implicitly differentiated the God of the Stoics, who himself goes
up in flames, from the Christian God, he can still go on to say
τῷ γὰρ λέγειν   ἡμᾶς ὑπὸ θεοῦ πάντα κεκοσμῆσθαι καὶ
γεγενῆσθαι Πλάτωνος δόξομεν λέγειν δόγμα τῷ δὲ ἐκπύρωσιν
γενέσθαι Στωϊκῶν. Only later (1.60) does he quote Deut. 32:22
to claim Judaeo-Christian supremacy: Ου τὰ αὐτὰ οὖν ἡμεῖς
ἄλλοις δοξάζομεν, ἀλλ' οἱ πάντες τὰ ἡμέτερα μιμούμενοι
λέγουσι. This is the argument also used by Minucius Felix in the
same context, when his Christian interlocutor, Octavius
Januarius, replies to the attack of Caecilius quoted above. Plato,
the Stoics and the Epicureans merely followed the divine
prediction of the prophets; and he adds a nice touch of Platonic
one-upmanship: 'Animadvertis, philosophos eadem disputare
quae dicimus, non quod nos simus eorum vestigia subsecuti, sed
quod illi de divinis praedicationibus prophetarum *umbram
interpolatae veritatis* imitati sint' (34.5). The philosophers, you
observe, use the same arguments as we; not that we have
followed in their footsteps, but that they, from the divine
predictions of the prophets, have borrowed *the shadow of a
garbled truth*.

In his second apology, 7.1-3, Justin returns to the subject of
the stoic ἐκπύρωσις and interprets it, thereby following the
order of events in 2 Peter, as the second destruction after the
Deluge with which his addressees, 'the Romans', must have
been familiar: he refers them to Deucalion and Pyrrha, and the
story known from Ovid, *Metamorphoses* 1.318-415, and
Apollodorus, *Bibliotheca* 1.7.2. Readers familiar with Ovid

would have remembered the passage *Met.* 1.256-58, preceding the deluge story, where Zeus plans a cosmic conflagration to follow the deluge at a later stage. The exact text is particularly interesting, as it would have connected Ovid with 2 Peter in the eyes of a discerning Roman who knew both texts:

> esse quoque in fatis reminiscitur, adfore tempus,
> quo mare, quo tellus correptaque regia caeli
> ardeat et mundi moles operosa laboret.

> He (Zeus) also considers that there should, according to the resolve of fate, come a time when the sea, and the earth, and the building of heaven shall burn, and the solidly crafted mass of the world shall be endangered.

Once again, Justin ever so carefully points at the discrepancies between stoicism and Christian eschatology, and he leaves the door wide open to those among his non-Christian readers who want to take the - apparently small - step from Greek philosophy groping after truth to Christianity as Truth revealed.[17] His technique is effective: he either quotes the oldest biblical authority that could actually claim to be pre-Platonic, i.e. Moses, or else he alludes to popular, contemporary Oracles of non-Roman, Judaeo-hellenistic origin. His readers would be able to relate to or at least to appreciate such references. In this context, a direct quotation by name from 2 Peter 3 might have been counterproductive: Peter, then commonly known to have lived and died in Rome, was, as it were, too close to home for comfort in an apologetic discussion on eschatological prophecy dedicated to Gentile Romans. So Justin omits a potentially irritating identification and leaves it to those who knew the letter to recognize its unmistakable appearance between the lines: dictum sapienti sat est, as Terence had put it in his *Phormio.*

V

Irenaeus and Origen, the two authors singled out by Riesner, do indeed differ from Justin's approach. Irenaeus, bishop of Lyons since 178, is the first plainly to dislike the conflagration concept. In *Adversus haereses* 1.7.1, he quotes the post-Petrine Valentinians as saying that the fire concealed in the world will

burst out, ignite, destroy all matter, will be annihilated with it
and will be transferred into nothingness. If that was so, he had
good reason to keep away from this heresy. Instead of
contrasting it with the biblical conflagration, however - and let
us remember, 2 Pet. 3:13 talks about the exact opposite of a
transferral into nothingness - he prefers to develop his own
theology: there would be no final conflagration, but a
transformation through fire - the result will be the new Heaven
and the new Earth, where man, in communion with God, will
abide (5.35.2 + 36.1). Irenaeus thus dissociates himself from
Peter's final cosmic conflagration, but agrees with him in the
idea of a new world: Isa. 66:22 and 2 Pet. 3:13 are both behind
6.36.1. In view of the one vital difference, however, it is
understandable that he does not use 2 Peter explicitly. His fight
against the Valentinian conflagration has moved him away from
any thoughts of a total destruction.

Origen, too, does not appreciate Peter's prophecy of a final,
destructive conflagration.[18] He is concerned not with
Gnosticism, but with Celsus' Ἀληθὴς λόγος of AD 178. Celsus,
writing at about the time when Irenaeus' *Adversus haereses* came
into existence, knew about the cosmic conflagration; we find
him mentioning the deluge in the time of Deucalion and the
conflagration in the time of Phaeton (*Contra Celsum*, 1.19-20).
Origen calls these stories myths which Celsus may have been
taught by the Egyptians, as the myth of world catastrophes was
put into the mouth of an Egyptian priest by Plato in his *Timaeus*
22.[19]

In 2.11-21, however, Origen is more precise and, having
quoted Celsus as saying that the Christians had misunderstood
the stoics by expecting a conflagration to follow on the deluge
of Deucalion, he counterattacks first by referring to Moses who
was much older than any of these authors who had presumed
cyclic occurrences of deluge and conflagration. Moses - he says
- and other prophets with him, had spoken of a forthcoming
cosmic conflagration, the others had misunderstood them and
invented the concept of cyclic ages. According to Origen, the
cosmic conflagration like the cosmic deluge is not caused by
cycles but by sin, which will be cleansed and purified by deluge
or conflagration.

The conflagration therefore does not result in annihilation, but in purification. And what is more, according to *Contra Celsum* 4.13, that fire is a figure of speech. The river of fire (Daniel 7:10, one of the several Old Testament passages quoted by Origen in this context) is therefore only metaphorical. Origen could not be further removed from 2 Peter 3 than he is in these passages. It is a conscious departure, since he knew the letter, but obviously felt uncomfortable about the consequences of its message. Celsus, on the other hand, seems to be closer to 2 Peter 3 than we normally give him credit for. Needless to say, his paraphrase is a caricature, but he correctly gives the order of events - after the deluge of Deucalion (already Philo had 'identified' Deucalion with Noah, taken up in this by Justin), a conflagration had to follow. This is the sequence of 2 Pet. 3:6-7; and as nowhere else in *Christian* documents prior to Celsus a parallel equally close to his rendering can be found,[20] we may assume that he is here indeed referring to 2 Pet. 3.6-7 (followed by Deut. 32:22), notwithstanding his total misinterpretation of its background and sources and his wilful confounding of it with the cyclic thinking of the stoics. Be this as it may, it should have become apparent that with Irenaeus and Origen and their turning away from 2 Peter we are already far removed from the world of Justin and, as we shall see again in a moment, of M. Minucius Felix.

VI

Minucius Felix presents the subject twice; and since this is not the place to discuss the whole dialogue, we should concentrate on these two occurrences, first during the cruel anti-Christian diatribe of Quintus Caecilius Natalis,[21] the pagan friend of Minucius, starting off the debate between him and the Christian Octavius Januarius, which has Minucius himself as the arbiter. All three may be of North-African origin, possibly from Citra (cf 2.1 with 9.6), but whereas Minucius and Caecilius are lawyers settled in Rome, Octavius is a visitor to the city, in the surroundings of which (the beaches of Ostia) the dialogue is actually set.

In 11.1-3, Caecilius recounts first the Christian conflagration concept (see end of III above) and, in the same breath, the belief in resurrection and eternal life.

> Anceps malum et gemina dementia, caelo et astris, quae sic relinquimus ut invenimus, interitum denuntiare, sibi mortuis extinctis, qui sicut nascimur et interimus, aeternitatem repromittere! (11.3).

One perversion and folly matches the other. Against heaven and the stars, which we leave even as we found them, they denounce destruction; for themselves when they are dead and gone, creatures born to perish, the promise of eternity!

As we have already seen, the words put into Caecilius' mouth in 11.1 by Minucius Felix appear to betray familiarity with 2 Peter 3; he also seems to be aware of the thinking behind 2 Pet. 3:11-13 (for 3:13, cf also Rev. 21:1!). *Octavius* would thus be an unequivocal attack against the cosmic conflagration of 2 Pet. 3; no other biblical or early Christian text could have offered Caecilius a similar precedent for the structure of his own diatribe.

When Octavius, the Christian, gets his say, he counters Caecilius's attack argument for argument and duly arrives at the conflagration in 34.1-5. Some editors have noted that Octavius follows biblical precedents.[22] This is not surprising, since he begins his reply by merely paraphrasing the argument of Caecilius which, as we have seen, betrays an acquaintance with 2 Peter. Octavius says, 'Ceterum de incendio mundi aut improvisum ignem cadere aut diffindi caelium non credere vulgaris erroris est'. 'As for the destruction of the world by fire, it is a vulgar error to regard such a sudden conflagration as incredible.' And he begins to turn the tables: not only is it a vulgar error not to believe in a cosmic conflagration - what is more, the Stoics, Epicureans and Plato have used the same concept:

> Quis enim sapienti dubitat, quis ignorat, omnia quae orta sunt occidere, quae facta sunt interire? caelum quoque cum omnius quae caelo continentur, ita ut coepisse desinere fontium dulcis aqua maria nutrire, in vim ignis abiturum Stoicis constans opinio est, quod consumpto umore mundus hic omnis ignescat; et Epicureis de elementorum

conflagratione et mundi ruina eadem ipsa sententia est.
Loquitur Plato partes orbis nunc inundare, dicit nunc alternis
vicibus ardescere et, cum ipsum mundum perpetuum et
insolubilem diceret esse fabricatum, addit tamen ipsi artifici
deo soli et solubilem et esse mortalem (34.2-4).

What philosopher doubts, or does not know, that all things
which have come into being die, that all things created perish,
that heaven and all things contained therein cease as they
began. (And, following the text of I. Vahlen, Ind,. Lect. Univ.
Berol semstr. aestiv. 1894, Leipzig 1907-08: So too the
universe, if sun, moon and stars are deprived of the fountain
of fresh water and the water of the seas, will disappear in a
blaze of fire.) And Epicureans hold the same about the
conflagration of the elements and the destruction of the
universe. Plato speaks of parts of the world as subject
alternately to floods and fire; and while maintaining that the
universe itself was created eternal and indissoluble, adds that
only God himself, who created it, can make it dissoluble and
mortal.

This is, as we noticed in **IV** above, the technique applied by
Justin in *Apol. I*, 60, with the difference that Octavius, or rather
M. Minucius Felix, is even less interested in correcting the stoics
that Justin. 'Animadvertis, philosophos eadem disputare quae
dicimus', he says in 34.5, and underlines the biblical superiority
by a mere unexplained, if witty dictum: '...illi de divinis
praedicationibus prophetarum umbram interpolatae veritatis
imitati sint'. 'The philosophers, you observe, use the same
arguments as we...they, from the divine predictions of the
prophets, have borrowed the shadow of the garbled truth.' As
in Justin, the similarities between the Greek philosophers and
Biblical teachings are, as a tool with which to 'open up' the
minds of the pagan readers, much more important than the
differences.[23] In other words, Caecilius should have known
better: through Greek philosophy, he already possessed a
glimpse of truth, now, in Christian eschatology, known to him
through 2 Peter, he would gain the full understanding of it, if
only he tried.

The *Octavius* ends in fact with the self-confessed defeat of
Caecilius: 'Vicimus et ita: ut improbe, usurpo victoriam. Nam
ut ille (Octavius) mei victori est, ita ego triumphator erroris'

(40.1). 'We are quits, as it stands, for I too have the face to claim a victory. If he (Octavius) has been victorious over me, I too have had my triumph over error.' The scene on Ostia beach ends in renewed and deepened friendship, and the author adds a realistic-sounding topos by letting Caecilius say that one or two minor problems do remain at the end of the debate, to be settled the following day: 'Etiam nun tamen aliqua consubsidunt non obstrepentia veritati, sed perfectae institutioni necessaria, de quibus crastino, quod iam sol occusui declivis est, ut de toto congruentes promptius requiremus' (40.2). 'But there remain still some minor difficulties, not contradictions fatal to the truth, but yet requiring more complete elucidation; these - for the sun is already dropping towards its setting - we shall do better to discuss tomorrow, in agreement on general principles.'

VII

The affinity of Minucius' approach with that of Justin points to a similar date, all the more so as both are markedly different from Irenaeus and Origen. Irenaeus and Origen shun the pagan parallels, while Justin and Minucius thrive on them. The possibility that Justin's *Apologia* and the *Octavius* are contemporary works is further corroborated by the reference to Marcus Cornelius Fronto in *Octavius* 9.6 ('id etiam Citrensis nostri testatur oratio' - ' it is also testified by the speech of our friend of Citra') and 31.2 ('Sic de isto et tuus Fronto non ut adfirmatur testimonium fecit' - 'In this way your own Fronto did not produce evidence as an affidavit'). Caecilius and Octavius are here referring to a lost anti-Christian *oratio*; although nothing is known of it apart from these two references,[24] Fronto himself is well-known and datable: he was 'consul suffectus' in AD 143, became tutor to the future emperors Marcus Aurelius and Lucius Verus and has become famous not least through his correspondence with these two and Antoninus Pius (the dedicatee of Justin's first *Apology*!), rediscovered in the early 19th century. The last extant letters can be dated in the year 166; he seems to have died then or soon after. Since both Octavius and Caecilius refer to him as a contemporary, the dialogue appears to be set in his lifetime.[25]

When Minucius wrote the *Octavius,*, Octavius himself had been dead for some years: '...non ea, quae iam transacta est decursa sunt, recondatione revocare;(...)nec immerito discedens vir eximius et sanctus immensum sui desiderium nobis reliquit' (1.1,3). 'I do not (intend to) recall to memory things over and done; (...)no wonder that on his departure so excellent and saintly a man has left behind him a measureless sense of loss.' Needless to say, this does not imply that Fronto was by then dead, also. The situation of the dialogue and the common ground it shares, in the conflagration debate, with Justin's *Apologies* over against Irenaeus and Origen make a date in the 160s plausible; and its reticence in *naming* Old Testament or New Testament authorities, as compared to Justin who here at least names Moses, seems to point to a still more careful; attitude within the pagano-Christian philosophical debate and therefore to a date even shortly before Justin's *Apologies*.[26] All this must therefore be mere conjecture, but there is certainly nothing in *Octavius* to *demand* a date much later than AD 143, the year when Fronto became a quotable public figure through his consulate.

Conclusion

To sum up, we must note that the cosmic conflagration of 2 Peter 3.7, 10-12 is firmly established in a scriptural context that makes a first-century date much more plausible than any date *after* the turn of the century; that both Caecilius in the writing of Minucius Felix and Celsus as quoted by Origen are likely to have known 2 Peter; and that the *Octavius* belongs to the period of Justin, prior to Irenaeus and his fight against the Gnostics. We also note that the cosmic conflagration was a matter of serious, not just popular or mythological concern in antiquity,[27] something we are beginning to understand again at the end of the twentieth century.

NOTES

1   R. Riesner, 'Der zweite Petrusbrief und die Eschatologie', in G. Maier, ed., *Zukunftserwartung in biblischer Sicht, Beiträge zur ‾Eschatologie*, Wuppertal 1984, 124-43.

2   Philo discusses the ἐκπύρωσις at length in the *De aet. mund.* 19.83-103 and attacks anti-biblical concepts in *Quis rer. div. her.* 47.228.

3   Riesner gives two: (a) 1 En. 1.5ff; 1 QH 3:29-36; 6:17ff; Jub. 9:15; Hippolytus, *Philos.* 9.27; Ass. Mos. 10.2ff; Vit. Ad. 49f; (b) Deut. 32:22; Am. 7:4ff; Isa. 1:24ff; Jer. 4:4; Zeph. 1:18; 3:8. The short sentence in Hippolytus (early third century) is interesting in that it ascribes the doctrine of ἐκπύρωσις to the Essenes (9:27.3); in 9.10 he mentions Heraclitus as the earliest source. And in his Ἀπόδειξις (De Antichr.) 64, David in Ps. 18:7-8 is credited with the ἐκπύρωσις idea.

4   E.M.B. Green, *2 Peter Reconsidered*, Leicester 1961.

5   Tertullian mentions the *conflagratio universitatis* literally in passing four times: *De bapt.* 8.5; *Ad. Marc.* 3.24; *De anim.* 54.1; *De spect.*30; but not in the *Apologeticum.* The leading exponents of a pre-Tertullian date of the *Octavius*, irrespective of the *conflagratio* (which is never discussed in this context) are A. Ebert, 'Tertullians Verhältnis zu Minucius Felix. Nebst einem Anhang über Commodians Carmen Apologeticum', *Abh. d. phil.hist. Kl. der Klg. Sächs. Akad. d. Wiss.,* 12, Leipzig 1870; E. Norden, *Antike Kunstprosa*, 1909, repr. Darmstadt, 1974, 605-606; J.P. Waltzing, ed., *Octavius de Minucius Felix*, Bruges 1909; G. Quispel, 'A Jewish Source of Minucius Felix', *Vig. Chr.*3, 1949, 113-22; id., 'Anima naturaliter christiana', *Latomus* 10, 1951, 163-69; S. Rossi, 'L'Octavius fu scritto prima del 161', *Giornale italiana di filologia*12, 1959, 289-304; H. von Campenhausen, *Lateinische Kirchenväter*, Stuttgart 1960, 12,17; C. Schneider, *Geistesgeschichte der christlichen Antike*, München 1970, 441-42; J. Daniélou, *The Origins of Latin Christianity*, A History of Early Christian Doctrine before the Council of Nicea, 3; London 1977, 411.

For a post-Tertullian date see among others: A. von Harnack, *Die Chronologie der altchristlichen Literatur bis Eusebius,* Leipzig 1904, 324-30; B. Axelson, *Das Prioritätsproblem Tertullian-Minucius Felix*, Lund 1941; J. Beaujeu, ed., *Minucius Felix Octavius,* Paris 1964; H. Chadwick, *The Early Church,* Harmondsworth 1967, 93; C. Becker, *Der 'Octavius' des Minucius Felix. Heidnische Philosophie und frühchristliche Apologetik,* München 1967; B. Aland, 'Christentum, Bildung und römische Oberschicht. Zum 'Octavius' des Minucius Felix,' in H.-D. Blume and F. Mann, eds., *Platonismus und Christentum. Festschrift für Heinrich Dörrie*, Münster 1983, 11-30; E. Heck, 'Minucius Felix und der römische Staat', *Vig Chr.* 38, 1984, 154-66.

The Fathers do not appear to be unanimous: Jerome seems to place Tertullian before Minucius, in passages, however, that are not quite clear (*De vir. ill.* 53; 58; *Ep.* 48.13; 60.10; 70.5; *In Is* 8, praef.). Jerome is known for his chronological nonchalance, and there is no reason to regard him as the higher authority in this matter over against Lactantius who is adamant about the priority of Minucius.

In *Inst. Div* 5.1.21-22 he even praises the apologetic mastery of Minucius over against Tertullian's lack of eloquence. C. Schneider (see above) also takes very much the same line: 'Tertullian hat diesen Dialog vergröbert, schroffer gemacht und manchen billigen Effekt nicht verschmäht. Doch schreibt er wohl auch für viel weitere Kreise als sein Vorbild Minucius', *op.cit.*, 442.

6   There are of course many more Old Testament passages using destruction by fire as a sign of God's judgment: Ps. 97:3-4; 2 Sam. 23:7; Isa. 4:4-5; Jer. 4:4; Ezek. 38:18-23; Dan. 7:11; Am. 7:4 (cf note 2). A good witness for this interpretation of Mal. 4:1 and Isa. 30:30 is Theophilus, Πρὸς Αὐτόλυκον (*Ad Autol.*, written some time after 180, since the death of Marcus Aurelius is mentioned in 2.117-28). In 2.37 he claims that Greek poets and philosophers who mention a destruction of the world by fire had only copied the Law and the prophets; and in 2.38 he actually quotes Mal. 4:1 and Isa. 30:30 verbatim as evidence that the ancients had said the same as the prophets. Unlike Justin and Minucius, however, Theophilus, writing in Antioch, is rather aggressive in tone against the Greek philosophers.

7   Here again, 1 En. 1:8 exempts the faithful from destruction. We could add Josephus, *Ant.* 1.2.3, published in 93/94, where he informs his readers of Adam's prophecy about a destruction by fire. Cf. also the late-first-century *Vita Adae et Evae* 49.3.

8.   J.N.D. Kelly, *The Epistles of Peter and Jude*, London 1969, 361.

9   Green, *2 Peter and Jude,* 2, note 4.

10   Of the LXX passages mentioning judgment by fire, Isa. 4:4, 2 Sam. 23:7 and Dan. 7:11 are using forms of καῦσις.

11   For further discussion of the subject, particularlyof the question whether Zoroastrianism could have influenced pre-Petrine Jewish thinking, see R. Mayer, *Die biblische Vorstellung vom Weltenbrand. Eine Untersuchung über die Beziehungen zwischen Parsismus und Judentum*, Bonn 1956. Cf also J. Cahine, 'Cosmogonie aquatique et conflagration finale d'après la *secunda Petri*', *RB* 46, 1937, 207-16.

12   'Εὑρεθήσεται in 2 Pet. iii.10', *ExpT* 32, 1920-21, 44-45.

13   *Jude, 2 Peter*, Word Bib Comm, 50, Waco, 1983, 319-21.

14   Prior to Justin, 2 Clem. 3:16 and Hermas, *Vis.* 4.4.3b, refer to a cosmic conflagration. 2 Clem. quotes Mal. 4:1 and 2 Pet. 3:12 and implicitly interprets the passage in favour of the disputed εὑρεθήσεται (see above, III). Hermas says that this world must be destroyed by blood and fire, which may or may not be an evaluation of 2 Pet. 3 - Hermas's acquaintance with 2 Peter becomes obvious, however, in the very next verse, where he alludes to 2 Pet. 2:20, and later in *Sim.* 8.11.1, where he refers to 2 Pet. 3:9. Although 2 Clem.

was probably written in the mid-second century, we can hardly use it in the context of a Roman ἐκπύρωσις-debate: it is more doubtful (*pace* Harnack and Bauckham) that 2 Clem. was ever connected with Rome before the fourth century; we have to reckon with an Egyptian origin (cf K. Wengst, *Schriften des Urchristentums, Zweiter Teil*, Darmstadt 1984, 227. And even if we assume its existence in mid-second-century Rome, the actual passage 16.3 gives us only an excerpt from Peter's prophecy and could not be the source of information behind the texts under discussion in this essay. The same applies to the half-sentence in Hermas, in spite of its early date and Roman origin.

15   For a man like Justin, at home in Greek philosophy, the (extant) references would have been: Heracl. Fr. 626, Chrysipp. Fr. 809, Cleanthes, Fr. 522 (cf *TDNT*, VI, 930-31.

16   For a discussion of this question, see H. Windisch, *Die Orakel des Hystaspes*, Verh. d. Koninkl. Akad. van Wetenschapen Amsterdam, Afd. Letterk., n.r. XXVIII, No. 3; Amsterdam 1929, here 26-40.

17   For Justin's attitude towards Greek philosophy, see H. Chadwick, *Early Christian Thought and the Classical Tradition*, Oxford 1966; repr. 1984, 9-23. Justin's disciple, Tatian, launches a heavy attack against the Greeks and mentions the ἐκπύρωσις in *Orat. ad Graec.* 25.2.

18   His teacher, Clement of Alexandria, quotes two excerpts from a tragedy in Pseudo-Sophocles, a post-Petrine, Jewish-Hellenistic writer, in *Strom.* 5.14,121.4-122.1; the flame from the aether will devour everything on earth and in heaven, but God will later save everything he had previously destroyed. See also 5.1.9.4-5.

19   Cf H. Chadwick, ed., *Origen, contra Celsum*, Cambridge 1965, note *ad loc.*

20   Melito of Sardis, who has the same sequence in his *Apology*, is almost certainly later than Celsus. This text, extant only in a Syriac version, is not an apology proper, but an *oratio*. It is commonly thought to be pseudepigraphic, in spite of the spirited defence of it by H. Ewald, *Göttingsche Gelehrte Anzeigen*, 1856, I, 655-59, in a review of the Syriac edition in W. Cureton's *Specilegium Syriacum*, London, 1855. Ewald proposed that this Syriac *oratio* is the text alluded to by Eusebius in *H.E.* 4.26.2 under the title of περὶ ἀληθείας. Harnack, *Die Überlieferung und der Bestand der altchristlichen Literatur bei Eusebius*, Leipzig 1893, 251, who thinks it is pseudepigraphic, nonetheless dates it to the first third of the third century: 'sie kann aber auch älter sein'. Since we have to assume that Syriac was its original language, its reception by Celsius, Minucius, *et al.* would appear to be unlikely, even if it were chronologically possible. However, the central conflagrational passage deserves quoting, as it highlights Melito's acceptance and

interpretation of 2 Peter 3: 'There once was a flood of water, and all men and animals perished in the mass of water, and the just ones were saved in the Ark (...). And likewise in the last days there will be a flood of fire, and the earth will þurn with its mountains, and men will burn with their idols which they had made and their scriptures which they worship, and the sea will burn with its islands, and the just will be delivered from its wrath as their fellows were saved from the waters of the deluge in the Ark(...)' (transl. from the Latin version on J.C. Th von Otto, *Corpus Apologeticarum Christianorum saeculi secundi*, IX, Jena 1872, 432.

21   Caecilius does not hesitate to call for the extermination of the Christians, 9.1; 'eruenda prorsus haec et exsecranda consensio'.

22   *Minucius Felix Octavius texte établi et traduit par J. Beaujeu,* Paris 1966, *ad loc.*; quoting M. Pellegrino 1, *Minucius Felix Octavius*, Turin 1947, *ad loc.*, with a reference to 2 Peter. Cf also J. Daniélou, *The Origins of Latin Christianity*, London 1977, 205.

23   Not that Octavius is always as reticent: in his refutation of Greek resurrection myths, 34.6-35.6, he actually says of Plato's *Phaidon* 82a, 'sed mimi convicio digni ista sententia est' (34.7).

24   We may, however, have a direct quotation from the *oratio* in 9.6-7.

25   G.W. Bowersock, 'The Date of Fronto's Death', in his *Greek Sophists in the Roman Empire*, Oxford, 1969, 124-26, tries to vindicate Th. Mommsen's position that Fronto must have died in 176 or after, as his reference in *De oratioribus* to a 'nummus Commodi' must mean the *nummus* struck for Emperor Commodus in 176. That it could allude to L. Verus, who was also called Commodus, that a *nummus* could in fact describe the medallion struck for him in 166, and that the lack of any correspondence safely datable after 166 must be taken seriously, has been held against this point of view; cf among others M.J.P. van den Hout , ed., *M. Cornelii Frontonis Epistulae*, Leiden, 1954, I, 242-43, and C.R. Haines, ed., *The Correspondence of Marcus Cornelius Fronto*, London, New York 1920, II, 282-84.

26   S. Rossi (cf note 4) has offered the most detailed argumentation for a date prior to 161, taking 18.7, the passage that appears to have been written prior to the diumvirate of L. Verus and Marcus Aurelius, as his starting point. He has since analysed further aspects of the text, such as the allusion to the Mithras cult in 31.3-4 in comparison with similar passages in Tertullian and Justin ('Minucio, Giustino e Tertulliano nei loro rapporti col culto di Mitra', *Giornale italiano di filologia* 16, 1963, 16-29, leading him to claim that the *Octavius* must have been written earlier than Justin's first *Apology*. An analysis of the *feriae* in 2.3-4 points in the same direction ('Feriae Vindemiales e Feriae iudiciariae a Roma (a proposito dell' *Octavius* di Minucio Felice)', *Giornale italiano de filologia* 15, 1962, 193-224). The laek of any reference to liturgical forms of a

Christian cult in 19.14.15 is another of his arguments for an early date ('Ancora sull' *Octavius* di Minucio Felice', *Giornale italiano di filologia* 16, 1963, 293-313). He sums his positions up as follows: 'Tenendo poi conto di ciò che s'è detto nei rignardi di Minucio e di Giustino, e considerando le nuove ed inoppugnabili prove addotte nei nostri studi precedenti, riteniano di potera legittimamente assegnare al decennio 140-150 l'ambientazione e la stesura dell' opera' (*op. cit.* 313). It should also be pointed out that none of the other - thus apparently later - Christian apologetes, such as Tertullian, refers to Fronto's anti-Christian diatribe again. By their time, it had lost the topical interest it had had for Minucius Felix.

27   One later Christian author should be added here - Commodianus. Commodianus, hitherto assigned to the third, fourth or fifth century, but increasingly likely to have been an early third-century if not late second-century author (cf the discussion in Daniélou, *The Origins of Latin Christianity*, London 1977, 100), treats the subject in two poems of his *Carmen Apologeticum*, 'De saeculi istius fine', *C.A.* 1.43 (2.2), and 'De die iudicii', *C.A.* 1.45 (2.4). Both are based on known Old Testament passages, contain obvious reference to 2 Peter 3, and parallels to Melito, on a background of millenarian thinking: e.g. *De saec. ist. fine*, 9-14:

> In flamma ignis Dominus iudicabit iniquos:
> Iustos autem non tanget ignis, sed immo delinget.
> Sub uno morantur, sed pars in sententia flebit.
> Tantus erit ardor, ut lapides ipsi liquiescant,
> In flumine cogunt venti, furet ira caelestis,
> Ut, quacumque fugit, impius occupetur ab igne.

and *id.,* 16-19:

> Flamma tamen gentis media partiturque servans,
> In annis mille ut ferant corpora sanctis.
> Nam inde post annos mille gehenneae traduntur,
> Et fabrica cuius erant cum ipsa cremantur.

Or *De die iudicii*, perhaps even more impressive:

> De die iudicii propter incredulos addo:
> Emissus iterum Dei do(mi)nabitur ignis;
> Dat gemitum terra rerum tunc in ultima fine,
> In ter(r)a gentes ut tunc incredulae cunctae;
> Evitat et tamen sanctorum castra suorum.
> In una flamma convertit tota natura,
> Uritur ab imis terra montesque liquiescunt,
> De mare nihil remanet, vincetur ab igne potente,
> Interit hoc caelum et ista terra mutatur.
> Componitur alia novitas caeli, terrae perennis.

Inde qui mereunt mittuntur in morte secunda,
Interius autem habitaculis iusti locantur.

For text see J. Martin, ed., *Commodiani Carmina*, Corpus Christianorum, series latina, 78; Tournhout 1950.

The strange and polemical attempt to link 2 Peter 3:7, 10-12 with a conflagrational text from Nag Hammadi (H.M. Schenke and K.-M. Fischer, *Einleitung in die Schriften des Neuen Testaments*, Gütersloh 1979, II, 325), however, is doomed to failure: the text incorrectly referred to by Schenke and Fischer, *NHC* 2.5 97.24-127.17 (here: 125-127), 'On the Origin of the World', dates from the late third/early fourth century and is a document of late Gnosticism that is too remote to be connected with 2 Peter in any meaningful way. (For the Coptic text see A. Böhlig and P. Labib, *Die koptisch-gnostiche Schrift ohne Titel aus Codex II von Nag Hammadi*, Berlin 1962, 107 (the ref. here is 174.6-35); cf M. Meyer, ed., *The Nag Hammadi Library in English*, Leiden, 1977, 178-79.

11

A Critic of the Critics: Dorothy L. Sayers and New Testament Research

Some people may believe that we have demythologized our world, but myths abound wherever one looks. There is the 'myth' of Europe, the 'myth' of German re-unification, and, closer to our own fields of study, the 'myth' of interdisciplinary research and debate. Needless to say, there are true Europeans, and fervent bridge-builders between 'East' and 'West' Germany, and even whole institutes dedicated to joint ventures of the arts and sciences - such as my own institute in Paderborn. Yet despite these attempts at co-operation between scientists and other academics, C.P. Snow's 'two cultures' - a term coined decades ago - have still not been reconciled.

New Testament research is a 'culture' in its own right, and by definition, it should also be the epitome of interdisciplinary work. For, to do it properly, you should be a classical philologist, a hebraist, a papyrologist, a textual critic, a historian, an archaeologist, and a few other things besides. Some people, by the vagaries of their academic endeavours, are qualified in more than one of these areas. One of the leading British theologians of the younger generation, Alister McGrath of Oxford, was a biologist with a doctoral degree before he took up theology - challenge him on the question whether Jesus really and physically died on the cross, and you will get an expert answer no mere New Testament critics could provide. Or, on a more personal note, I myself have been trained as an historian, literary critic and papyrologist and, by virtue of being a trained and licensed 'Reader' in the Church of England, I am also a qualified theologian of sorts - more of a strain than a strength, of course, for sometimes, one might be tempted, tongue in cheek, to set up a few mirrors in front of one's desk to do one's interdisciplinary research with oneself. Yet even doing it with others has been known to lead to the occasional identity crisis. New Testament critics are not known to accept the opinion of outsiders, and when you tell them that, for example, as far as the textual tradition of the documents is concerned, they should listen to people whose daily work it is to study them comparatively, not just within the closed world of New Testament documents, their eyes tend to glaze over. The ongoing debate about Greek New Testament papyri among the Dead Sea Scrolls is a case in point. Papyrologists and classical philologists all over the world have stated that there is, in Qumran Cave 7, a Greek papyrus fragment belonging to the Gospel of Mark, to be dated to about AD 50. With a handful of exceptions, New Testament critics have so far refused to accept this analysis. To them, the detailed research into one tiny item must not override the generally received and pre-conceived knowledge (so-called) that the Gospel of Mark cannot have been written that early, and that there cannot have been a Christian text among the Essene documents at Qumran, anyway.

I shall not bore you with the 'Documents in the Case', but you will have noticed that we have reached the point where Dorothy L. Sayers makes her entry. For not only was she, too, a rank outsider while being a true and acknowledged expert in a field necessary for New Testament studies - that of literary history - but she also tackled the question of sources: Who wrote them and when, and how reliable are they?

Her Oxford-trained mind had given her the scope to study and penetrate aspects of church history and classical textual criticism for stage plays like *The Zeal of the House*, 1937, and *The Emperor Constantine*, 1951, or for radio plays like *He That Should Come*, 1938, and *The Man Born to be King*, 1940. Even in her play on the threadbare German legend of Dr Faustus, *The Devil to Pay*, 1939, her theological insights are vastly superior to those of, say, Christopher Marlowe or Johann Wolfgang von Goethe; and *The Just Vengeance* of 1946 could not have been written without a profound knowledge of medieval and modern theology and doctrine. It is, however, to two of her works in particular that I want to turn for a closer description of her attitude towards New Testament criticism, of the type which used to be called 'lower criticism', or, equally misleadingly in German, *Einleitungswissenschaft*.

I am referring to the twenty-four page introduction to the printed version of her series of radio plays, *The Man Born to be King*, and to her essay 'A Vote of Thanks to Cyrus'. The latter is part of her collection of essays *Unpopular Opinions* of 1946. The copy I own is the second impression of 1951, subtitled 'First Cheap Edition', and I got it for four shillings and sixpence in 1976. Unpopular opinions do not come that cheap any more, but there was a price to pay even then: the price of ignoring the substance of what Dorothy L. Sayers wrote. Whole shelves particularly of learned German *Einleitungswissenschaft* would have looked different had Karl Barth decided to translate, rather than 'The Greatest Drama Ever Staged' (*Das größte Drama aller Zeiten*) or 'The Triumph of Easter' (*Der Triumph von Ostern*), her introduction to *The Man Born to be King* and 'A Vote of Thanks to Cyrus', and had he put his authority behind the opinions expressed in them. But then of course, Karl Barth would not have dreamed of doing so. In his introduction to the edition of his translations, Barth speaks of '*bemerkenswerte historische Studien und auch spekulative Erwägungen*' ('remarkable historical studies and speculative considerations as well') and notes '*daß sie sich die Aussagen des Evangeliums in atemlosen Erstaunen über ihren zentralen Gehalt schwungvoll zu eigen gemacht*' ('that she zestfully adopted the statements of the gospel in breathless astonishment at their central content') and one feels that his interest in her doctrinal essays was probably mitigated by a mild irony towards her historical position. Just in passing, he also accuses her of mild bouts of semipelagianism which he thinks were due to the influence of Erasmus on English Christianity.

Barth's conscious indifference towards her historical and textual-critical position was of course typical of the brotherhood. In all fairness, though, it must be kept in mind that *The Man Born to be King* with its introduction was first published in 1943, at a time when, to put it mildly, no German theologian was encouraged to obtain, study and publicly debate the work of a British author. Even Karl Barth, a Swiss who had by then returned to Switzerland from his German professorship, delayed the publication of his translations for - well, let's say diplomatic reasons. When the *Unpopular Opinions* were published in 1946, Rudolf Bultmann's school of demythologization, begun during the war with his *Offenbarung und Heilsgeschehen*, had reached public attention. Taking the New Testament seriously as authentic historical information, written down by eyewitnesses and investigative historians living as real people in a real world within a generation or two of the events they recorded - that had become well-nigh impossible in respectable circles. Thus, there was no audience for Dorothy L. Sayers the critics' critic in post-war Germany. In fact, my translation of 'A Vote of Thanks for Cyrus', published by Manfred Siebald in a collection of her essays, is the first German translation ever. In Britain (needless to say) the reception granted to her critical contributions was more positive, if only in the sense that there always is a market for idiosyncratic attitudes in yon merry Albion. But let us look at her own words, and I must ask you to bear with me for a few minutes while I quote from her introduction to *The Man Born to be King*:

The Man Born to be King, London 1943, Author's Introduction:

> God was executed by people painfully like us, in a society very similar to our own - in the over-ripeness of the most splendid and sophisticated Empire the world has ever seen. In a nation famous for its religious genius and under a government famed for its efficiency. He was executed by a corrupt church, a timid politician, and a fickle proletariat led by professional agitators. His executioners made vulgar jokes about Him, called Him filthy names, taunted Him, smacked Him in the face, flogged Him with the cat, and hanged Him on the common gibbet - a bloody, dusty, sweaty, and sordid business.

> If you show people that, they are shocked. So they should be. If that does not shock them, nothing can. If the mere representation of it has an air of irreverence, what is to be said about the deed? It is curious that people who are filled with horrified indignation whenever a cat kills a sparrow can hear that story of the killing of God told Sunday after Sunday and not experience any shock at all.

Technically, the swiftest way to produce the desirable sense of shock is the use in drama of modern speech and a determined historical realism about the characters. Herod the Great was no monstrous enemy of God: he was a soldier of fortune and a political genius - a savage but capable autocrat, whose jealousy and ungovernable temper had involved him in a prolonged domestic wretchedness. Matthew the Publican was a contemptible little quisling official, fleecing his own countrymen in the service of the occupying power and enriching himself in the process, until something came to change his heart (though not, presumably, his social status or his pronunciation). Pontius Pilate was a provincial governor, with a very proper desire to carry out Imperial justice, but terrified (as better men than he have been before and since) of questions in the House, commissions of inquiry and what may generically be called 'Whitehall'. Caiaphas was the ecclesiastical politician, appointed, like one of Hitler's bishops, by a heathen government, expressly that he might collaborate with the New Order and see that the Church toed the line drawn by the State; we have seen something of Caiaphas lately. As for the Elders of the Synagogue, they are to be found on every Parish Council - always highly respectable, often quarrelsome, and sometimes in a crucifying mood.

So with all of them. Tear off the disguise of the Jacobean idiom, go back to the homely and vigorous Greek of Mark or John, translate it into its current English counterpart: and there every man may see his own face. (p.23)

Which brings us to the records themselves.

They were not compiled by modern historians, nor yet (needless to say) with an eye to the convenience of a radio-dramatist some nineteen centuries later. The Evangelists, particularly the Synoptists, are concerned to write down what Jesus said and did; not to provide 'local colour' (which their readers knew all about) or sketches of contemporary personalities. Nor are they as much interested as we should be in a precise chronology - except, of course, as regards Holy Week. That was the important date, and there they are substantially united about the outline of events. St Luke also takes a good deal of pains to fix the birth-date. But between these points, as Archbishop Temple has pointed out,[1] only St John has any real chronology at all. Frequently the material seems to have been arranged according to subject-matter rather than to the logical or chronological succession of events. (pp.28-29)

With the discourses and public disputations, the case is different.

Most of these, such as the great passage about the Bread of Heaven, the dispute at the Feast of Tabernacles, and the long discourse and prayer after the Last Supper, we owe to St John, and their style is so unlike that of the parables and sayings that some people have found it hard to believe that they were spoken by the same person, and that St John did not invent them out of his own meditations. But the difficulty is more apparent than real. It must be remembered that, of the four Evangels, St John's is the only one that claims to be the direct report of an eye-witness. And to anyone accustomed to the imaginative handling of documents, the internal evidence bears out this claim. The Synoptists, on the whole, report the 'set-pieces'; it is St John who reports the words and actions of the individual, unrepeated occasion, retrieving them from that storehouse of trained memory which, among people not made forgetful by too much pen and ink, replaces the filed records and the stenographer's note book. It is, generally speaking, John who knows the time of year, the time of day, where people sat, and how they got from one place to another. It is John who remembers, not only what Jesus said, but what the other people said to him, who can reproduce the cut-and-thrust of controversy, and the development of an argument. It is John who faithfully reproduces the emphasis and repetition of a teacher trying to get a new idea across to a rather unintelligent and inattentive audience. It is he again who has caught the characteristic tricks of manner and delivery - the curious outflanking movement of the dialectic, capturing outpost after outpost by apparently irrelevant questions, and then suddenly pouncing upon the main position from the rear; and the amen, amen, lego hymin ('indeed and indeed I tell you') which ushers in the most important statements.[2]

Indeed, when John is the authority for any scene, or when John's account is at hand to supplement those of the Synoptists, the playwright's task is easy. Either the dialogue is all there - vivid and personal on both sides or the part of the interlocutor can be readily reconstructed from the replies given. And it is frequently John who supplies the reason and meaning for actions and speeches that in the Synoptists appear quite unexplained and disconnected. Thus, after the Feeding of the Five Thousand, there seems to be no very good reason why Jesus should have withdrawn Himself and sent the disciples across the lake by themselves; but John supplies the missing motive, and also the answer to one or two other practical questions, e.g. how the disciples were able to see Jesus coming across the water (it was near Passover, therefore the moon was full) and how some of 'the multitudes' turned up next day at Capernaum (they followed as soon as the boats had put across from Tiberias to fetch them). It is John who gives us that dramatic moment when Pilate, suddenly deciding not to ratify the sentence of the Sanhedrin without enquiry, disconcerts the priestly party with the formal invitation to state their case ('What accusation bring ye against this man?'), thus leading up to the question, 'Art thou the King of the Jews?' which, in the Synoptists, is launched without preliminary and without any explanation of how so fantastic an idea could ever have entered Pilate's head.[3] It is John who knows that, at the Last Supper, he and Judas were seated so close to Jesus as to permit of whispered conversation and the handing of the sop; John also, and John only, who knows about the interrogation before Annas, thus clearing up the where and how of Peter's denial, and explaining how it was that the Lord could 'turn and look upon Peter' as He was led through the courtyard of the High Priest's house to his trial before the Sanhedrin.[4]

All through, in fact, the Gospel of St John reads like the narrative of an eye-witness filling up the gaps in matter already published, correcting occasional errors, and adding material which previous writers either had not remembered or did not know about. Usually, he passes briefly over events that were already adequately dealt with and stories which everybody knew by heart; sometimes he omits them altogether: the Birth-story, for example, the Temptation, the Parables, the words of the Eucharistic Institution. There is no reason to suppose that a thing is inauthentic because he does not mention it, or, on the other hand, because nobody else mentions it. In modern memoirs written by real people about another real person we should expect just that sort of diversity which we find in the Gospels. If it surprises us there, it is perhaps because we have fallen out of the habit of looking on Jesus and His disciples as really real people. (pp.33-35)

The playwright, in any case, is not concerned, like the textual critic, to establish one version of a story as the older, purer or sole authoritative version. He does not want to select and reject, but to harmonize. Where the two versions are really incompatible (as in St Mark's and St John's dates for the Cleansing of the Temple), he must, of course, choose one or the other. But what he really likes is to take three or four accounts of the same incident, differing in detail, and to dovetail all these details so that the combined narrative presents a more convincing and dramatic picture than any of the accounts taken separately. And in doing this, he is often surprised to find how many apparent contradictions turn out not to be contradictory at all, but merely supplementary. Take, for example, the various accounts of the Resurrection appearances at the Sepulchre. The divergences appear very great at first sight; and much ink and acrimony have been expended on proving that certain of the stories are not 'original' or 'authentic', but accretions grafted upon the firsthand reports by the pious imagination of Christians. Well, it may be so. But the fact remains that all of them, without exception, can be made to fall into place in a single orderly and coherent narrative without the smallest contradiction or difficulty, and without any suppression, invention, or manipulation, beyond a trifling effort to imagine the natural behaviour of a bunch of startled people running about in the dawnlight between Jerusalem and the Garden. (p.35)

A few pages further on, she names some of her sources, Archbishop Temple's *Readings in St John's Gospel* and Frank Morison's enduring bestseller *Who Moved the Stone?* among them. But it is quite obvious that she did her own thinking, and we discover at least three strands that have been extremely unfashionable for a very long time - strands that were unfashionable even when she wrote, and still are in most circles today: first, the socio-topographical world of Jesus and the Disciples and its accurate portrayal in the gospels; second, the priority of John in the sense of its chronological and historiographical reliability; and third, the mere idea of a possibility of harmonizing the gospel accounts.

In Germany as well as in Britain, the study of the social phenomenon of the world of Jesus and his followers was made popular by Gerd Theissen of Heidelberg University, whose academic monographs were supplemented by the cleverly devised epistolary bestseller *The Shadow of the Galilean* of 1986. Other, more conservative scholars like Rainer Riesner of Tübingen, Howard Marshall of Aberdeen and Richard T. France of Oxford have contributed recent studies which underline Dorothy L. Sayer's position. It is slowly, but inevitably, becoming ever more obvious that the gospels are generally trustworthy and accurate in their portrayal of contemporary customs, attitudes, people and places. Funnily enough, even recent 'Qumran' bestsellers such as Baigent and Leigh's *The Dead Sea Scrolls Deception* or Barbara Thiering's *Jesus the Man*, ridiculous as they are, have inadvertently contributed to a better understanding of our sources - for even scholars who would not normally defend the historicity of the New Testament have felt obliged to state publicly that such pseudo-investigative inventions as are offered by that lot cannot in the least be reconciled with the existing evidence. Dorothy L. Sayers, who never comments on the Dead Sea Scrolls even though the first of them were published nine years before her death, would today have been reminded of something she wrote at the end of her introduction to the radio plays. There she comments on the opposition to her play by people who felt it inappropriate to put Christ on stage or to let an actor playing his role speak His very Gospel words as though he actually was Christ, or to use the modern English vernacular instead of the venerable, sacred language of the 'Authorized Version'. She writes:

> These doughty innocents secured for us a large increase in our adult audience and thus enabled the political and theological issues in the most important part of the story to be treated with more breadth and pungency than might otherwise have seemed justifiable. Their beneficence is none the less real for having been unintentional.

Her second tenet, the superiority, as it were, of the Gospel of St John, was a courageous position to take up. Only five years before she wrote *The Man Born to be King*, it was possible to regard John's Gospel as a mid-to-late second century work influenced by post-apostolic hellenism, and far removed from anything historically reliable. The discovery and publication of papyrus p^{52} (or John Rylands 457) in 1935 changed this view for good: here was a Greek papyrus fragment from a codex which preserved parts of chapter 18 of the gospel on both sides; and for palaeographical reasons, it had to be dated to the first quarter of the second century. Since it was a copy found in Egypt, the original gospel itself had to be earlier still, and hence one arrived at the commonly accepted date of c. 100 at the latest for the completion of that gospel.

No problem for an 'octogenarian divine', as Dorothy L. Sayers calls the gospel author in her essay 'A Vote of Thanks to Cyrus', to write his eyewitness account himself, with the help of his trusted friend, John the Elder, at such a late - or should we rather say early? - date. But the real audacity in her position is to be seen in the unequivocal clarity with which she regards John's gospel as the document of an eyewitness belonging to the innermost circle of Jesus. As late as 1984, none other than John A.T. Robinson - the very John A.T. Robinson who had shocked the fraternity twice before, first by his *Honest to God*, then by *Redating the New Testament* - provided the detailed arguments for Dorothy L. Sayer's position. 'The Priority of John' was the title given to his Bampton Lectures, published posthumously in 1985. In the published version, their 443 pages bristle with material shaking up the scholarly consensus and underlining the first-hand authenticity of this gospel. Others have followed his path, and there now is a considerable literature opting for what Dorothy L. Sayers used as a starting point for her radio plays.

In brackets, I should like to add that the actual dates of the gospels were of minor importance to her. As I said, she does not see a comparatively late date, such as just prior to AD 100, as an explicit or implicit argument against the historicity of the accounts. She knew, of course, that a report written at a later stage, say, some fifty or sixty years after the event, could well be more accurate, more objective than one written down under the immediate impact of what had just taken place.

Were it otherwise, no eyewitness accounts of the rise of Nazism or the Dambusters Raid or what have you could be gathered and published today. Dorothy L. Sayers would probably not have been surprised to see John Robinson arguing convincingly for a date of pre-AD 70 for John's gospel. But to place it that early was certainly not necessary for her own kind of argument.

What about her third strand then, harmonization? This is arguably unpopular, even though it has been tried again and again throughout the history of the church. Indeed, she does know that there appear to be incidents where harmonization in the usual sense of the word is ruled out. She names one herself - the chronology of the Cleansing of the Temple in John over against that in Mark. Or to give just one more example, the healing of the centurion's servant in Capernaum. Did the centurion come to Jesus himself (Matthew 8:5 ff) or did he merely send the elders of the Jews (Luke 7:1 ff)? Did Jesus go (Luke), or did he work a long-distance miracle (Matthew)? But, as Dorothy L. Sayers must have sensed when she advocated the general feasibility of harmonization, solutions may still be found of which we are, as yet, completely unaware. For example, the chronological differences between the Passion Week accounts of John and the Synoptics have been solved by the discovery of the Essene Calendar among the Dead Sea Scrolls in Cave 4. We now know that there were three different calendars in use at the time, the Roman one, the official moon calendar of the Temple and the Sadducees, and the sun calendar of the Essenes. Mark, followed by the other Synoptics, but not by John, clearly used the Essene sun calendar. Such variations of choice may have been influenced by their different target groups or personal backgrounds; but whatever the reason, it is a question which irritated generations of readers and critics and which can now be answered satisfactorily.

As another aside, it may be interesting to note that Sayer's insights into the dramatic structure of John's gospel have recently been supplemented by archaeological excavations and surveys. We can show that there were theatres all over Galilee, Judaea, Samaria, and in Jerusalem. One of them, the theatre of Sepphoris in Galilee, was actually built while Jesus was living a mere four miles away in Nazareth. It has been suggested that

Jesus and Joseph, whose New Testament 'job description' *tekton* does not mean carpenter, but builder and even architect (*archi-tekton*), would have been involved in the construction of the theatre, and that Jesus picked up some of his vocabulary, such as 'hypocrites', which literally means 'actors', or his quotation from Aeschylos in Acts 26:14 (talking to Paul on the road to Damascus) while watching plays at Sepphoris as a young man, eager to imbibe the culture of the people he was to address with his message only a few years later.

As for Mark, G.G. Bilezikian, in his *The Liberated Gospel - a Comparison of the Gospel of Mark and Greek Tragedy* (1977), tried to demonstrate that this gospel is constructed like a Greek tragedy. Mark, too, could easily have been influenced by the culture of the theatre in Roman Palestine, or he may have studied its structure years later in Rome, where he wrote his gospel. With her dramatist's eye, what Dorothy L. Sayers realized, almost instinctively, is being borne out by recent interdisciplinary research. 'A Vote of Thanks to Cyrus' of 1946 continues the line of constructive criticism exemplified in *The Man Born to be King*. The basic argument is simple enough: Cyrus the Persian and Ahasverus or Xerxes may be Bible people, but contrary to pseudo-enlightened popular opinion, that does not make them legendary people. They are also people straight from Herodotus, the Greek historian, and thus, they demonstrate, to quote Sayers, 'that history was all of a piece'. The critique behind this observation is simple yet far-reaching. There is a tendency today, not least among New Testament critics, to regard nonbiblical sources as more reliable than biblical ones. To go back to the New Testament; if Josephus contradicts or appears to contradict Luke, as for example in the dating of incidents surrounding Theudas (Acts 5:36), credence is given to Josephus. Or, since Herod's infanticide at Bethlehem is not mentioned by Josephus, it cannot have taken place. If historical events, such as the census of Quirinus, are not mentioned outside the New Testament, they are disregarded as non-historical - not by historians, but by New Testament scholars. And so on, *ad nauseam*. Never mind that historians and archaeologists have shown time and again that the data of the gospels can be trusted even if there is no corroborative evidence elsewhere, never mind that it has been shown that Caesar's crossing of the Rubicon or countless details of his campaigns in Gaul are unsupported propaganda - Caesar's writings are history, Luke's, or Mark's, or John's are pious eulogies. Dorothy L. Sayers cut through this unscholarly prejudice by doing what she had learned to do as a student of literary history at Oxford - by taking her sources seriously as documents of their time, with all that this entails. Let me end by quoting from 'A Vote of Thanks for Cyrus' (in *Unpopular Opinions*, London 1951, 23-28):

> How much more readily we may accept discrepancies and additions when once we have rid ourselves of that notion 'the earlier, the purer', which, however plausible in the case of folk lore, is entirely irrelevant when it comes to 'real' biography. Indeed, the first 'Life' of any celebrity is nowadays accepted as an interim document. For considered appreciation we must wait until many contemporaries have gone to where rumour cannot distress them, until grief and passion have died down, until emotion can be remembered in tranquillity.

> It is rather unfortunate that the 'Higher Criticism' was first undertaken at a time when all textual criticism tended to be destructive - when the body of Homer was being torn into fragments, the Arthurian romance reduced to its Celtic elements, and the 'authority' of manuscripts established by a mechanical system of verbal agreements. The great secular scholars have already recanted and adopted the slogan of the great archaeologist Didron: 'Preserve all you can; restore seldom; never reconstruct.' When it came to the Bible, the spirit of destruction was the more gleefully iconoclastic because of the conservative extravagances of the 'verbal inspiration' theory. But the root of the trouble is to be found, I suspect (as usual), in the collapse of dogma. Christ, even for Christians, is not quite 'really' real - not altogether human - and the taint of unreality has spread to His disciples and friends and to his biographers: they are not 'real' writers, but just 'Bible' writers. John and Matthew and Luke and Mark, some or all of them, disagree about the occasion on which a parable was told or an epigram uttered. One or all must therefore be a liar or untrustworthy, because Christ (not being quite real) must have made every remark once and once only. He could not, of course, like a real teacher, have used the same illustration twice, or found it necessary to hammer

the same point home twenty times over, as one does when addressing audiences of real people and not of 'Bible' characters. (pp.27-28)

'The synthesis of history and the confutation of heresy' - this, in fact, is the legacy of Dorothy L. Sayers as the critics' critic. She would, I suppose, be quite disappointed to see - in her terminology - a heretic as (former) Regius Professor of Divinity at Oxford, and another one as former Bishop of Durham. But she would be delighted to see many among today's younger generation of scholars learning the lessons she had learned when she researched her plays and essays.

NOTES

1   *Readings in St John's Gospel*: Introduction. [D.L.S]

2   The same trick of speech, reduced to a single 'amen', is found in all the synoptists: John certainly did not invent it, though his version is more picturesque and individual. We also have the rather unexpected appearance in Matt. XI.27 of a sentence so exactly in John's style that it might have come direct from one of the Johanine discourses. [D.L.S.]

3   For a more detailed discussion of this point, see Frank Morison: *Who moved the Stone?* [D.L.S.]

4   Mark and Matthew place Peter's denial during and after the trial before Caiaphas in the Sanhedrin. Then they both start off again to mention a fresh 'consultation', at the end of which Jesus is condemned, bound, and taken away. That is, they both seem to know that there were in fact two enquiries, though they do not say why. John straightens out this confusion and gets the events into their right order, besides explaining the simultaneous existence in Jerusalem of two 'High Priests' - Annas (High Priest 'Emeritus', appointed by the Jews in the usual way and deposed by Rome), and Caiaphas (the 'collaborating' ecclesiastic set up by Rome in his place). His narrative is perfectly lucid, though it may not seem so at first sight, owing to his confusing habit of communicating vital information in a parenthesis (John VIII 24 - cf the style of John VI 22-23, XI.2 and XVIII 13-14). [D.L.S.]

12
Dating Ancient Manuscripts: Why We Need to Work Together

Like most academic endeavours papyrology operates as an independent discipline with its own techniques, literature and history, and it is taught as such at colleges and universities. Yet whilst papyrologists can be jealous of their territory, there exists in the minds of most exponents, an awareness of the considerable benefits to be had from working in conjunction with other disciplines such as Ancient History, Classics and Theology. Operating as an ancillary science papyrology can provide scholars working in these areas with written records and safe reliable sources.

Given the above, and given the distinctive nature of many of the techniques used by papyrologists, the interface between papyrology and other subjects provides a particularly good example of the benefits and pitfalls to emerge from this kind of interdisciplinary work. For it is a sad fact that whilst the potential for genuine cooperation exists, particularly in the area of complementary working methods, it has not been entirely fulfilled, and the actual record of interdisciplinary cooperation is much less impressive than all parties may have hoped for[1]. In what follows I will attempt to map out what I believe is possible, and what could be achieved, using one of the most contentious areas for cooperation - the dating of ancient manuscripts.

The most common method used for dating ancient manuscripts employs a technique called 'Comparative Palaeography'. Basically this technique involves taking a manuscript for which one has some rough parameters regarding its date and origins, comparing it with other documents which would appear to be similar and which have been more fully dated, and thus arriving at a more precise date for the original document.[2] The closer the general type and appearance of the writing in the test document is to the benchmark document, the more certain we can be of its likely date and origin.

These benchmark manuscripts may well contain internal evidence which can enable them to be more firmly dated. For example a petition, which was later amended by a significant deletion to be a *Damnatio Memoriae* of Emperor Geta who was murdered on either the 19th or 26th of December AD 211, can be confidently dated to 28.10.211, as it contains the line, 'On the 30th Phaophi in the 20th year of Imperatores Caesores Lucius Septimus Severus Pius Pertinax Arabicus Adiabenicus Parthicus Maximus, and Marcus Aurelius Antoninus Pius, both Augusti and Publius Septimus Geta, Caesar Augustus'.

If one wishes to compare a document to this manuscript, or to another manuscript of a similarly certain date of composition, then as we have stated above there are key conditions which must apply. However the problem for palaeographic comparison does not lie with comparisons between documents such as that above and other test documents. Far more serious is the uncritical confidence with which some practitioners of the current palaeographic dating method date test documents by reference to other documents of much less certain attribution than the Greeting to Geta above.[3] Clearly we do not live in a perfect world, and the peoples of the ancient world did not arrange their affairs for our convenience. We will not always have perfect benchmark documents on which to base our decisions.

Yet in allowing for this we must not lose sight of the tenuousness of our grasp.

When using such materials one must continually justify what it is that one is doing, lest one fall into the pit identified by the theologian Austin Farrar who warned of the dangers inherent in connection with dating historical texts: 'The datings ... are like a row of revellers going home linking arms; everyone is kept upright by the others, and no-one has solid ground under his feet. The whole row can lurch on for another five years without colliding with a solid obstacle.'[4]

Working with documents for which there is external evidence for their dating is always a safer procedure, than working on the basis of comparative palaeography alone. Examples of such manuscripts include those found in the ruins of Pompeii and Herculaneum, since we can say categorically from other evidence that these towns were destroyed by the eruption of the volcano Vesuvius in AD 79. Any texts uncovered by archaeologists there - providing that we can be confident that the archaeological strata have not been compromised, which would be unlikely given the weight of ash, and in the case of Herculaneum, lava - can confidently be said to have been written prior to that year.

In the case of Pompeii we have additional external evidence in the form of the accounts tablets of the banker L Caecilius Iucundus which were discovered in the house and which are dated AD 15-62.[5] The ancient town of Pompeii as we now know it was built in 89 BC [6] as a luxury development for Romans, and we therefore know that all documents found in the city - even those which cannot be so precisely dated as the tablets of Iucundus - were almost certainly written in the period between 89 BC and AD 79. Clearly we cannot be absolutely precise about the earlier date, since it is possible that the inhabitants may have brought with them or imported earlier texts - yet in the vast majority of cases this date should hold.

Similar problems in establishing an earliest date for materials apply at Herculaneum, and indeed at Qumran where we are also able to assign a last date for composition. The settlement and the adjoining heights at Qumran were overrun by the 10th Roman Legion in AD 68,[7] and we therefore know that all the Qumranic texts - whether written in Hebrew, Aramaic or Greek - must have been deposited in their caves prior to that date. For the earliest possible date of the documents' composition the archaeological evidence is far less certain. There is some evidence on which to base such a decision - the rebuilding and resettling of Qumran after the earliest settlement was damaged by fire and earthquake in 31 BC - but not enough to make a certain judgement. As in Pompeii one would not wish to use this date uncritically, as it is more than possible that manuscripts may have survived the fire, or indeed that older manuscripts may have been brought into the site from elsewhere after the conflagration.

To conclude, archaeology provides a number of useful criteria for use in dating manuscripts, but it is not a panacea.

When deciding the history of the gospels, the assigning of a *latest possible date* is particularly important, as the earliest possible date is fixed by the nature of the documents themselves. They simply cannot have been written before AD 30 - the year of the last events included in the texts.[8]

The latest possible date for composition can also be of paramount importance in non-Christian texts, when the relationship between the internal meaning of the document and outside historical events needs to be established.

One example of such a case are the Aramaic and Hebrew Qumranic fragments, which the controversial American orientalist Robert Eisenman has claimed contain coded information and names from Christian history. His bestselling book based on this thesis[9] received world-wide publicity, particularly after he brought in two journalists to propagate his thesis more effectively. In order to categorically disprove the Eisenmann thesis archaeological dating was not enough, as prior to AD 68 there would theoretically have been enough time for 'Christian' encoding to permeate 'Essene' documents. Eisenmann rejected the data provided by comparative palaeography - which had for a long time dated the Qumranic fragments to a period between the 2nd Century BC and the 1st Century AD - and declined to accept theological arguments against his thesis, as it was these very arguments which his thesis had set out to overturn. At Eisenman's request these documents were therefore subjected to Radiocarbon dating using the C14 isotope.

Radiocarbon dating theoretically can be applied to manuscripts as the papyrus, leather or parchment can be dated by its carbon content. Early on the data produced by radiocarbon dating were subject to a wide margin of error, and there was a fluctuation of plus or minus 200 years. This meant that were a document assigned a mean value of '0' under the test, it could well have been written at any time between 200 BC and AD 200. For the purposes of finding a solution to the kinds of questions raised by Eisenman, these early forms of radiocarbon dating would have been completely useless. However with the development of the Accelerated Mass Spectrometer the accuracy of the process has considerably improved, and we are now able under ideal circumstances, to reduce the plus or minus error margin to less than 50 years in either direction.[10] However before such accurate results can be obtained certain pre-conditions have to be fulfilled.

These pre-conditions are dealt with at greater length in another essay in this volume, but briefly stated they are that the materials to be assessed have not been corrupted by exposure to external influences from later centuries (traces of burning, repairs, contamination from storage materials etc.), and that a large enough sample of the material can be provided. Thus it is that in the case of the Magdalen Papyrus which forms the basis of two of the chapters in this book, and which I have palaeographically dated to circa AD 70, radiocarbon dating cannot be used, as the samples are both too small and too light.[11]

One final caveat must also be entered. Radiocarbon dating can only determine the date of the material on which documents were written. It cannot determine the date of the actual writing, and it is therefore always possible - although unlikely - that the document was written on an older piece of papyrus etc.

In 1991 at the Zurich Institut fur Mittelenergiephysik, fragments of eight Qumran scrolls drawn from three different caves were examined using radiocarbon dating techniques. Mindful of the pre-conditions for successful radiocarbon dating given above, all the fragments were of adequate size and weight, and none of them contained either text or remnants of ink. In all cases but one the results of these tests confirmed exactly the conclusions garnered from palaeographical dating - namely that the scrolls could be dated to between the 2nd and 1st centuries BC. Only in one case could a fragment even possibly have originated from the beginning of the 1st century AD, and in this case such a dating was at the outer limits of the possible plus/minus variance.[12]

As a result of this dating not only could the Eisenman thesis be confidently rejected - not that this persuaded its originator to abandon it - but more importantly the techniques of palaeographical dating had received an unqualified endorsement from an external source. To put it another way the results of the Zurich tests showed that when all due care was taken to ensure accurate results by two totally different methods - one depending on a good eye, experience and a comprehensive knowledge of styles of handwriting on the part of the papyrologist, and the other, a 'scientific' method carried out under laboratory conditions - complementary and mutually substantive results can be obtained.

Even when archaeology and radiocarbon analysis are able to make a contribution to the process of dating a manuscript - and there are many cases in which they cannot - palaeological investigation still remains a decisive stage in the dating process.

New possibilities for interdisciplinary cooperation are developing in this area, but before becoming too enthusiastic it is worthwhile recording the criteria which need to be borne in mind in comparative palaeology if reliable results are to be obtained.

First, where manuscripts cannot be dated by using a date or substantive reference from within the document itself, or where they cannot be dated by comparison to documents that have such a fixed date, considerable caution must be taken. A comparison with a document that has in its turn been dated by using a comparison with another benchmark document, cannot provide more than supportive evidence.

Secondly, to allow classification to take place there must be at least two major shared characteristics within the test and benchmark documents which are identical to a lesser or greater degree. We should examine both the general appearance - the orientation of characters and words, the linking of letters (ligatures) or lack of same etc., as well as the specific formation of individual characters (descenders, oval or round shapes etc.) and try to find points of similarity in both areas.

Thirdly, the author's individuality must also be taken into account. Is the work an example of the handwriting of a young man or an old one? If the former, has he written in an archaized form - the equivalent of a modern teenager writing in 'copper plate' handwriting. When an old man is he writing at the end of his career? Are we dealing with an Early, High or Late style?

Clearly such criteria are to some degree subjective and can lead to significantly different assessments. It is because of this that critics often like to lay stress on the problems associated with comparative palaeography. Whilst a certain amount of subjective intelligence will always be necessary in this process - comparative palaeography is no different in this regard than radiocarbon data - one should not overestimate the extent to which this is the case.

For example, as can readily be verified through self-experimentation, an individual's style does not remain consistent throughout his or her life. A twenty year old does not write like a forty year old, and with an eighty year old the handwriting is different again. Yet all three phases belong to the same person. Individuals are not likely to write in an archaic style unless such a style was obligatory as was sometimes the case in scriptoria, offices or monasteries. Even in Qumran, which obviously had a scriptorium, such a practice is not standardized across the range of documents, as it is clear that some of the texts found in the caves had not been written in Qumran, but had been brought in from outside. Whilst it must be admitted that in the early Christian era there were from comparatively early on, technical and dogmatic guidelines for preparing a text,[13] a fully co-ordinated style for writing documents according to obligatory style patterns did not emerge until AD 330 - during the time of Emperor Constantine - when the Emperor ordered Eusebius his court historian to have 50 codices of the Greek Bible made up (none of which is still extant).[14]

Despite these points, it is the case that most of the difficulties encountered when attempting to assess the general appearance and characteristic appearance of letters, arise not principally as a result of the indiscriminate nature of the material presented, but from the imprecise and unreliable reproductions used for comparison. Not all papyrologists are able to view the manuscripts they are working on in the original. The around one hundred New Testament papyrus manuscripts are spread throughout the world in museums and universities from Philadelphia and Ann Arbor, to New York, Princetown, Oslo, Dublin, Glasgow, Manchester, Oxford, Cambridge, London, Barcelona, Milan, Trieste, Florence, Cologne, Paris, Ghent, Leuven, Strasbourg, Heidelberg, Berlin, Vienna, St Petersburg, Jerusalem and Cairo. Important non-Christian papyri, which are often used for comparison, are held in archives throughout the world - often not in the same city which keeps the relevant biblical documents. For the sake of convenience, and to be able to accomplish the work within the often limited funds available, much research is therefore done on the basis of photographs. If these photographs are poor then the chances of good work emerging are consequently much lower.

An example of the kinds of problems that can be caused by poor reproductions is provided by the research that has so far been done on the oldest fragment of Luke's gospel (p^4) which is kept in the Bibliothèque Nationale in Paris (= BN *Supplementum Graecum* 1120/5). The reason that it is inconclusive, with one or two exceptions (cf note 17 below) is that those studying the fragment are dependent upon a truly dreadful illustration from 1938 unless they are prepared to go to Paris and study the original.[15] The view, still widely held today, that this codex fragment originally belonged to the same early Christian codex as the Oxford Matthew fragment p^4 and its counterpart in Barcelona p^{67},[16] could only have been tenable if those forming such a view were unable to study the fragment clearly.

An examination of the Paris fragment in the original shows quite clearly that whilst there are certainly affinities between the papyri, there are a number of details which provide compelling reasons why they could not have formed parts of the same p^4, p^{64} or p^{67} codex.[17]

Many of these details would no doubt have been visible had scholars been using carefully prepared and carefully reproduced photographs. If comparative palaeography is to move forward, the first step is therefore a systematic review of all existing illustrations and the re-shooting of any documents which have not previously been adequately photographed. It should be evident to anyone that such an exercise could not be done piecemeal, and sponsors need to be found who would be prepared to release funds to ensure that the benefits of this project were widely available to anyone who wished to view them. Before any of this can happen however a pool of specially trained photographers needs to be developed. Had such a group of qualified persons been available it might not have taken no less than three attempts to produce useable photographs of the three fragments of the Oxford Matthew papyrus.[18] Here is another example of the need for interdisciplinary endeavour. Photography is a serious discipline, and papyrology depends more and more upon it for its own results. Ideal photographs of manuscripts can only emerge from a co-operative endeavour on the part of well-equipped and trained professional photographers, and expert papyrologists who know the uses to which the photographs will later be put.

There are a number of photographic techniques - amongst which can be numbered infra-red photography - which have been known about for some time and which are well tried and tested. In recent years advances have been made in photography by linking together the latest stereo microscopes with video printers. By this process every stage in an examination can be recorded in picture form in the most minute detail, and can then be printed out as a good quality photographic reproduction.[19] In order for this process to be improved yet further, there needs to be additional work done on the evaluation process as well as on the microscopes themselves, and this is work which the papyrologist can encourage, but is mostly not in a position to develop on his or her own part. Such developments include Infra-Red Reflectography - which will be particularly useful for looking at medieval codices - and Multi-Spectral Imaging (MSI), which has already been used on Qumranic fragments of scrolls written on leather.

Yet even such new and exciting techniques have limits to what they can achieve. For example the effectiveness of Reflectography is impaired by the glazing common to most papyri, and MSI, whilst it can penetrate surface dirt and dust, is sometimes unable to differentiate between dirt and stray fibres and the ink in which the documents are written. Even so when all these limitations are admitted these new techniques can make an important contribution to decisions on the reading and dating of manuscripts.

Nevertheless answers to the important questions raised by the style of the writing on a particular document - the positioning of the pen, or the manner in which characters made up of more than one stroke were composed - can only really be answered with authority once the author of a particular document has been assigned to a given school of writing and epoch.

The answers to such questions are the goal of a new method being developed by myself and my co-worker the biologist George Masuch. This method uses a new optical process for the detection of the surface structures of documents on an x and y axis, and the depth structure of the document on the z-axis, and does so by using digital picture recording and three-dimensional representation. This new development has been introduced to the scholarly world at the 21st International Congress of Papyrologists held in Berlin in August 1995, and the process can be used to facilitate the technique for completing fragmented characters, as well as for assessing the damage to ancient papyri as a prelude to taking decisions on the most appropriate measures for the document's preservation[20].

Improvements in the tools we have at our disposal to date ancient manuscripts are on-going. Whilst much has been achieved - particularly in recent years - I have no doubt that in order for further progress to be made we need not only to develop new techniques *within* disciplines, but also to foster a greater awareness of the need for co-operation *between* disciplines. For if we abandon the guard posts and tear up the fences that mark off our particular academic territories, there is a whole world of knowledge which is open to us to discover.

NOTES

1   Hans-Albert Rupprecht, *Kleine Einführung in die Papyruskunde*, Darmstadt 1994, mainly pages 1-42; see also E. Pöhlmann, *Einführung in die Überlieferungsgeschichte und in die Textkritik der antiken Literatur*, Volume 1 (Classic), Darmstadt 1994.

2   For fundamental questions see mainly W. Schubart, *Griechische Paleographie*, Munich 1926; reprinted 1966, 8-155; see also I. Gallo, *Greek and Latin Papyrology*, London 1986 82-89, O. Montevecchi, *La Papirologia*, Milan 1988, 52-70, and P. W. Pestman, *New Papyrological Primer*, Leiden 1990, 6-41.

3   The classic example of schematizing is the classification of the origins of the codex, which for a long time had been assumed to be a phenomenon of the latter part of the 3rd century AD or the early years of the 4th century AD. Because of this assumption and using the palaeographic criteria which flowed from it, manuscripts from the last third of the 1st century AD were assigned a date some three and a half centuries later than their true date, simply because they

had been handed down in codex form (see chapter 1). For a long
time the possible existence of Christian scroll fragments in a
Qumran cave was systematically refuted. It was simply assumed
that that there had been no Christian scroll fragments, that no
materials from the Gospel of Mark (later found and identified as
7Q5) or the First Letter of Timothy (7Q4) could have been present
there, and that indeed no Christian texts could have been found in
such close proximity to the Qumran 'Essenes'. (See C.P. Thiede,
*The Earliest Gospel Manuscript? The Qumran Fragment 7Q5 and
its Significance for New Testament Studies*, Exeter 1992; see also O.
Betz/R. Reisner, *Jesus, Qumran and the Vatican. Clarifications*,
London 1994, 114-124.

4   A.Farrer, *The Revelation of St John the Divine*, Oxford 1964, 37; see also
J.A.T. Robinson, *Wann enstand das Neue Testament?*
Paderborn/Wuppertal 1986, 354-55. A good example of how one
can fall into this trap is provided by A. Schmidt, 'Zwei
Anmerkungen zu P. Rhyl III 457', in *Archiv für Papyrusforschung
und verwandte Gebiete* 35, 1989, 11-12, who attempts a late dating
for papyrus fragment p^{52}, without noticing that the dating of the
material he is comparing is unreliable and written on. For
fundamental questions see S. .R Llewelyn, *New Documents
illustrating Christianity*, Volume 7 Sydney 1994, 243-244.

5   C. Zangmeister, 'Tabulae ceratae Pompeis repertae annis 1887 et 1887,
in *Corpus Inscriptionum Latinarum*, 4 Suppl, 1898.

6   See amongst others Cicero, *Phillipicae* 12, 11, 27; see also Cicero, *De
Divatione* 1,33, 72 and Orosius, *Historiae adversum Paganos* 5, 18,
22-28.

7   The archaelogical date for the conquest by the Romans and the end of
Jewish settlement, AD 68, has been considered a reliable *communis
opinio* for research since the head of the excavation team R. de
Vaux presented an extensive research report on the excavations
(*Archaeology and the Dead Sea Scrolls*, London 1973) . For the
latest summary of information see J.Murphy O'Connor,
''Qumran', in *The Anchor Bible Dictionary*, Volume 5, New York,
Doubleday 1992, 590-94. Occasionally groundless doubts have
been expressed with regard to the archaeological or historical facts,
see O. Betz/R. Reisner, *Jesus, Qumran und der Vatikan*,
Gießen/Freiburg 1995, 67-800.

8   It is conceivable that an exceptional case can be made for Matthew's
Aramaic source of logia as is assumed by Papias (in Eusebius,
History of the Church 3,39,16), as these may have been in the form
of tachigraphical (ie short hand) notes take by the evangelist (see
amongst others E. J. Goodspeed, *Matthew, Apostle and Evangelist*,
Philadelphia 1959, 16-17; R. H. Gundrey, *The Use of the Old
Testament in St Matthew's Gospel*, Leiden 1967, 182-84; C. P.
Thiede, 'Schrift VII. Tachygraphie/Kurzschrift', in *Das Große*

Bibellexikon, Volume 3, Wuppertal/Zurich 1990, 1401-1403. Here near or total contemporaneity of speeches is assumed.

9   R. Eisenman, *Maccabees, Zadokites, Christians and Qumran,* Leiden 1983; R.Eisenman, *James the Just in the Habakuk Pesher,* Leiden 1986; M. Baigent/R. Leigh, *Verschlußsache Jesus. Die Qumranrollen und die Wahrheit über das frühe Christentum,* Munich 1991.

10   On the radiocarbon method in general see R. Switsur, 'Radiocarbon dating', in P. Mellars (ed.), *Research Priorities in Archaeological Science,* London 1987, 44-44. see also, ibid, J.A.J. Gowlett, 'Radiocarbon accelerator dating', 45-46, as well as the specialist magazine *Radiocarbon* which has been published since 1958.

11   A minimum of 20-25 milligrammes of material is necessary, and since this material is consumed in the analysis it is no longer present afterwards. The three Oxford fragments weigh 45 mgms, 25 mgms and 21 mgms respectively, and it is therefore clear from this that all or a significant portion of the manuscripts would have gone completely and such a test would therefore be both counterproductive and damaging for later research. See chapter 4 of this book.

12   G.A. Rodley, 'An Assessment of the Radiocarbon Dating of the Dead Sea Scrolls', in *Radiocarbon* 35, 1993, 335-338.

13   The decision to use the scroll in the early phase of the development of Christian writing, and to change to the codex form no later than AD 70, would have been related to missionary strategy, just as in the early introduction of the abbreviation of 'holy names' (*nomina sacra* eg IS for *IhsousI,* KS for *kyrios* etc, which stress the divinity of Jesus) could not have been imagined without the authority of a leading local congregation; the papyrologists C.H. Roberts and T.C. Skeat who place this development before AD 70, concentrate on Jerusalem, but have considered Antioch as possible too. C.H. Roberts/T.C. Skeat, *The Birth of the Codex,* London 1983, 58-59. In the same context Roberts and Skeat also assume that the authority of Jerusalem or Antioch backed the introduction of the codex. See also C. P. Thiede, 'Magdalen Papyrus' (see note 3), and C. P. Thiede as in note 11.

14   Eusebius, *Vita Constantini* 4, 36, 2; see also F.F. Bruce, *The Canon of Scripture,* Glasgow 1988, 203-205.

15   J. Merell, 'Nouveaux Fragments du Papyrus 4', in *Revue Biblique* 47, 1938, 5-22, plates I -Vii.

16   See chapter 1.

17   See Philip W. Comfort, 'Exploring the Common Identification of Three New Testament Manuscripts: p^4, p^{64} & p^{67}' in Tyndale Bulletin

46/1, 1995, 43-54. Comfort agreed that the Paris codex is considerably older than accepted so far, and that it belongs to the end of the 1st century, or at the latest the beginning of the 2nd century.

18   As yet no entirely satisfactory illustration has been published, even the plate in *ZPE* 105, 1995, plate IX, still leaves something to be desired. Some early illustrations had been made on a dark base so that it was not obvious in various places whether there were remains of ink or holes in the papyrus. In the meantime the professional photographers John Gibbons, of Uffington, Oxfordshire, and Alain Le Toquin, Paris - the latter in the presence of the author - had made a set of colour photographs which are exemplary. The photographs by Gibbons have not yet been published, and the pictures by Le Toquin have so far only been published in sections of the magazine *Le Figaro* 14.4.1995, (Paule Selig, 'Et si les Évangiles étaient un"'reportage"'?), which made a further risk factor obvious: even the best photographs may lose their quality in a reproduction, when individual steps, spaces and boundaries have not been clearly defined. As a result of the work of the page compositor the fragments were backed with blue which gradually got darker from top to bottom, so that it was impossible for the viewer to distinguish between ink and a hole in the papyrus.

19   In this way it was possible to document the examination of Qumran fragment 7Q5 (= Mark 6:52-53) in the forensic laboratory of the Israel National Police Force's Department of Investigation in Jerusalem, making visible the remains of a diagonal down stroke, which decided the argument about the reading of a decisive, badly damaged Greek character (I or N) definitely in favour of its being an N, and thus allowed for the Mark identification. See chapter 17 of this book.

20   C.P. Thiede/G. Masuch, 'Neue mikroskopische Verfahren zum Lesen und zur Schadenbestimmung von Papyrushandschriften', to be published in G. Poethke, (ed.), 'Akten des 21. Internationalen Papyrologenkongresses 1995', Supplement to *Archiv für Papyrusforschung*, Stuttgart/Leipzig 1996.

13

Babylon, 'The Other Place': Thoughts on the Whereabouts of Peter[1]

Amongst the many controversies to emerge from modern studies of the Petrine literature are two closely interconnected questions regarding the whereabouts of Peter himself. The first of these concerns whether or not Peter made his way to Rome after being freed from Herod Agrippa's prison, and if he did so whether his whereabouts are referred to in the phrase 'another place' , or 'elsewhere' (*Revised English Bible*) found in Acts 12:17. That this was the case was assumed by both Eusebius and Papias[2] and there is therefore the weight of tradition behind the argument. Secondly, was the First Letter of Peter begun in Rome, and if it was, was the sender referring to Rome when he used the term 'Babylon' found in the First Letter in chapter 5, verse 13? In what follows we will attempt to find solutions to these questions by drawing on evidence from within the Bible as well as from secular Roman literature of the period.

Contrary to the tradition identified with Eusebius, there is today a generally held consensus amongst scholars that the 'other place' referred to in Acts 12:17 is not in fact Rome, but is rather an unidentified hiding place outside the sphere of influence of Herod Agrippa.[3] Much of the credit for this consensus must go to C.H. Hunzinger who put together a persuasive argument that there was no evidence for equating Rome with Babylon in Jewish literature before AD 70 - that is during Peter's lifetime - and that the use of Babylon as code for Rome in the Book of Revelation 14:18 and chapters 16 to 18, was also clearly post-Petrine. Furthermore if the use of Babylon as a sobriquet for Rome was without a known Jewish-Christian precedent, then Hunziger argues, is it really plausible that Peter would have used a term which would have been impossible for his correspondent to decode? And of course it follows on from this that if he did indeed use such a term, then the First Letter of Peter could not have been written before the end of the first century AD.[4]

Hunziger's work is thorough and persuasive, however it contains within it all the deficiencies to be found in arguments based on negative evidence. To come nearer to a solution that is based on positive evidence, we need to return again to the key texts of 1 Peter 5:13 and Acts 12:17. At the same time we must challenge Hunziger's chosen mode of argument and begin from the premise that the absence of Jewish evidence for the equation of Babylon with Rome does not of itself say anything about the historical Peter's intentions in this regard. It cannot surely be permissable to assert with any confidence that the first Christian use of a given term can never predate the corresponding usage in Jewish literature.

We know from both linguistic research and from our own experiences, that patterns of linguistic use cannot be crudely delineated using *a priori* assumptions. In any event the Old Testament - which modern scholarship has shown to provide both the bedrock and building blocks for so much to be found in the New Testament - provides more than enough material to provide the basis for such an allusion. It is not difficult to believe that a Christian author would have been led on some occasion to compare the capital of the Roman Empire with that of the Babylonian Empire. If in one of his most famous poems D. H. Lawrence could expect his readers to understand an implicit comparison between the Roman and Etruscan civilisations on the one hand, and the modern day United States and Mexico on the other, could not the author of 1 Peter expect a similar mental leap on the part of his readers?

Any Jew or Christian who had come from the Jewish Diaspora - and there were at times more than 50,000 such people [5] - would have lived with the awareness of the injunction contained in Micah 4:10 - 'Zion /You must go to Babylon;/ there you will be saved' [6] - and would have measured the ever present signs of moral decay and of the oppression of power politics, against the writings of Isaiah chapters 13 to 14 and 43:14-21, and Jeremiah chapters 51 to 52. It would have been only natural for Christians to compare these two periods - the one historical and the other contemporary - given the turbulent nature of life under the Emperors Caligula (AD 37-41), Claudius (AD 41-54) and Nero (AD 54-68).

Even for non-Jews in Rome and the Roman Empire, Babylon had achieved a symbolic and metaphorical meaning, such that the Roman 'man on the Clapham omnibus' can be shown to have made use of it.

In Terence's popular comedy *Adelphoe*, staged in AD 160 and closely related to an earlier play by Menander which has been lost (traces of this play can be found in 1 Corinthians 15:33 where Paul, quoting Menander, writes that 'Bad company ruins good character'), the Athenian character Micio is called a 'Babylonian' in allusion to his extravagant life-style (*iube nunciam dinumeret ille Babylo viginti minas* or in English 'Let the Babylonian pay his twenty mines').

In this phrase Babylonian luxury is transferred to a non-Babylonian. In a comedy written and staged in Rome, an Athenian has become a Babylonian, and the epithet 'Babylonian' has thus acquired a metaphorical meaning to go alongside its purely geographical one. In order for the author to have believed that such an allusion would have been comprehensible to an audience drawn from across the social strata, it must surely have been in common use at the time.[7]

The Romans had many sources of information regarding the legendary luxury of Babylon, and the decadence and excesses which were considered to have gone on there. The writings of Herodutus whose *Histories* (see Book I, 180-203) contain such material had been available from the earliest days of Rome's history and would certainly have still been available during the Christian era. During the reign of the Emperor Claudius (or to use a variant dating, during the reign of the Emperor Vespasian) the *History of Alexander the Great* by Quintus Curtius Rufus, contained details of the Babylon encountered by Alexander in the process of his conquests and in which he died. For an inhabitant of the Roman Empire it was perfectly possible, and indeed quite natural, to compare the ancient Babylonian Empire with that of Rome in terms of their respective size, splendour and power, and equally in a negative sense, in relation to their decadence and declining morals. Biblical examples and secular sources both make it clear how obvious such an equation of Rome and Babylon would have been.

II

In Peter's lifetime, during the years prior to Nero's persecution of the Christians, we find further evidence for this symbolic use of Babylon. In *Cena Trimalchionis,* the central fragment of Petronius' *Satyricon,* which was written no later than AD 61,[8] but which was set some years earlier, the central character Trimalchio recites lines from a poem which is ascribed to the obscure writer Publius or Pubilius:

> Luxuriae ructu Martis marcent moenia:
> Tuo palato clausus pavo pascitur
> Plumato amictus aureo Babylonico

> The city of Mars (= Rome) weakens in the belching of affluence,
> for your palate a peacock is being fatted in a cage,
> enveloped by a Babylonian, golden coat of feathers

(*Satyricon* 55)

These lines characterize the decadent luxury of Roman life at the period by using the epithet 'Babylon' as a metaphor for corruption, and are followed by further verses listing other decadent delicacies and attacking with merciless derision bejewelled adulteresses and those married women who would wear see-through clothing in public. Clearly Petronius assumes here that 'Babylon' would hold a currency for his audience when used in the context of Rome's moral decay. This usage which was clearly common by the middle of the first century when Petronius was writing, may be even older still if the lines do indeed come from Publilius, a first century writer of mime farces.[9]

To return to our central argument, where does this new evidence leave us in relation to the use of Babylon in First Peter 5:13? Whilst we still have no compelling evidence for the belief that Babylon does equal Rome in this passage, we have at least begun to collect some positive support for our hypothesis. If as is clear from the above, there is a considerable body of evidence to suggest that such a link was made in the Roman Empire prior to and during Peter's life, is it really such a leap to posit that the passage in First Peter is in fact the first example of such a transference occurring in the Jewish-Christian literature of the period?[10]

III

Now we have established at least a prima facie case for the historic Peter having used the cryptogram Babylon for Rome in the First Letter of Peter, let us perhaps move on to consider the suggestion made by J.E. Belser that the passage in Acts 12:17 mentioned at the beginning of this essay, actually refers to Ezekiel 12:3 - 'You must pack what you need, O Man, for going into exile, and set off by day while they look on ...' *(REB)* - and thus from Babylon to Rome.[11]

Papias, Eusebius and Hieronymus, all concluded that Peter arrived in Rome for the first time during the second year of the reign of the Emperor Claudius, that is to say in around AD 42.[12] However long he stayed in the city, [13] we know that he returned to Jerusalem for the Council of Jerusalem no later than AD 48, and that he may well have begun the return journey to Jerusalem at around the end of AD 44, when following the death of Herod Agrippa, his freedom of movement was restored. Given that his name is missing from the greetings, Peter probably arrived back in Rome soon after the writing of the Letter to the Romans, but it is no more possible to discuss here in detail whether or not the First Letter of Peter with its troublesome passage 5:13[14] was written from there, than it is to discuss in detail the date and geographical origin of the Acts of the Apostles - this despite the reference in Acts 28:14ff to the fact that the writer had spent at least some time in Rome. What can be determined with some accuracy however, is that the author of the Acts of the Apostles - who was also present in Rome at some time between AD 58-63, must have had access to the same information as the writer of the First Epistle of Peter. It is even possible to posit that the two of them might have met, although this latter thought must remain no more than speculation.

Given that Luke should have been *au fait* with an equation of Babylon and Rome, that the First Letter of Peter was in all probability available to him at the time of his writing,[15] that the use of Babylon for Rome would have been an obvious way of coding important information regarding Peter's presence in and absence from the capital of the Empire at a time when there was a definite need for tactical political reasons to have such a code that could be readily decipherable by someone who had the requisite background and knowledge, and that we know from Isaiah 13 to 14; 43:14-21, Jeremiah 51:1-58, Micah 4:10 and other passages[17] that there were well known Old Testament 'models' for the usefulness of a Babylon cryptogram, it is not unreasonable to assume that Luke would have used another Old Testament passage connected with Babylon - Ezekiel 12 - as a code for unlocking the true meaning of the phrase 'the other place' in Acts 12:17.

In Ezekiel 12 the narrator receives the word of the Lord (12:1-2) - 'The word of the Lord came to me. O man, you are living among a rebellious people' *(REB)* - and is given orders to pack his belongings for exile, and to move 'to another place'. The word used here in the Septuagint to indicate 'another place' is exactly the same as the word used by Luke in Acts 12:17.

The narrator in Ezekiel follows his orders and leaves the city by night (12:7).[18] Whilst so far the meaning of the phrase 'other place' can be decoded, it has not formally been identified by name. A few lines further on the reference is made explicit. Here in verse 13 the Lord speaks for a second time saying - 'But I shall throw my net over him, and he will be caught in the meshes. I shall take him to Babylon, to the land of the Chaldeans, where he will die without ever seeing it'. *(REB)*.

Without needing to consider the concrete historical and theological framework of Ezekiel 12, it is clear that should Luke have required such a device for his coding in Acts 12:17, Ezekiel 12 could have more than adequately provided it.

To recap, what do we have here? We know that Peter was in Rome. There is also a strong possibility that Luke may have known Peter's whereabouts and have wished for political reasons to have conveyed them in code. We have seen that Babylon was in common usage at the time as a metaphorical epithet for Rome. Ezekiel 12 provided a useful and commonly recognized coded reference to Babylon and Luke deliberately chose to mirror the Greek used in the Septuagint for the Ezekiel passage in his own description of Peter's whereabouts in Acts. Can we go further than this?

IV

It is a fact that has only recently been fully recognized that the Christian outlook remained predominantly a Jewish one until many decades after the period we are discussing. Christians who were for the most part culturally Jewish, if not personally former Jews themselves, would have viewed the departure from their own country using the same vocabulary of experience as Jews from the Old Testament period. For them departing from one's own country, whether it be to go to Babylon or to Babylon-Rome, would be to go into exile; any experience of exile would have brought to mind the greatest period of exile for the Jewish people. The fact that at the time of Peter Roman Jews would doubtless have felt in this way (and that given the political situation would have had every reason for doing so) only confirms the efficacy of a code such as is found in Acts 12:17 and the cryptogram in 1 Peter 5:13.[19] Such codes contained the added advantage of combining practical utility, with deeper and more profound resonances.

The Book of Ezekiel was well known to early Christians. Nestle/Aland in their *Novum Testamentum Graece* (26th edition), list no fewer than 195 passages referring to Ezekiel in the New Testament, amongst which are some six direct quotations.[20] Since it is fair to assume that both the Acts of the Apostles and the First Letter of Peter were written during the apostolic period there is no need to go on to consider the many references to Ezekiel to be found in the Fathers of the Church or in the New Testament Apocrypha. Were we to do so it would only serve to indicate the continued influence of Ezekiel on later generations. In the same way we know as a result of the diligence of Hunziger, that there can be little doubt that later generations also used Babylon as a cryptogram to indicate Rome on many occasions.

What is crucial to our enquiry is whether or not the writers of the First Epistle of Peter and the Acts of the Apostles, writing in the early AD 60s, could have assumed that an initiated reader of their time would be able to work out and decode their meaning. From all that we have read above it should be clear that for the author of First Peter the use of Babylon to indicate Rome - a usage which would have formed a part of everyday language - would have provided a valuable circumlocution in difficult times, whilst for the Luke of the Acts of the Apostles the rare repetition of the word used in the Septuagint Ezekiel passage to mean 'another place', would have provided a welcome opportunity to inform without the possibility of the information falling into the wrong hands. To the careful reader his words would have been more than enough incentive to research his meaning more deeply, if not to recognize it straightaway.

V

It would seem as unlikely that Luke did not know of Peter's whereabouts when he left Jerusalem, as that Peter would not have known where he was when he wrote his First Letter.

The authors of the New Testament set puzzles that continue to baffle us, but the solutions do not always emerge with the relentless efficiency of Hercule Poirot marshalling his arguments in front of the suspects in the last chapter. The key, it seems to me, is that we come to accept that these authors - though not academically educated - were not of low intelligence, and that they were capable of being skilful and sophisticated communicators. If we are truly able to place ourselves in their shoes - to think through what they knew and what was most important to them - then we have in our hands the possibility of working with them, to find solutions to even the hardest questions.

NOTES

1   This essay emerged from studies for my book *Simon Peter: From Galilee to Rome,* Exeter,1986. I would like to thank Rainer Riesner of Tübingen and I. Howard Marshall of Aberdeen for their helpful suggestions.

2   See Chronicle of Eusebius Volume II,/*Eusebi Chronicorum Libri Duo* Volume I, Berlin 1866, 152-57, and Hieronymus *de Viris Illustribus*

8, and S.Dockx *Chronologies neotestamentaires et Vie de l'eglise primitive,* Leuven, 1984.

3 ·   I. Howard Marshall, *Acts,* Leicester, 1980, 211

4   C.H. Hunziger, 'Babylon as a code-name for Rome and the Dating of the First Epistle of Peter' in H. Graf Reventlow's (ed.), *Gottes Wort und Gottes Land. A Festschrift for H W Hertzberg,* Göttingen 1965, 67-77. Hunzinger wishes to exclude the possibility that First Peter was written in Rome at all, however he offers no arguments against the evidence marshalled by Papias in this regard (Eusebius *K G* 2,15,2), preferring instead to refute the work published by J.A.T. Robinson in the latter's *Redating the Gospel,* London 1976. Goppelt in his *Der erste Petrusbrief,* Göttingen 1978, has also disagreed with Hunzinger's conclusion.

5   See J. Juster, *Les Juifs dans L'empire Romain,* Paris 1914, 209-10, and J. Leipold and W. Grundmann (ed.), *Umwelt des Urchristentums* 1, Berlin 1982, 292-98.

6   'Zion, writhe and shout like a woman in childbirth/for now you must leave the city/and camp in open country./You must go to Babylon;/there you will be saved;/there the Lord will deliver you from your enemies.' Micah 4:10.

7   That Babylon became *the* term to describe objects of extravagance is shown by both Plautus *Stichus* 378: '*Tum Babylonica et peristroma tonsilia et tappetia advexit, nimium bonae rei* and Lucretius, *De Rerum* natura 4, 1029, '*Cum Babylonica magnifica splendore rigantur*'.

8   See G. Bagnani, *Arbiter of Elegance: A Study of the Life and Works of Petronius,* Toronto 1960.

9   H.C. Schur (ed.), *Petronius' Satyricon*, Stuttgart 1968, 64 and 213, reads the name as Publilius rather than Publius, since this reading makes explicit a witty comparison inherent in the scene between Publilius Syrius and the great Cicero himself.

10   For further biblical material see E.G. Selwyn, *The First Epistle of Peter,* London 1947, 303-5, and for material on the equating of Babylon with Rome in the late rabbinical period see *ibid,* 243. See also L. Goppelt, *Der erste Petrusbrief,* Gottingen 1978, 350-54. To disprove the speculation, occasionally still advanced, that Peter stayed at a small Roman garrison Babylon Fossatum on the Nile, or even the Mesopotamian Babylon, see J.N.D. Kelly, *The Epistles of Peter and Jude,* London 1969, 217-220; see also O. Cullman, *Petrus, Junger-Apostle-Martyrer,*Zürich 1960, 93-97. That Peter was himself the writer of the First Epistle has been fairly conclusively proved by F. Neubauer, 'Zur Deutung und Bedeutung des 1 Petrusbriefes', in *New Testament Studies* 26, 1980, 61-86.

11   J.E. Belser, *Einleitung in das Neue Testament,* Freiburg 1901, 197-98;
      see also J.E. Belser, *Die Apostelgeschichte,* Vienna 1905, 156; E.
      Seydl, 'Alttestamentliche Parallele zu Apg 12.17', in *Der Katholik*
      79, 1899, 481-83, and also S. Lyonnet, 'Ministerio romano S Petri
      ante adventum S Pauli', in *Verbum Domini* 33, 1955, 143-54.

12   See Dockx, note 2 above.

13   The historian K. Buchheim has given some reasons why Peter may
      have been in touch with Rome as early as AD 41-42 in 'Der
      historiche Christus', in *Geschichtswissenschaftliche Überlegungen
      zum Neuen Testament,* München 1974, 110-46.

14   See note 2 above.

15   For the date of the First Letter of Peter see F. Neugebauer above; C.P.
      Thiede, as in note 1. For the date of the Acts of the Apostles, see
      I.H. Marshall, as in note 3.

16   See K. Buchheim as in note 13. Luke is careful when reporting events
      which could be interpreted as being in opposition to the political
      authorities, and which hence could have been of embarrassment to
      the recipient of his dedication to the high Roman official
      Theophilus (see Geldenhuys, *Commentary on the Gospel of Luke,*
      53, London 1950. The escape *from* Herod Agrippa's prison is
      noted, but the escape *into* the capital of the empire is given in code.
      In his Gospel Luke also refrains from identifying Peter as the man
      who cut off the ear of the servant of the High Priest (Mark writing
      from Rome also similarly refrains, as does Matthew whom it is
      generally assumed was dependent upon Mark for his account here).
      At the very least Theophilus had taken on the task of publishing
      Luke's work at his expense as was customary in the ancient world
      when accepting a dedication (see E. Haenchen, *Die
      Apostelgeschichte,* Göttingen 1977, 143 note 4 - 'The one named in
      the dedication is permitted to make copies and to see that they were
      circulated'; see also M. Hengel, *Die Evangelienuberschriften,* pp
      31-32 (Heidelberg 1984), and it is therefore clear that Luke would
      have taken considerable care not to cause him unnecessary
      difficulties.

17   For further passages see E.G. Selwyn, as in note 10; See also L.
      Goppelt, as in note 10.

18   The latest interpretation of the historical context lying behind the
      composition of Ezekiel can be found in B. Tidiman, *Le Livre
      d'Ezekiel,* (Vaux-sur-Seine 1985, 176-80.

19   See J. Juster, as in note 5 above; see also H.J. Leon, *The Jews of
      Ancient Rome,* Philadelphia 1960.

20   The use of the Septuagint version of the Book of Ezekiel by Luke has
        been reconfirmed by M.R. Strom, 'An Old Testament Background
        to Acts 10-23', in *New Testament Studies* 32, 1986, 289-32.
        Interestingly this is the same chapter 12 which also refers to Ezekiel
        in verse 13.

14

Papyrus Bodmer L: The New Testamental Papyrus Fragment p^{73} First Edition

Amongst the ninety-five known New Testament papyri contained in J.K. Elliott's 'A Bibliography of Greek New Testament Manuscripts',[1] only one remains unedited. This papyrus, p^{73}, was recently given the name 'Papyrus Bodmer L'[2] by the Trustees of the Bibliotheca Bodmeriana. The fragment is known to users of the Greek NT Nestle-Aland[26], because of its inclusion in the continuous list of 'Codices Graeci et Latini in hac editione adhibiti' (p. 684ff).[3] Whereas the date of the papyrus is still an open question, the content was given as 'Mt. 25:43; 26:2-3'. The obvious fact that this papyrus was a codex fragment is not dealt with in the only comment quoted by Elliott, an essay on New Testament papyri by K. Aland.[4] While in his earlier work Aland classifies the fragment as 'relatively late' and the lack of a photo is noted, twenty years later he ascribes to it a date in the 7th century in a 'descriptive list' of the papyri[5] - a commitment he had not yet made in the Greek NT Nestle-Aland[26] (1979), and which he did not insert until the tenth amended reprint (1988). The description of p^{73} in *Repertorium der griechischen christlichen Papyri, I, Biblische Papyri*[6] published by K. Aland and not referred to by Elliott, appeared between the two references mentioned above. It is a four line summary of details, provided by R. Kasser. Kasser had edited the Papyrus Bodmer XVII (p^{74}) in 1961;[7] the fragment p^{73} was found amongst its folios 39 and 40.

Kasser had described the similarities and differences between p^{73} and p^{74} precisely.[8] The 'petit fragment de papyrus' p^{73} was 'visiblement étranger à notre manuscrit' (that is to say p^{74}). Admittedly it was correct that 'l'écriture de ce morceau paraît être d'un style assez semblable à celui que nous retrouvons dans tout le codex: on ne saurait exclure absolutement que les deux ouvrages soient de la même main'. yet Kasser emphasizes the 'différences frappantes': the characters of p^{73} are 'plus petite, le calame plus fin, l'encre plus noir'. Kasser asks nevertheless whether this is a 'codex frère' of p^{74} and observes that the enclosure of p^{73} between two folios of p^{74} 'date d'avant l'époque ou ils ont été amalgamés l'un a l'autre par l'agent dissolvant'.

Whilst Kasser promises that the fragment will be published at a later date, the above is a fair statement of the position at the current time. What follows is the first edition promised by Kasser of the fragment made on the basis of my study of the original in the Bibliotheca Bodmeriana Cologny-Geneve with constant reference to the enlarged photographs.

Text Edition

The identification of Papyrus Bodmer L as Mt. 25:43 (*recto*) and Mt. 26:2-3 (*verso*), has always been assumed since the description of the papyrus by R. Kasser can be verified by the following description.

On the *recto* we can see three perfectly preserved letters forming part of a complete word in line 2: $ουκ$. Following the $κ$ is a character which could be an $ε$ or an ϑ. The fact that the upper curve bends sharply downwards and to the right which might indicate a ϑ, is acutally just as characteristic of an $ε$ in p^{74}, the brother codex. The decision in favour of an $ε$ can be made when comparing it with the typical sequence of both characters in p^{74} (e.g. Kasser p. 107, line 10 $πλησϑεις$). The lower curve of the $ε$ is more pronounced than the upper, more open to the right than the one of the ϑ ; although the fragment breaks off at the important point, nevertheless a detailed study of the original clearly commends the parallel to $ε$ of p^{74} . The $ε$ is followed by further remains of a character. It is the left portion of an upper part of a character starting with a point-like thickening, which in p^{74} is characteristic for the letter π, less distinctive also for the υ (compare υ in p^{73} three characters further left). The o of $o\upsilon\kappa$ is preceded by traces which cannot be interpreted reliably in comparison with what is well preserved in p^{73}. Again a comparison with p^{74} helps here. these are the lower remains of the characteristic join of α and ι (see e.g. Kasser p.107, lines 16 and 20, in $\kappa\alpha\iota$). Line 2 therefore looks like this:

$$\alpha\iota o\upsilon\kappa\varepsilon\pi$$

There are also remains of characters recognizable in line l. Above the ε there are unmistakable traces of a ν (a reliable comparison made on the basis of the ν in p^{74}), above the κ, or to be more precise between the υ and the κ, there are faint remains of the lower curve of a character which could be a ϑ, a ε, α, o, or a s. A decision in favour of ϑ is only possible when one uses the accepted identification Mt. 25:43 which in this place assumes an ϑ. Under the κ and the ε of line 2 the photo of the papyrus shows a black stroke where the top margin of the third line of text should be. This stroke does not correspond with any trace on the original papyrus in its present form.

Continuing to the left with this stroke, under the α of line 2, the remains of a curve are discernible, just as it occurs in p^{73} and p^{74} with the character α, yet according to the evidence from p^{74} it could just as easily belong to a s. Of both these possibilities the ε remains the most likely when identifying the fragment with Matthew 25:43. After this final remnant of a letter, no further traces of characters can be discerned even in the original. It might perhaps be attractive to attempt a search for traces of further characters with the help of the Lund Beam Set-Up Proton microprobe,[9] recently developed by G. Lövestam. This is able to show up even the smallest remnants. The gap at this point certainly makes sense on the basis of the identification with Mt. 25:43, as verse 43 ends here with a $\mu\varepsilon$. We would be dealing with a spatium following on the end of verse 43. This would be consistent in as far as this verse ends a distinct passage of Jesus' thought.

]ϑ[..]ν[
]αιουκεπ[
]ε̣

Thus we have the following for Matthew 25:43

βαλετεμεασ]ϑ[ε]ν[ησκαιεν	20 characters
φυλακηκ]αιουκεπ[εσκ	17
εψασϑεμ]ε̣ [τοτεαπο	8

Line 3 contains 8 characters plus spatium. With a possible continuation this line may perhaps contain 19 characters including spatium.

On the *verso* the characters on the two lower lines are easily recognizable. Above these lines however the situation is the same as on the *recto,* and the characters in the first line are only present in an extremely fragmented and damaged form.

Line 2 has the three characters υρω in an undamaged state . The character preceding the υ, though damaged, is clearly recognizable on the basis of a comparison with p^{74} as an α. The ω is followed by the remnants of a character which may equally well be a ϑ, ο, ς or ε. By using a comparison with p^{74}, however, the reading ϑ emerges as the most likely, as the curve bends sharply to top right while on the ε it runs more openly to the right (compare also with the ε of the *recto,* line 1). The characters ο and ς are excluded in the process of making the identification with Mt. 26: 2-3. Line 2 therefore reads:

αυρωϑ

In line 3 there are three letters, the third of which though damaged, is also perfectly legible: νηχ. The third character is followed by the upper curve of a character which could be either a ϑ, ε, ο or ς . Based on the identification with Mt 26:2-3 this has to be read as an ϑ. Line three therefore reads:

νηχϑ

Line 1 which as we have seen above is also difficult to interpret on the *recto*, on its own offers few possibilities. Above the ρ of line 2 nothing can be seen except the darkening of the material. An interpretation of these letters can only be made if based on a reconstruction of lines 2 and 3 and their stichometry.

The three lines in Mt. 26:2-3 read:

πουπ]αραδ[ιδοταιεις   17
τοστ]αυρωθ[ηναι   13 (plus spatium)
τοτεσυ]νηχθ[ησανοιαρ   18

Both sides of the fragment show spatia, and spatia are also frequent in the comparable codex in p^{74} and they can be of considerable length. Kasser (p. 106) shows that the average for spatium within a line in Acts 13:1-12 verse 11 is followed by a spatium five characters long. End spatia can be up to twelve characters long (see Kasser p. 124, Acts 15:36), but may be only five or fewer letters long (see same, p.106, Acts 13 after καιρου). The spatia assumed for p^{73} in the present edition are therefore of a comparable size.

On the *recto* we are faced with a situation where working in accordance with the stichometry for line 1 which has 20 characters, the spatium in line 3 is no more than twelve characters long. It is, however, conceivable that the text of verse 44 in the lost part of the fragment commences after a spatium of five (or more) characters. The spatium on line 2 of the *verso*, should be at least four characters long, but could also be up to seven (basing it again on the longest reconstructed line, line 1 of the *recto*). The maximum stichometrical variation (without spatia), 17/20, in the present reconstruction stays within familiar boundaries and is comparable with the result.

The reconstruction which we have made for both sides of this fragment shows no textual deviations from Mt 25.43/26 2-3 as in Nestle-Aland[26] (with apparatus).

Time and Place of Origin

As the above comparisons have shown, p^{73} and p^{74} are closely related. Beyond the observations already recorded, this close relationship can also be observed in the formation of the characters η, κ, χ, ο, ρ and ω. p^{74} itself is not always consistent in its character formation (κ, η and χ vary slightly), however, given the presence of more than one exact parallel with the characters on p^{73}, and the overall resemblance, it would seem to be fair to suggest that the the writers are the same.

The differences between the types of handwriting are not important and can easily be explained: the material of p^{74} is of a slightly thicker consistency, and thus the characters of p^{73} appear somewhat finer. Furthermore, R. Kasser has already observed that the writer of p^{73} might have used a finer 'stylus'. Nevertheless the size of the letters of both papyri varies only marginally (0.5-1 mm); the slightly higher characters of p^{74} may be mainly due to the difference in papyrus material and 'stylus'. When compared using the the original fragments the ink of both papyri was identical (*pace* Kasser p. 10), a slightly [lightened] black turning russet.[10] As the colour of both papyri is a dark brown, letters that are very damaged or faded are relatively difficult to read.

That the writer of both papyri is the same can therefore be assumed. In the edition of p^{74} this writer had already been identified as a user of the Coptic type of uncial of the 6th or 7th century, with a slight tendency in favour of the earlier date.[11] Concerning the likely place of origin for the fragments no more is revealed than a hint that they may have been produced in a Coptic language area.

As to whether p^{73} was part of a larger codex originally, perhaps even containing all four gospels, or indeed whether it could have been a lectionary codex (compare with p^{44}) there is simply not enough evidence to say. Nor can we say whether the place where p^{73} was found between folios 39 and 40 of p^{74} was simply a coincidental dislocation among two codices stored next to each other.

In its present form p^{74} starts with the Acts of the Apostles and also contains Jas, 1 Pet, 2 Pet, 1 Jn, 2 Jn, 3 Jn and Jude - that is to say Acts and the 'Catholic Letters'. According to Aland, p^{74} belongs into the top category I[12] 'because of the quality of its text'.

Although no statement can be made as to the quality of the text of p^{73} because so little of it is available, it is possible to see in this fragment of Matthew's gospel the minute remnant of a high grade codex, which was written in direct connection with the codex available to us as Papyrus Bodmer XVII (= p^{74}).

The Papyrus Bodmer p^{73} is one of 18 known papyri of Matthew's gospel. Together with papyrus p^{44} (Metropolitan Museum of Art, New York, Inv. No. 14.1527) it represents what we have from the Coptic writers' tradition of the 6th and 7th century.[13]

NOTES

1   Cambridge, 1989.

2   This number has not been recorded in Elliott's bibliography.

3   Whilst the Greek New Testament 1 UBS {3 }corr., omits it (S.XV).

4   'Neue Neutestamentliche Papyri II', in *NTS* 9 1962/63, 303-316, here 303 and 308.

5   K. and B. Aland, *Der Text des Neuen Testaments*, Stuttgart 1982, 110.

6   Berlin/New York 1976, p.305.

7   *Papyrus Bodmer XVII. Actes des Apôtres. Epître de Jacques, Pierre, Jean et Jude*, Cologny-Geneve 1961, Bibliotheca Bodmeriana.

8   P. 9f. Identification of text and description of p^{73} with announcement 'Ce texte sera publié ultérieurement.'.

9   G. Lövestam/E. Swietlicki, 'An External Beam Set-Up for the Lund Proton Microprobe', in G. Lövestam/E. Swetlicki, *Development of a Scanning Proton Microprobe - Computer-control, Elemental Mapping and Applications*, Lund 1989, 49-63.

10   Really black ink can only be shown in some corrections in p^{74} (see Kasser p. 11 and 15)

11   See note 7, p. 11

12   See note 5, p. 105

13   Possibly the Coptic-Greek Papyrus at the Austrian National Library, Vienna, K7244 (p^{96}) of the sixth century, containing Matthew 3:10-12/13-15, as yet unedited, will complete the picture.

15
Speaking in Tongues: On the Multilingualism of the Essenes and Early Christianity

There have been a great many sensational stories concerning Qumran and the people who lived there. Such has been the prevalence of rumours, legends and 'discoveries', that it is difficult not to forget that such stories are not new. Thirty years ago John Allegro attempted very similar 'creative' interpretations of the scrolls, and his more controversial publications stirred up similar interest - and similar consequences - as shown in the books of Baigent, Leigh and Eisenman.[1] One constructive consequence of this earlier controversy was an intensification of the solid scientific work of identifying the documents.

Now given that we have all been here before, it seems at first glance even more surprising still that the new bestsellers could be so successful. Specialists from around the world agree that the core arguments in these books are not in any way supported by facts that are verifiable.

Jesus the Man, a book by the Australian scholar Barbara Thiering, offers a classic case of how the process of sensationalizing the academic controversies associated with this period has intensified.[2] According to Thiering not only do the Qumran Texts reveal that Jesus did not die on the cross, but they also indicate that he married twice and had three children.

For anyone harbouring a wish to return to the texts themselves, it must be said that the fact that all the important

Hebrew and Aramaic Qumran Scrolls date back to the 1st and 2nd centuries BC (evidence provided by *both* radio-carbon-dating and comparative palaeography), does tend to put a damper on things. Only the most farsighted scholars can provide historical statements on early Christianity, based on documents that date from one or two hundred years earlier. But leaving aside the problems of the date attributable to the key documents, Thiering's ideas - as well as those of Baigent, Leigh and Eisenman - cannot be drawn from the texts which they wishfully refer to, not even allegorically.

Yet the public interest in Qumran and Early Christianity raised by such books, shows that there is a demand for information. This applies not only to the content of the scrolls and fragments alone, but also to their environment, the history of Jewry and of early Christianity in the period of Jesus and the first congregations. The central question can be put simply: What actually happened in Palestine and the surrounding areas during that period, and with what degree of certainty can we find out?

Beyond all doubt the Aramaic and Hebrew Qumran texts do offer an insight into the faith and thought of at least one of the great Jewish movements at this turning point in history. If one looks at the wider picture from the right perspective - and after all the people who left us the Qumran documents represented only one of the major movements; from the Sadducees and Pharisees, for example, we have no contemporary documents - then it is possible to draw conclusions about the spiritual climate in which the early Christians, obeying Jesus' instructions, became active as missionaries.

In the continuing debate about the Qumran texts the conspicuous Greek fragments have so far played a peculiar role: on the one hand they are not mentioned in Baigent, Leigh and Eisenman's 'bestsellers' and are therefore rarely taken into account in the refutation devoted to them. On the other hand between 1972 and 1976 and then again since 1984, some Greek papyri from the 7th cave have been the occasion of a number of lively controversies. These controversies have centred around the possibility of whether or not New Testament texts were present in Qumran. In this context it was mostly overlooked that not only are there nineteen fragments in cave

7, but also six Greek fragments in cave 4. Admittedly there is a numerical imbalance here, as cave 7 contained exclusively Greek language fragments on papyrus and formed a collection or 'library' on its own, whereas the four parchment and two papyrus fragments in cave 4 seem to be foreign bodies among the hundreds of Aramaic and Hebrew texts. But the fact that Greek texts were not only kept in cave 7 demands further considerations.

A new stimulus to this debate came from the complete publication of Greek fragments in cave 4 by Patrick W. Skehan, Eugene Ulrich, Judith E. Sanderson and Peter J. Parsons.[3] Some of these six texts had already become known, and P.J. Parsons in 1990 had used the opportunity of his contribution to Emanuel Tov's edition of the 'Greek Minor Prophets Scroll from Nahal Hever' to comment briefly and apodictically on the Greek fragments of both caves.[4] Parsons however had not advanced matters much further than had J. van Haelst, whose first perspective on Greek biblical papyri that appeared fourteen years earlier, seemed similarly brief and provisional.

This being the case I believe that when examining both this material and other textual questions pertaining to the Qumranic documents, it is helpful to keep in mind the following points.

First, not only Hebrew and Aramaic documents were kept in Qumran caves. Twenty-five Greek texts have been preserved or have become known to date: six in cave 4, nineteen in cave 7.

Secondly, the nineteen fragments of cave 7 are eighteen papyri and a reversed imprint on hardened soil. The six fragments in cave 4 are two papyri and four leather texts.

Thirdly, all fragments come from scrolls.

Fourthly, all twenty-five Greek fragments can be dated to the period from the middle of the first century BC to the middle of the first century AD. This means that the Greek texts are the most recent of all manuscripts found in Qumran.

Fifthly, to date only a small number of the fragments have been reliably identified. In this regard the situation in cave 4 is more satisfactory than that in cave 7. The following are considered as having been reliably identified:

1. Q LXX Leviticus {a} (leather) (= van Haelst 49) = Lev: 26.2-16

2. pap 4QLXX Leviticus {b} *papyrus* = thirty-one items with particles from Leviticus 1-6.

(These two fragments are 400 years older than the Greek Leviticus manuscripts previously known.)

3. 4QLXX Numbers leather (van Haelst) 51) = Numbers 3: 40-43 and little remnants from 4:1, 5-9, 11-16; perhaps also 3:39, 50-5.

4. 4QLXX Numbers leather = Deuteronomy 11:4; only five lines, with 38 letters.

5. 7Q1 (van Haelst 38) *papyrus* = Exodus 28.4-7

6. 7Q2 (=van Haelst 312) *papyrus* EpistJer (Baruch 6), 43-44.

These six fragments generally recognized as reliably identified consist of three papyri and three leather texts. Two are exceptionally small - 4QLXX Deuteronomy with 38 letters on 5 lines, 7Q2 = Epistula Jeremiae 43-44 with 20 letters on 5 lines. In addition 7Q2 = EpJer is the only evidence for this apocryphal or deuterocanonical work in Qumran, whether in Greek, Aramaic or Hebrew. Furthermore, a growing number of international papyrologists and classicists are of the opinion that two New Testament texts in cave 7 have been reliably identified: 7Q4=1 Timothy 3:16 to 4.3 and 7Q5 - Mark 6:52-53.[6]

Without claiming that the attributions had a sufficient degree of reliability to be wholly convincing, the Spanish papyrologist José O'Callaghan had connected some additional minute fragments of papyri in cave 7 with the New Testament. He justified these suggestions with the observation that they cannot be placed in the Septuagint and therefore he was at least justified in hypothesizing that there were in addition to the large NT fragments 7Q4 and 7Q5 further NT texts kept in this cave.

It was in this context that he referred to the following as being possible addenda:

7Q6$_1$, = Mk. 4:28;
7Q6$_2$ = Acts 27:38;
7Q7 = Mk. 12:17 ;

7Q8 = Jas. 1:23-24;
7Q9 = Rom. 5:11-12;
7Q10 = 2Pet. 1:15;
7Q15 = Mk. 6:48.

These fragments are so small that a reliable classification is unlikely to be possible, even if technical methods of analysis improve greatly. Only fragment 7Q9 which it has been suggested can be identified as a passage from Rom. 5:11-12, seems to worthy of further examination. This suggestion is reinforced by the fact that for socio-topographical reasons, it makes sense that a fragment of the Letter to the Romans would be present in cave 7.[7]

Yet even if one were to follow all the possible identifications suggested for 7Q, several fragments would remain without plausible identifications - just as was the case with cave 4. The situation can therefore be set out as follows.

Undoubtedly not of biblical origin are two cave 4 fragments: Greek parchment fragment Unid(entified)gr, which consists of pieces of differing sizes, and Greek papyrus fragment pap4Q Para Exod gr., which has been identified, as comprising 86 individual pieces offering unconnected paraphrases of Exodus passages, although because of their condition they cannot be reconstructed to give a complete message that makes sense.

In cave 7 those fragments which are also undoubtedly not of biblical origin are 7Q3 and the reversed floor imprint 7Q19. This negative identification has been possible because both fragments are of sufficent size to be used in elimination tests (7Q3 consisting of 26 characters on 4 lines and 7Q19 of 34 characters on 5 lines). It has not been possible to identify either of these fragments in preserved Greek literature even allowing for a margin of differential caused by the inclusion of variants or different possible readings for disputed characters. An attempt at identifying 7Q3 with Jeremiah 43.28-29 was made but to no avail. [8]

Moving beyond this to other fragments in cave 7 there are no suggestions at all for fragments 7Q11, 7Q13,   7Q14, 7Q16-7Q18, which are minuscule and would appear not to be biblical.

From the little evidence that can be gleaned the position is therefore as follows.

The Greek scroll fragments of Qumran include part of the Torah (Exodus, Leviticus, Deuteronomy), a deuterocanonical text (Epistula Jeremiae), in all probability at least two New Testament texts (Mark and 1 Timothy), a paraphrase (on Exodus) and sundry extrabiblical texts which are so far unknown and cannot be reconstructed.

It is this last statement which is relevant to both caves which has the greatest consequences. For many reasons, historians have no difficulty in accommodating the suggestion that Greek versions of the Old Testament and copies of early Christian texts - which were after all also written by Jews, and at a time when Christianity had not fundamentally severed its links with Judaism - had reached as far as Qumran. To collect ancient and new religious texts of Jewish concern in the lingua franca and everyday language of the eastern Empire would not have been unusual for a movement like the Essenes. Only the sad fact that pre-AD 70 Sadduccean or Pharisaic libraries have not been preserved (unless one follows the old thesis that the Qumran texts are the stock of the temple library evacuated prior to AD 70 during the Jewish uprising^9), prevents us from substantiating that all other major groups would have also been likely to have established such collections.

But the mere existence of 'unknown' Greek texts is evidence that cannot be overlooked. Not only the standard texts, the sanctioned documents as it were, were considered, but also accompanying material. The discovery of texts such as the unidentified Greek document and the Exodus paraphrase in cave 4, prove that when the Qumran Essenes collected Greek texts they were not only interested in possessing the Torah and so forth in the language of the Septuagint. They also took note of theology, exegesis and secondary literature in the Greek language. Surely therefore it would not be unnatural for Christian texts to find room in a Qumran cave also.

All this goes to show that the Greek language played an important role among the Qumran Essenes, and helps us to complete the model we have been constructing of the Essenes and 'Christians' prior to AD 70. It is certain that during that period both Jesus and his disciples, as well as many Jews in general, spoke Greek as much as Aramaic. Now we must also put on record that this applied to the Essenes also. They too were a part of their contemporary multicultural society, despite their initial isolation from the temple cult in Jerusalem. We see more and more clearly that even quite a remote area by the Dead Sea, apparently isolated and referred to as desert,[10] attracted men who, quite independent of their political or theological viewpoint, were quite naturally at home in more than one language, and in more than one culture. Let me demonstrate the basis of this assertion with three examples.

In New Testament times, during the middle of the 1st century AD, a Greek manuscript was written in iambic trimeters, which was later discovered not far from Qumran. This could be a fragment of a Greek comedy (Colin Austin 1973, the first publishers at the École Biblique saw it as a philosophical text[11]).

Only a little later, also found in the Wadi Murabba'at, there is a Greek tachygraphic manuscript - a short hand text[12] - which has not yet been decoded.

As for the text in iambic trimeters, it is furthermore to be noted that palaeographically it may be related to the same Greek style of writing (so-called Herodean ornamental style) as most of the Greek fragments in the 4th and 7th caves at Qumran (naturally a similar statement is impossible for the Greek tachygraphy fragment). The knowledge of tachygraphic writing among Greek speaking Jewry is documented in the Septuagint text of Psalm 45:2.[13] Thus the Murabba'at discovery confirmed what was already known.

Whilst a discovery that indicates that there was amongst Jews of this period at least some knowledge of tachygraphy may be unastonishing, a discovery that indicates that a Greek comedy text was present and known in this area really is thought-provoking news. If Paul can quote from the comedy author Menander (1 Cor. 15:33 = Fr. Thais), we may assume that he could have been acquainted with this type of literature since his school and student days. Often Paul's knowledge of Greek texts (usually only Arat is acknowledged, but he also knows Aeschylus and Epimenides, perhaps also Euripides) is connected with his teacher Gamaliel. The more we know about Greek language competence among Jews of all theological orientations the more credible this supposition becomes.

It should be pointed out in passing that there are good arguments for the assumption that Jesus himself had come into contact with the theatre and Greek drama in his younger days.[14]

Finally, good evidence for the spread of Greek in the New Testament world is provided at Masada - evidence which is made more interesting for our present context because of the connection between Qumran and Masada. Qumran texts like the Sabbath Songs have also been found at Masada, and it can be regarded as certain that Qumran Essenes fled the Romans to this fortress before they, too, were conquered by the occupation force in AD 73/74.

Not only Aramaic and Hebrew texts were found at Masada, but Greek and Latin texts also. The Latin texts - which incidentally include the oldest preserved fragment of Virgil's, Aeneid 4.9[15] - can be related to the Roman occupation; they were found at a separate location and present an individual typology.

However, the Greek papyri and ostraca were not only found where Aramaic ones were; more than that, they belonged to the same group of texts. They comprise information about quantities of water and provisions to be shared among the defenders of the fortress. Proper names are also quoted. Everything happens at random in Greek or Aramaic. The numerical proportions approximately correspond to the scroll fragments at Qumran: hundreds of Hebrew-Aramaic ostraca compare with a few dozen Greek ones. [16]

This is not surprising as no-one doubts that Aramaic was the mother tongue, and would therefore be the first to be used in everyday speech. Yet the undoubted fact that texts of identical content and purpose were also written in Greek - not for external communication, but for internal purposes - underlines the ease with which Greek could be used. Perhaps the situation can be summarized more appositely: not only were there Hellenists amongst the Early Christians around Stephen, Philip, Prochorus, Nicanor, Parmenas and Nicholas,[17] but there were also Greek speakers amongst the Qumran Essenes and the Masada Zealots, whom the Qumran Essenes joined. This group of Essenes were able to communicate in Greek among themselves and if necessary with others. At any rate the evidence from Qumran caves 4 and 7 and the sites at Masada show that it was not exclusion, but multilingual togetherness which was taking place.

For this reason it is no coincidence that the indirect verse about the Essene priests who converted to Christianity, Acts 6:7, appears in that part of the Acts of the Apostles which reports on the Hellenists and Stephen. It seems as if the writer did not insert something foreign by accident, but as if he particularly intended to signal how well even the Essene leadership could be integrated into a Christian environment in which Greek too was spoken.

One consequence of the current Qumran debate could well be a detailed investigation of the multilingualism of first century Palestine. After the Greek fragments of the fourth cave at Qumran have been published and been shown to be comparable to those of the seventh cave, there can be no doubt about the trilingualism of the Essenes (Aramaic, Hebrew, Greek). In addition, the more apparent it has become that the use of Greek, even amongst nationalistically minded Jews, was common - especially after publication of the papyrus and ostraca discoveries at Masada - the more we have to bid farewell to the old prejudices about the linguistic competence of Jews and Jewish Christians.

The Early Christians were not poor, uneducated 'underprivileged' people in an outlying region of the Roman Empire. They shared the same multicultural environment as their Jewish fellow citizens. This shared cultural identity operated regardless of their political attitude to their time. Even during periods of 'resistance' against Roman occupation - such as the Zealot uprisings in AD 66 and 73, or 'inner resistance' - the culture of the empire with its cultural language, Greek, was used naturally as an everyday tool.

And one can go further. The Masada discoveries indicate clearly that even during a period of tension, this group of Jews were naturally and voluntarily in communication with each other in another tongue. This would seem to take the matter beyond multilingualism, and indicate instead at least a degree of multiculturalism.

The scope of early Christian 'conversion successes' is much more easily understood against such a multicultural background. Such reported success cannot now be adequately understood as either a coincidence, or a result of bias on the part of the reporter (Luke). That the first newly converted Christians we hear of were an Ethiopian Minister of Finance, a Roman centurion and Essene priests now fits perfectly into the picture which was beginning to emerge from research in recent years, at least since Hengel,[18] and which is confirmed by the latest studies of Qumran.

Right from the start early Christianity took advantage of the positive factors to be found in its environment and used them for its own ends. One such factor was that the environment in which it operated was without significant language barriers. To this extent classical antiquity was an ideal breeding ground for a Christian point of view.

NOTES

1   M. Baignent/R.Leigh, *The Dead Sea Scrolls Deception*, London 1991; R. Eisenman/M. Wise, *The Dead Sea Scrolls Uncovered*.

2   B. Thiering, *Jesus the Man: A New Interpretation from the Dead Sea Scrolls*, New York 1992.

3   *Discoveries in the Judean Desert IX, Qumran Cave 4 IV*, Oxford 1992.

4   *Discoveries in the Judean Desert VIII, The Greek Minor Prophets Scroll from Nahal Hever (8 Hev XtI gr)*, Oxford 1990, 19-26.

5   J. van Haelst, *Catalogue des papyrus littéraires juifs et chrétiennes*, Paris 1976.

6   For a summary of the discussion see: C.P. Thiede, *The Earliest Gospel Manuscript?*, Exeter/Carlisle 1992, *Christen und Christliches in Qumran?* Regensburg 1992; O. Betz/R. Riesner, *Jesus, Qumran und der Vatikan - Klarstellungen*, Gießen/Freiburg [H{5}] 1994, 139- 150.

7   See also chapter 18 in this book. Even if one were to follow all 7Q-suggestions, even in this cav1e several fragments would remain without suggestion of identification, as is the case with two of the six fragments in the 4th cave.

8   For a summary see, J. O'Callaghan, *Los papiros griegos de la Cueva 7 de Qumrân*, Madrid 1974, 89-91; re 7Ql9 see also chapter 18.

9   K.H. Rengstorf, *Hirbet Qumran und die Bibliothek vom Toten Meer*, Stuttgart 1960, 22-23 and 34. This theory has recently been regurgitated by N. Golb in a number of publications, which depart from orthodox archaeology, and which may be considered methodologically unsound.

10   Thus already in Luke 1:80, but also the title of the Qumran edition, *'Discoveries in the Judaean Desert'*.

11   C. Austin, *Comicorum Graecorum Fragmenta in papyris reperta*, Oxford 1973, no. 360; cf: Discoveries in the Judaean Desert II, *Les Grottes de Murabba'at,* Oxford 1961, 234; plate 81.

12   *DJD* II, as in note 11, .275-277, plate 164.

13   See also chapter 7 in this book.

14   See also R.A. Batey, 'Jesus in the Theatre', *in New Testament Studies* 30, 1984, 563-74; C.P. Thiede, *Jesus - Life or Legend?* Oxford 1990, 23-27; B. Schwank, 'Sepphoris', in *Das große Bibellexikon*, Wuppertal/Zurich 1990, vol. 3, p.1429.

15   H. M. Cotton/J. Geiger, *Masada II: The Greek and Latin Documents*, Jerusalem 1989, 31-35, plate 1.

16   As above, 113-129, plates 13-16; *Tituli Picti*: 179-198, plates 30-39.

17   Acts 6.5.

18   M. Hengel, *Juden, Griechen and Barbaren. Aspekte der Hellenisierung des Judentums in vorchristlicher Zeit*, Stuttgart 1976, and subsequent literature.

16

Christianity and Qumran: Cave 7 in its Papyrological Context

It goes without saying that making comparisons is a central part of papyrological work. No ancient manuscript can be reliably classified unless it is capable of being compared with other documents which we think will provide a 'match', or will at the very least establish certain parameters.

In order to make valid comparisons we have to be prepared to respect the evidence we find, and not to spend our time searching for ways in which to explain away any difficulties that may arise. Problems of comparison can be found at their most acute when one is seeking to examine the relationship between Qumran and early Christianity. One of the key textual battlegrounds in this debate concerns the identification of certain of the minute fragments from cave 7 with passages from Christian texts.

Given the centrality of comparison as a technique, it is perhaps somewhat surprising that it has played a largely secondary role in the debate on the key fragment from cave 7 at Qumran: fragment 7Q5, Mark 6:52-53.

Kurt Aland did use comparison as part of his *ad hominem* argument against José O'Callaghan's Markean identification of the fragments in cave 7. Aland wrote that if this fragment and the other three 'Mark' fragments in cave 7 (7Q6=Mk 4:28; 7Q7= Mk 1:.17; 7Q15=Mk 6:48) listed by O'Callaghan were indeed all from Mark, then given that they were written by different authors, it would mean that there were at Qumran four copies of Mark's gospel all dating from the same period, a suggestion that Aland found inconceivable.[1]

Leaving aside the fact that it is by no means certain that the four fragments do indeed come from different authors, it is possible that what we are actually dealing with here are different authors within a single scroll, as can be found both in other Qumran scrolls and elsewhere.[2.] Yet why was Aland so confident that there could not have been a number of different copies of all or part of this short gospel in and around Jerusalem before AD 68 which were then deposited in cave 7? Aland produces no evidence to support his dismissal of this possibility, and indeed it is difficult to think of a way in which his hypothesis could ever be substantiated.

If we proceed with this kind of partly false and quite unverifiable assumptions, and are deaf to the possibility of meaningful comparisons from the outset, we shall swiftly fail and we will deserve to do so.

I would like to suggest a different *modus operandi*. Using other manuscripts of a similar date and geographical origin, and drawn from biblical and non-biblical source material, I would like to investigate whether the distinctive features of fragment 7Q5 are so exceptional that they render any comparisons meaningless, or whether the fragment can be seen to be a part of a given milieu, in which case comparisons will be possible.

In what follows I will attempt to give a summary of those distinctive features of 7Q5 which are most often mentioned as hindering identification, or which are offered as providing decisive arguments against the identification with Mk 6:52-53. For the purposes of this argument I do not propose to consider the so-called 'disputed characters' as they have been subjected to an extensive analysis elsewhere.

The first point brought up in critical studies, is the change in consonants from δ to τ in δ/τιαπεράσαντες after the και parataxis (i.e. a complete sentence beginning with 'and', such as Mark 6:53).

The second point is the omission, assumed by the stichometric measure, of the words ἐπὶ τὴν γῆν after τιαπεράοντες in line 3, or at the beginning of line 4. Without these three words line 3 has twenty characters and line four twenty-one. By way of comparison line 1 has twenty characters, line 2 twenty-three and line 5 twenty-one. This regularity would be disrupted by the presence of ἐπὶ τὴν γῆν, and therefore whilst it is not entirely compelling it would appear to make sense to omit these words.

Thirdly, apart from the conspicuous sequence of characters *ννης* only one complete word - *και* - is present in line 4, which in spite of its obvious paratactical function is very common. To examine the first point, the very presence of the parataxis *και* in the middle of line 3 as well as the spatium proceeding *και*, both exactly correspond with the new narrative unit beginning in Mark 6:53, and do in fact offer definite help in establishing an identification with Mark 6:52-53. Here the character *η* proceeding the spatium, which is only present in part but which has not been disputed, is the same as the last letter of the passage Mark 6:52. This interpretation is given additional help by the rare sequence of characters mentioned in line 4, as well as by the small deviations from *scriptio continua*, found exactly where gaps would be expected in case of a proper identification with Mark 6:52-53 - that is between the final characters of line 2 which belong to *αὐτῶν ή* (*ν* and *η* with a small gap in between), as well as *Iotas* and *Tau* in line 3 which form the *ι* of *και* and the *τ* of *τιαπεράσντες*.

For present purposes, I intend to ignore the numerous positive indications to be found in any examination of fragment 7Q5, and concentrate instead on analysing the disputed phenomena. What are the deviations from the standard text - the sound shifts and omissions - and what inconsistencies can be found in an examination of the topographical and chronological environment of 7Q5? How problematic would the omission of *ἐπι τὴν γῆν* be, even if as I have shown elsewhere such an omission not only fits internal New Testament usage of constructions with *διαπεράνω*, but is also an absolutely consistent variant for the early palaeographical classification of this fragment? To put it another way, how close does the text found in 7Q5 have to be to standard readings of the gospel, in order for it to be counted as Markean, taking into account its environment and size?

The Immediate Environment

All fragments found in cave 7 are small in size. 7Q4, the largest fragment found in the cave, only measures 7.2 x 3.5 cm, whilst other fragments 7Q19 (4.3 x 3.4cm), 7Q1 (4.7 x 2.3 cm), 7Q2 (3.5 x 3.2 cm), 7Q3 (3.2 x 2.8 cm) and 7Q5 (3.3 x 2.3 cm), though even smaller still, are large when compared to the remaining fragments in the cave.

Now the size of a preserved papyrus does not necessarily relate to the number of lines and characters to be found on it, nor in particular to its state of preservation and legibility, but it can be indicative of the former at least. One fragment from a different source that can be used as a benchmark (and to which we will return later), is a fragment from Menander's *Samia* (P Oxy XXXVII 2831), which measures 2.4 x 3.3 cm and which is thus smaller than several of the fragments from cave 7 described above, and only a millimetre larger than fragment 7Q5.

Two of the fragments from cave 7 were identified in 1962 by the editors of the 'Petits Grottes de Qumrân', in *Discoveries in the Judean Desert of Jordan* Volume III,[5] as being Exodus 28:4-6 and 28:7 (7Q1), and the Letter of Jeremiah/Baruch 6:43-44 (7Q2). Both identifications are still quoted without criticism by all relevant commentaries on the Septuagint text, and yet it may be of interest to look at them again in order to demonstrate the way in which comparative techniques have been used in less contentious identifications, and to draw some conclusions as to where to set the guidelines when making such identifications.

Despite the general acceptance of the 7Q1 and 7Q2 identifications, it becomes apparent upon even the most superficial examination of the supportive analysis, that neither is entirely unambiguous or without problems. Fragment 7Q1 includes some nine lines (+ two for the separate scrap) and some 54 characters. However, of the characters which are readily identifiable in the fragment, and excluding καɩ and το which are little everyday words of no distinctive meaning, there is only one entirely legible passage of words - τοχϱυσίον - which is not specifically biblical. Diacritical marks or other distinctive palaeographical features are also absent from the text with the exception of the spatium in front of κα [ɩ] at the beginning of verse six.

Boismard, who was responsible for making the identification, had already stated that 'le text est en général plus proche du TM que la LXX2'.[6] Amongst other omissions he pointed out that in verse 4 the fragment differs from the Septuagint by not including εις το in front of ιερατευειν. Here we quickly encounter an omission of exactly the sort which others have used to rule out the Markean attribution of 7Q5, yet miraculously in this case it presents no problems to the commentators. In addition to this omission the fragment also includes two words which are in turn 'omissions' from the standard text LXX.[7]

Having accepted these points - the divergences from the standard text in terms of both omissions and inclusions - it is still possible to construct a stichometrical solution which will make the attribution of the passage to Exodus 28:4-7 possible. But whatever the truth of this identification, it should be clear by now that the difficulties in the attribution of 7Q5 are no greater than those in the case of 7Q1.

In anticipation of later argument I should add at this point that Boismard notes a further deviation in the fragment 7Q1. In order to increase the area of text he could interpret he chose to add to the fragment itself another fragment of 1.1 x 1 cm which he considered to be contiguous with it. This second fragment contains in the first line the barely discernable characters σον, and in the second line the clear characters τε followed by the less accessible ρα. By doing this he is able to add to the number of discernible characters such that he can postulate the presence of the word ἑτέραν in the second line. Boismard notes that with the character 'ρ' 'le boucle revient croiser le trait vertical, donc un peu différent de ceux du f.I'.[8] Indeed the difference is so remarkable, that one may ask whether the two fragments are the products of the same author.

Turning to the fragment 7Q2 it is clear that matters are little better. Benoit and Boismard jointly identified this fragment as part of the Letter of Jeremiah, that is Baruch 6:43-44. Here we have five lines with twenty-two characters of which five are merely assumed. In other words we have here the same number of lines, and only two more characters, than are found in fragment 7Q5. In 7Q2 two words are complete - οὖν and αὐτούς - neither of which are specific to the Bible, and neither of which is unusual or in any way helpful to an identification. In order to come to any sensible reading of the text Benoit and Boismard have to assume a ϑ after αὐτούς in line four. To get to their eventual identification therefore Benoit and Boismard have been forced to favour one out of a number of potentially equal interpretations. To make such an interpretive leap is a legitimate scholarly technique, but if it is legitimate to do so in the context of an Old Testament or Deuterocanonical 'text' it must also be legitimate to use an identical technique when examining a putative New Testament text later on.

Of more significance than the interpretation of the single character ϑ is the omission of no fewer than five words of verse 44. In order to make the identification with Baruch 6:43-44, it must be assumed that between νομιστέον (of which only νο has been preserved) and ὑπάρχειϖ (which could only be made accessible by stichometry anyway), the sequence of words ἤ χλητέον ὥστε θεοὺς is absent, and further that the continuation is not with verse 45 (Ὑπὸ τεκτόνων), but with a totally different wording which Benoit and Boismard have derived from the Lucian Review and the Syrian text.

Given the size of fragment 7Q2 it is legitimate to ask whether Benoit and Boismard have not made too many exceptions and assumptions. On the other hand one may ironically consider that such a working technique is entirely legitimate for analysis of a Qumran fragment providing that in working in this way no-one gets the idea that the fragment could have originated in the New Testament. P.J. Parsons recently took as read the identification of fragment 7Q2 as 'EpistJer', whilst in the next sentence turning down fragments 7Q4 to 7Q9 as 'unprofitable scraps'.[9]   Double standards are operating here, and they prevent us from reasoning objectively.

For the purposes of extending the scope of our comparison, let us look at another fragment found in the immediate environment of 7Q5: 7Q4. Here O'Callaghan had suggested a New Testament text, 1 Timothy 3:16 to 4:1 and 4:3.[10] In our examination of this text we must forget about what the confirmation of this identification would mean for our understanding of the New Testament in general. For in the view of a growing number of scholars, not all of whom are drawn from the ranks of conservative exegetes, there is no evidence so convincing that it rules out the existence of this Pastoral Letter prior to AD 68 (irrespective of the Letter's author), and there is therefore no certain theological reason why this identification cannot be postulated.[11]   This identification of 7Q4 with 1

Timothy is also of interest for papyrological reasons, as, if accurate, the fragment would represent the only known papyrus of this letter.

When we examine 7Q4, one distinctive feature sticks out immediately which delineates this fragment from the others found in cave 7. Not only is it the largest of all 7Q fragments, but more importantly the main fragment and the smaller piece related to it, are quite obviously from the right hand margin of the text. It is therefore certain how the preserved lines end. With small fragments this is naturally an invaluable aid to identification.

Five lines in the main fragment have been preserved, and a further two lines in the small piece related to it. Line one of the main fragment has one character which is illegible and has been badly affected by a piece of adhesive tape. Line one of the smaller piece is also no longer legible. In line five of the main fragment there is some considerable damage which has led to two characters being moved sideways. But despite these problems, of the total number of twenty-one characters on seven lines, eighteen are easily legible.

Besides the distinctive feature of the fragment coming from the right hand margin of the text, the following points are also aids to identification: clearly recognizable verb endings in line three ($ov\tau\alpha\iota$); a clearly recognizable ending to a noun in line two ($\eta\tau\omega v$), and important parts of a further more noteworthy word in line 4 ($\pi v\varepsilon v$). Also worth noticing is the sequence of characters in the small fragment line 2 ($o\vartheta\varepsilon$), which are without doubt attributable to the same scribe and which again refer to a noun, this time with an article. The obvious assumption is $\acute{o}$ $\vartheta\varepsilon\grave{o}\varsigma$, which is also the reading used by O'Callaghan.

To recap, it is true that with the exception of the article $\acute{o}$, no complete word has been preserved, yet this fragment still offers an exceptional wealth of palaeographical and textual characteristics, which are absent from fragments 7Q1 and 7Q2.

O'Callaghan's interpretation only varies in one place - at the bottom where the fragment is extremely damaged - from that of Baillet, the first editor, who had not attempted an identification. Further examination of the original confirms that the remnant thought to be an *Iota* by Baillet is in fact the horizontal stroke of an *Eta,* and we have here one torn character, H, rather than ΓΙ. There is indeed no clue for a *Gamma* in the original.

What about deviations from well known texts, variants which are after all the norm and not the exception in 7Q1 and 7Q2? These are present here too, and though naturally they are different from the variants in 7Q1 and 7Q2, they have to be fitted into the same familiar conditions. For example in line two ῥητῶς must be read instead of ῥητῶν. The sound shift *s* to *v* is found extensively in Greek papyri. Mayser, Völker and Rademacher have all produced proof of this transposition in both the pre-New Testament and New Testament periods. On the other hand it could be a genuine variant. The adverb ῥητῶς appears only in this one place in the New Testament, and not at all in the standard text of the LXX. The adverb ῥητῶν can replace it without difficulty.

The writer of the fragment could therefore quite easily have put the familiar noun ῥητῶν in the place of such a rare adverb. The passage would therefore read τὸ δὲ πνεῦμα τῶν ῥητῶν - 'the spirit of words'. This reading would fit into the context quite well, as here we are indeed talking about the Holy Spirit working prophetically.

Certainly this passage, if it is to be read as O'Callaghan would argue, contains a deviation. Yet this deviation is quite different from those in fragment 7Q2, as it is derived from the text itself and is in any event only a marginal alteration from the usual interpretation.

In line 3 the omission of the usual ὅτι ἐν has to be assumed for stichometrical reasons. We have already come across the tendency to omit words in this way in fragment 7Q1. What was no obstacle to an interpretation there, should not be one here - even less so since the omission causes no problems of grammar or content.

In line 5 O'Callaghan presumed that the portion of the fragment which was not preserved contained πλάνοις rather than πλάνης. The one character difference naturally influences the stichometry, but only marginally and it is of no real importance. If one nevertheless accepts this variant, and O'Callaghan has been extremely meticulous in his analysis, there are no fewer than twenty-nine examples of this variation in biblical manuscripts.[12]

Finally in the fifth and last line of the fragment the word ημο suggests δημονίων rather than the more common δαιμονίων. This itacism is found so often that it is not really worth us discussing here.[13]

Let us summarize the position so far. None of the variants postulated by O'Calllaghan changes key points in the text, where the work of identification has to start. The fragment 7Q4 can be regarded as both identifiable and identified, not only by the standards of 7Q1 and 7Q2, but also on its own terms. It is the only papyrus of the First Letter of Timothy; it must be dated on palaeographical grounds to the middle of the first century AD.

Let it be said in passing that an attempt to identify 7Q4 as Enoch 10:.3f,[14] failed mainly because the small fragment with the second line οϑε cannot be taken into consideration, unless the order is reversed and bigger gaps are assumed. Only in Enoch 98:11 could characters be found which might be made to fit with this. In addition the assumption that της is divided after η is a cornerstone of this identification. With inscriptions, nearly anything is possible, but not in literary papyri. Then there is a question as to whether the word της should be present at all. According to Enoch 103:3 it should read ταις. An itacism αι to η is assumed elsewhere by O'Callaghan, but whilst his δαιμονίων/δημονίων transposition is normal, the variant assumed by the Enoch reading of της/ταις would be more than exceptional in literary papyri. In addition the probability of this identification being correct is further reduced by the fact that assuming that the passage is from Enoch, a 'wrong' της would follow on immediately from a 'correct' ψυχαις. If this should be believed to be the case we can only assume an extremely muddled author, but in any event given that the Timothy identification of the passage does not call for such an inconsistency, it must be preferred to this somewhat laboured attempt to identify 7Q4 with Enoch.

G.W. Nebe has in his work on 7Q4 cleared away at least some of the undergrowth, and it now becomes clear that in order to break the identification of the fragment with 1 Timothy 3:16-4:3 one has to employ methods and hypotheses which do not have a reference point within a comparable environment.

In my own book on fragment 7Q5[15] I have compared this fragment extensively with the codex papyrus p^{52}, which is still generally regarded as the oldest text fragment of the New Testament, although Young Kyu-Kim has recently held that codex p^{46} is older and dates from the late first century AD.[16]

In this context I shall not comment on either p^{52} or p^{46} as in both cases they are codex fragments - in any case papyri that are written on both sides - whilst in cave 7 we are dealing with scroll fragments which are much harder to identify as there is no possibility of using both the front and back (*recto* and *verso*) in comparisons. Because of this difference in the kinds of documents under discussion, I feel that it is only worth mentioning in passing that the phenomena found in the papyri fragments of cave 7 - especially the omission of one or more words and the use of variant characters - are also common amongst those papyri whose identification is beyond doubt. In the case of p^{52} I would refer to the example given in my book, of the omission of the repetition of εἰς τοῦτο in John 18:37, in the second part of the verse. Amongst all the manuscripts of John this stichometrically unalterable omission is only found in p^{52}. Strangely this variant has not found its way into Nestle-Aland or any of the other editions of the New Testament in Greek.

It is also of interest that changes to the standard word order and numerous itacisms are further distinguishing features of p^{52}.

At this point it may also be useful to look at an edition of New Testament papyrus fragment p^{91} (P.Macquarrie Inv 360=Acts 2;30-37; 2:46-3:2), which Stuart Pickering - an opponent of the identification of 7Q5 with Mark 6:52-53 - has prepared.[17] In line 2 of this fragment (= Acts 2:31) there is a considerable omission. The words τοῦ Χριστοῦ are entirely absent from the text. This omission is only found in this single manuscript. Such an omission is clearly more important than either ἐπὶ τὴν γῆν in 7Q5, or ὅτι ἐν in 7Q4. Apart from this example p^{91} also includes the following omissions: in line 4 (= Acts 2:32) it would appear that both ἐσμεν and ἡμεῖς are missing. In line 11 (= Acts 2:36) ὅτι is absent after the καὶ. In addition to these omissions there are a number of further variants which can be found in Pickering's edition.

Given the extent to which this fragment departs from the standard reading of the passage, one has to ask the question why Pickering would choose to comment critically and at such length upon the 7Q5 omission in the polemical treatise that he prepared with R.R.E. Cook ('Has a Fragment of the Gospel of Mark been Found at Qumran ?'[18]). Despite their polemic, however, both authors do in fairness concede that 'such an omission, or primitive shorter text, is not impossible',[19] and this is after all what we are talking about.

The Environment Outside the Bible

During a survey of Masada an interesting fragment was found which despite its very different content may help to provide an interesting comparison. Written a little later than either 7Q4 or 7Q5, it was subsequently dated to a timeframe 'shortly before Spring of 73 or 74 CE'.

Although published in 1989, this fragment has still not yet received the full measure of attention which is its due.[20] The fragment, which measures 16cm x 18cm, is quite substantial in comparison with some of the other fragments we have been discussing. Its *recto* contains fifteen discernible characters - two of which are fully legible - in a single line. The *verso* also contains fifteen characters on a single line, of which three are present only in fragments.

Whilst the text on the reverse cannot be decoded even by using *Ibykus* (the advanced computer programme which contains texts from Greek and Roman literature which can be accessed for comparative purposes) - this despite the fact that it contains the word *titubantia* which is an unusual one - the line of text on the front has been identified by Joseph Geiger as being part of Virgil's Aeneid 4.9: *Anna soror quae me suspensam insomnia terrent*.

The legible part of this text are the characters:

]NA[]OR[]RQUAEMESUSP[

Both of the R's have been reconstructed from barely legible remnants. In other places the ink is no longer visible, even when using infra red enlargement. Apart from the 'NA' proceeding the 'O', only the everyday words *quae* and *me* are fully legible, along with the noticeable beginning *susp.*

Yet despite the paucity of material this combination of letters is enough for an identification. The characteristics of the line are specific enough, such that no other text could be considered, even if one would only use the minimal amount of text that is present on the right of the line.

From a scholarly point of view this identification is important for two reasons.

First, it shows what can be done with the smallest of fragments, even when as is the case with this document, the material did not form part of a full text, but was only a writing or memory exercise.

Secondly, to find a portion of a Virgil text at Masada where no-one would have necessarily expected to find it, and to be able to date it to the period just after the taking of the fortress by the Romans (thereby making it the oldest known manuscript of Virgil), and to do so on the basis of a mere fifteen characters is sensational. And here again we meet those double standards. Virgil on Masada is happily (and rightly) accepted, with less evidence to show for it than the disputed Mark identification at Qumran.

In this context it is revealing that the same *Ibykus* computer programme which contributed to the identification of this Masada fragment (721a), and which could not place the *verso* (721b) as being present in the preserved Latin literature despite the presence of a complete word, identified the combination of characters in 7Q5 as read by José O'Callaghan and others as being Mark 6:52-53. [21] If it is accepted that O'Callaghan made an accurate transcription of the characters found in 7Q5 (as was confirmed by Herbert Hunger, Orsolina Montevecchi and many others), then it holds true here just as it did with the Virgil fragment, that these characters can only belong to one text of preserved Greek-Roman literature, and that text is Mark 6:52-53.

This identification can be made with even greater confidence given that none of the repeated attempts to question O'Callaghan's interpretations in difficult areas of the papyrus, and to replace them with other suggestions, have led to a constructive result. All attempts at finding and combining variants as plausible alternatives to those originally suggested by O'Callaghan have without exception failed - even those experimentally controlled by O'Callaghan himself following a subsequent computer analysis.[22]

Furthermore one other instructive point can be derived from the Masada fragment.

Following Kurt Aland[23] it is generally considered that the text on the reverse of a fragment makes identification easier, or in the case of very small fragments, more probable.

I myself have used this 'rule of thumb' in my first edition of the New Testament papyrus p^{73} (Bodmer L=Mt 25.43 to 26.2-3).[24] However the Masada fragment 721 warns us of the dangers inherent in following this premise too rigidly, because as we have seen from our review of Geiger's analysis, in the case of this fragment what is written on the back does not contribute anything to its identification. For demonstrably the characters on the *verso* of 721 do not belong to the same text as those on the *recto*.

Let me end this chapter by returning to one final fragment which I have previously mentioned in passing. My reason for introducing this fragment is that I believe that it perfectly complements the Latin Virgil fragment as it is an extra biblical *Greek* literary text from a period that is again only marginally later than the 7Q fragments - that is around the end of the first century AD or the beginning of the second. [25] It is the fragment from Menander's *Samia* which was identified by Edgar Lobel, the great old man of Oxyrhynchus papyri. With his characteristic genius and unsurpassed knowledge of texts, Lobel had identified the scroll fragment which measured a mere 2.4 x 3.3 cm in size and on which the ends of six lines (five of which had visible characters) with nineteen legible or partially legible letters were present, as a passage from the third act of *Samia* (*Samia* 385-390). In making this identification he may well have been helped by the edition of the big *Samia* codex papyrus (Bodmer XXV) published the previous year (1968) by Rodolphe Kasser and Colin Austin, as it may well be that the context of the text was still fresh in his mind's eye when he held the minute Oxyrhynchus scrap in his hands.

Yet even so it is obvious that this fragment offers fewer reliable clues for identification than does 7Q5. It offers only the nondescript word τί in line 2, and ἰδού in line 5, together with νή in line 1, a word which previously one would not have thought to have existed in a literary text of that time. E.G. Turner who edited the fragment[27] wrote that 'νή used absolutely, has been commonly held to be unacceptable Greek. It has, in fact usually been emended away, to ναι or something else'.[28] In the years since Lobel's identification other evidence has been found to support this usage.[29]

Two nondescript words and one that according to the usual rules should not have been present at all, did not prevent Lobel, Turner and Austin also, from reliably identifying the fragment, nor did the paucity of the evidence lead others to question this interpretation. It is the wealth of individual characteristics, including the ending κνει of the word which is assumed to be δακνει in line 3, as much as the evidently dialogic construction which is marked twice by a dikolon (in lines 1 and 3, the second of which however is a spelling mistake), which not only make it clear that the passage is from a dramatic text, but also that it is from precisely that section of *Samia*.

On the other hand which *Samia* is this? Clearly it is recognizably comparable with the text, as we know it from other manuscripts, yet there are deviations . The apparatus of F.H. Sandbach's edition of *Menandri Reliquiae Selectae* 2nd edition, Oxford 1990, 248, offers variants for every verse from 385 to 390 of the Oxrhynchus fragment which is kept here under Siglum O 16, and these variants go so far that for fragment 385 to 387 they offer a sequence of text different from the usual reading.

The classicist may remember with a good conscience the *delectat varietas* (as we find it in Phaedrus, *Liber Fabularum II*, prol. 10, although in doing so we should note with amusement that here again we have an example of transformation, as the current form in which this phrase is commonly quoted, *variatio delectat*, is not paralleled in ancient literature).

The New Testament scholar however will be left to ponder anew, as in the case of fragment 7Q5 the many questions which have been asked of the text with regard to its immediate and wider environment have resulted in answers that are in no way unusual, but rather well tested and accepted among the experts, and which have indeed been exactly in line with what might have been expected. None of the deviations in 7Q5 is unusual, and there are none which cannot be adequately accounted for on the basis of evidence from the document's textual environment; none leaves unanswered or unaswerable questions.

This applies even to the conspicuous change in consonants which is used as an argument against the identification of 7Q5 with Mark 6:52-53 and which was has not been discussed so far in this paper. The τ which replaced a δ in the word τιαπερἁσαντες in line three, is not only a sound shift that has been substantiated elsewhere many times, but also underscores the origin of the author as being from the Jerusalem area, since the most obvious contemporary proof for this change is the stone placed in the Temple of Herod warning non-Jews not to advance beyond the boundaries. A complete example of this stone is kept in Istanbul and fragments of it are in Jerusalem. On this stone the word for closing off, δρύφακτον, is here written with a τ rather than a δ. [30]

One of the 7Q5 critics, H.U. Rosenbaum, embarrassingly tried to eliminate the importance of this discovery. With considerable nonchalance he wrote the discovery off as a coincidence [31], as if the coincidence involved in a discovery (and this is not in any case a coincidence anyway), was an argument against the consequence of its having been found. The fact remains that even if literary material from within biblical texts or from outside sources is not used in our comparisons, conclusive evidence is available from other sources to classify 7Q5 in its time and environment.

Naturally enough when we look further there are literary examples of the change from *Delta* to *Tau* prior to an *Iota*. F.T. Gignac has listed several relevant examples in his *Grammar of the Greek Papyri of the Roman and Byzantine Periods, I Phonology*, Milan 1976, 80-83. For example in a document from the year AD 42 we find τίκης rather than δίκης, and again in a document from AD 132 we find τιακοσίας rather than διακοσίας . José O'Callaghan has offered further examples of where this occurs in biblical papyri;[32] even so the inscription on the Temple stone of Jerusalem remains the most exciting and revealing.

By way of showing how some people try to wipe out such definite evidence by hollow arguments, it may be worth returning to the work of the aforementioned H.U. Rosenbaum.

His essay of 1987 quoted above has happily received little attention, and even critics of the O'Callaghan identification have been so put off Rosenbaum by his occasional *faux pas* and errors of fact, that mention of his work is usually relegated to footnotes. With regard to the *Delta/Tau* sound shift in τιαπεράσαντες, Rosenbaum's rhetoric could only have had the effect of confusing those of his readers who were less familiar with the texts. Although he clearly knows Gignac's *Grammar of the Greek Papyri* he witholds its reference to the δι/τι transposition in a contemporary manuscript of AD 42. Then the twenty biblical references from four manuscripts are not enough for him, for as he points out there are after all two hundred and sixty-five biblical papyri and O'Callaghan was only able to prove that the shift occurred in 1.5% of them.[33] What is Rosenbaum trying to say? That such shifts are only significant if they appear in a given percentage of papyri, whether it be 10%, 50% or 100%? Does the exception have to become the rule before it is allowed to be the exception?

Similarly Rosenbaum's statement that the confusion of *Delta* and *Tau* was mainly an Egyptian phenomenon and was not established in the Semitic language area[34] is as methodologically flawed as it is inaccurate. Recently Peretz Segal proved that the Temple boundary stone with the word τρύφακτον rather than δρύφακτον, is by no means a Roman product (as Rosenberg, supported by Mommsen and Dittenberger, would have it), but is genuinely from Jerusalem.[35] As we have seen above, Rosenbaum attempts to get out of his difficulties by dismissing the Temple stone as a coincidence and then invokes Wilhelm Dittenberger's *Orientis Graeci Inscriptiones Selectae* (OGIS) no. 598 which quotes Herodianus Technicus, a grammarian of the second century AD. Herodianus knows about the shift from *Delta* to *Tau* and notes that δρύφακτον is derived from δρῦς. According to Herodianus those knowing the origin of the word still wrote with *Delta,* but otherwise the use of *Tau* was becoming more common. Herodianus' summary may or may not be accurate, but if so it is no different from similar examples which anyone studying any language will encounter to this day. But what is it that Rosenbaum wants to say? That for Herodianus sound shifts had nothing to do with local pronunciation, but were instead connected with etymology? If so he may well be right. But none of this contributes anything to a discussion of the Jerusalem Stone which was some two centuries earlier. The fact of the inscription does not disappear simply because one chooses to use as a key to interpretation the much later work of Herodianus.

One explanation suggested by Clermont-Ganneau to deal with the Jerusalem Stone variation , is that it may result from a special local Greek pronunciation.[36] This may be a hypothesis, but Rosenbaum fails to refute it. His use of Herodianus as the cornerstone of his argument is useless. We must hold on to the fact that in Jerusalem - and thus within the field of view of the Early Church from among whose members Mark's Gospel came, irrespective of our view as to where the Gospel was written - the change from *Delta* to *Tau* is documented. It is a simple as that. [37]

The task I gave myself at the beginning was to verify the fragment 7Q5 in the light of other ancient papyri (biblical and non-biblical) from its environment. Thus I have not discussed other questions pertaining to the identification of this papyrus. I hope however I have gone beyond this aim and have demonstrated that it is possible to do this fragment justice provided it is handled with the same rigorous methodological processes which are generally used in papyrology. It may well be the case that the consequences of identifying the Qumran fragments 7Q4 and 7Q5 as scraps from the First Letter of Timothy and St Mark's Gospel may have far greater impact than the identification of other scraps in the same cave with passages from the Greek Old Testament, and the Apocrypha, Virgil on Masada or even Menander at Oxyrhynchus. Yet the fact of an identification's subsequent importance must not lead us to change the way we look at the evidence, even if to do so may mean abandoning cherished hypotheses and traditional interpretations. The rules of a game do not change when the stakes are raised.

NOTES

1   K. Aland, 'Neue Neutestamentliche Papyri III', in *NTS* 20, 1974, 375-381; an unrevised reprint with the title 'Die Papyri aus Höhle7 von Qumran und ihre Zuschreibung zum Neuen Testament duch J. O'Callaghan', in K. Aland, *Supplementa zu den neutestamentlichen*

und den kirchengeschichtlichen Entwürfen, Beate Köster (ed.) , New York 1990, 142-157.

2   See E.Würthwein, *Der Text des Alten Testaments*, Stuttgart 3rd ed. 1988, 40.

3   J. O'Callaghan, 'The Identifications of 7Q', *Aegyptus* 56, 1976, 287-294.

4   C. P. Thiede, *The Earliest Gospel Manuscript? The Qumran Fragment 7Q5 and its significance for New Testament Studies*, Exeter 1992, 29-32.

5   Oxford 1962, 142-43.

6   Ibid, 142.

7   Ibid, 143.

8   Ibid, 143.

9   P.J. Parsons, 'Introduction', in E. Tov, *The Greek Minor Prophets Scroll from Nahal Hever*, Oxford 1990, 25.

10   J. O' Callaghan, '1 Tim. 3,16; 4,1-3 en 7Q4?' , in *Biblica* 53, 1972, 362-367.

11   See J.A.T. Robinson, *Redating the New Testament*, London 1976,82-85; G.E. Fee, *1 & 2 Timothy, Titus*, San Francisco 1984, xx-xxiii, xxxiv-xl; M. Prior, *Paul the Letter Writer and the Second Letter to Timothy,* Sheffield 1989, 13-59; D. Guthrie, *New Testament Introduction*, Leicester 1990, 607-55; see also J.Jeremias, 'Zur Datierung der Pastoralbriefe', *ZNW* 52, 1961, 101-104; J. van Bruggen, *Die geschichtliche Einordnung der Pastoralbriefe*, Wuppertal 1981.

12   So already H. v. Soden, *Die Schriften de Neuen Testaments II,* Göttingen 1913, 827, with list.

13   J. O'Callaghan, 'El cambio $\alpha\iota > \eta$ en P Chester Beatty XIII', *Biblica* 60, 1979, 567-569.

14   G.W.Nebe,'7Q4 - Möglichkeit und Grenze einer Identifikation', in *Revue de Qumran* 13, 1988, 629-633.

15   See above, note 4.

16   Y. K. Kim,'Palaeographical Dating of p^{46} to the Later First Century', *Biblica* 69, 1988, 248-57.

17   S.R. Pickering,'P. Macquarrie Inv. 360:(+P. Mil. Vogl. Inv. 1224): Acta Apostolorum 2.30-37, 2.46-3.2, in *ZPE* 65, 1986, 76-78 + plate 1b,c.

18   S. . Pickering and R.R E. Cook, 'Has a Fragment of the Gospel of Mark been Found at Qumran ?', *Papyrology and Historical Perspectives,* 1, Sydney 1989.

19   Ibid 13.

20   H. M. Cotton/J. Geiger, *Masada II: The Latin and Greek Documents,* Jerusalem 1989, 31-35 + plate I,721 a/b .

21   A. R. Millard, Liverpool, in a letter to the author dated 12 December 1990. See also my book*The Earliest Gospel Manuscript? The Qumran Papyrus 7Q5 and its Significance for New Testament Studies Exeter 1992, 40-41.*

22   J. O'Callaghan,'El Ordenador, 7Q5, y los autores griegos', *Studia Papyrologica* 13, 1974, 21-29; 'The Identifications of 7Q5', *Aegyptus* 56/1-4, 1976, 287-94.

23   K. Aland, 'Über die Möglichkeit der identifikation kleiner Fragmente neutestamentlicher Handschriften mit Hilfe des Computers', in J.K. Elliott (ed.), *Studies in New Testament Language and Text,* Leiden 1976, 14-38, in particular 21-22 and 32-33; uncorrected reprint in K. Aland, Supplementa (as in note 1), 117-141. It mars the otherwise quite valuable essay that Aland cites O'Callaghan's suggestions and tries to dismiss them with allegations that are plainly wrong and contradictory to the indisputable facts.

24   C.P. Thiede, 'Papyrus Bodmer L. Das neutestamentliche Papyrusfragment p^{73} = *Mt 25.43- 26.2-3',* in *Museum Helveticum* 47/1, 1990, 35-40 + plate.

25   E.G. Turner, 'Menander, Samia 385-390 Austin (170-175 Koe)', *Aegyptus* 47/3-4, 1967, 187-90 + plate, here 187. In spite of the official publication date '1967', the volume was only published in December 1969 (according to the imprint); this explains notes and references to publications of 1968 and 1969 in Turner's article.

26   R. Kasser/C.Austin, *Papyrus Bodmer XXV Ménandre, La Samienne,* Genf 1968.

27   See above note 25.

28   Ibid 189.

29   Ibid.

30   The first, and still most detailed commentary can be found in C. Clermont-Ganneau, 'Une stèle du temple de Jerusalem', in *Revue Archéologique,* 23, 1872, 215-34.

31   H.-U. Rosenbaum, 'Cave 7Q! Gegen die erneute Inanspruchnahme des Qumran-Fragments 7Q5 als Bruchstück der ältesten Evangelien-Handschrift', *BZ* 31, 1987, 189-205, here 200.

32   J. O'Callaghan, 'El cambio δ −τ en los papiros biblicos', *Biblica* 54, 1973, 415-416.

34   Ibid 200.

33   As above note 31, 198.

35   P. Segal, 'The Penalty of the Warning Inscription from the Temple of Jerusalem', *IEJ* 39, 1989, 79-84.

36   As above note 30, 222.

37   A detailed refutation of Rosenbaum's polemics and factual errors can be found in F. Rohrhirsch, *'Markus in Qumran ? Eine Auseinandersetzung mit den Argumenten für und gegen Fragment 7Q5 mit Hilfe des Methodischen Fallibilismusprinzips*, Wuppertal/Zurich 1990; see also C.P. Thiede, *'The Earlist Gospel Manuscript? The Qumran Fragment 7Q5 and its Significance for New Testament Studies*, Exeter 1992.

17

Greek Qumran Fragment 7Q5:Possibilities and Impossibilities

The Greek scroll fragments from Qumran present a curious phenomenon: whereas the one Greek Old Testament papyrus from Cave 4 (supplemented by four Greek parchment scraps and one Exodus paraphrase on papyrus from the same cave) does not appear to belong to a separate collection, but to a general, motley 'library' preserved in that cave, the neighbouring Cave 7 includes a collection in its own right - nothing but nineteen Greek fragments, eighteen of them on papyrus, and another one preserved as an imprint in the hardened soil of the cave. Recently, the international scholarly debate about this cave was given a new twist. Vittoria Spottorno, the new editor of the Spanish journal *Sefarad*, published an article which claims to shed new light on the most important Greek papyrus fragment from Cave 7, '7Q5'. In it, she proposes 'una nueva posible identificatión de 7Q5', Zechariah 7:4-5.[1]

Her paper appeared a couple of months after the publication of the Eichstätt University Qumran symposium, 'Christen und Christliches in Qumran?'[2] At Eichstätt, it had become apparent that there are more arguments in favour of the identification of 7Q5 as Mark 6:52-53 - a *New Testament* identification first suggested as long ago as 1972 by the Spanish papyrologist José O'Callaghan[3] - than had previously been supposed by a majority of scholars. Above all, it was the detailed analysis presented by the Vienna papyrologist Herbert Hunger in favour of the Markean identification which did not fail to impress the participants.[4] As an aftermath of the symposium, fragment 7Q5 was analyzed in the forensic laboratory of the Department of

Investigations at the Israel National Police in Jerusalem. The upper remnant of a decisive diagonal stroke could be made visible in line 2 and further contributed to the solidity of the Markean identification.[5] It is thus highly likely that 7Q5 = Mark 6:52-53 will have to be added to the official list of New Testament papyri sooner or later. On the other hand, attempts to suggest alternative identifications remain legitimate, even if - or perhaps precisely when - they are carried out in the ignorance of the results obtained at Eichstätt and Jerusalem. To try and find an Old Testament (LXX) passage for 7Q5 is neither new nor original,[6] not least in view of the fact that a fragment from Exodus (7Q1 = Exod 29:4-7) and one from the deuterocanonical Letter of Jeremiah (7Q2 = EpistJer 43-44) - two texts of some importance to early Christianity - had already been identified among the 7Q papyri.[7]

It is, however, not only Hunger's paper and the forensic analysis in Jerusalem that have recently added to the arguments in favour of 7Q5 = Mark 6:52-53; O'Callaghan's identification was checked by the *Ibykus* computer programme with the result that there is no other text than Mark 6:52-53 in extant Greek literature which fits the papyrological evidence of 7Q5.[8] Any alternative suggestion must therefore be expected to come up with corrections or improvements of at least equal value and importance as those represented by the Markan *status quo*. As this tiny scroll fragment offers a mere twenty letters on five lines,[9] the scope for convincing alternative readings is understandably limited.

A juxtaposition of the *editio princeps*, O'Callaghan's reading and Spottorno's alternative highlights the problem:

editio princeps	O'Callaghan	Spottorno
].[	]ε[	]τ.[
].τῷ α.[	]υτωνη[	]εγωνε[
]η και τω[	]η καιτι[	]ς καιπ[
ἐγε]ννησ[εν	]ννησ[	]ννησ[
].θηεσ.[	]θησα[	]ωηεν[
		]ε[

O'Callaghan's dot underneath the *Nu* in line 2 may now be deleted; the Jerusalem analysis has proved its existence beyond

the shadow of a doubt. However, this *Nu* is not part of
Spottorno's suggestions, anyway.

The extremely damaged letter in line 1 was not even
tentatively identified in the *editio princeps*,[10] even though the
working hypothesis of an *Epsilon* was admitted. On the other
hand, it cannot possibly be a *Tau*. This is obvious from a
comparison with the undamaged *Tau* in lines 2 and 3. Should
one want to look for an alternative to *Epsilon* in line 1, it might
just conceivably be *Sigma*.

It is thus equally impossible to read *Gamma* instead of *Tau*
in line 2. The *Tau* of 7Q5 is above suspicion and has been so as
early as in the *editio princeps*. The first and last letters of this
line are severely damaged; even so, O'Callaghan's *Upsilon* had
been accepted as a possibility by the original editor.[11] The *Eta*,
on the other hand, has gained further plausibility by the forensic
analysis in Jerusalem.[12] Therefore, Spottorno's variants are
highly unlikely, if not downright impossible.

As for line 3, both O'Callaghan and Spottorno read *kai* after
a *spatium*, i.e. paratactically. O'Callaghan's *Eta* is confirmed by
the *editio princeps* and indeed by all published enlargements,
including an infra-red photograph.[13] By definition, Spottorno's
Sigma must be ruled out as impossible. Prior to Spottorno, only
Aland had thought of reading *Pi* instead of *Tau* + ... at the end
of this line,[14] but without any serious argument in its favour.

In line 4, there are no differences suggested by Spottorno;
however, she wants to find a justification for her reading of *ea]n
nês[teúsête* (as in Zech. 7:5) by seeing 'las dos v de linea 4' as
'discontinuas'. Fragment 7Q5 does in fact offer two exceptions
to the rule of *scripto continua*; they indicate small gaps between
words - on line 2 (*autôn hê* of Mark 6:52) and in line 3 (*kai ti* of
Mark 6:53). The small gap in line 3 is part of the undamaged
centre of the fragment; thus it can be compared accurately to
the writing of the two *Nu* in line 4. It should be obvious to the
naked eye, even without the analysis of enlargements, that the
'gap' between the two *Nu* in line 4 is anything but a proper
spacing. Otherwise, even the undisputed *kai* in line 3 could not
be a *kai*, since the 'space' between *Kappa* and *Alpha* is as wide
as, if not wider than, between the two *Nu*.

In line 5, O'Callaghan and Spottorno have only one letter in
common, the second one, *Eta*. It might just be possible to admit

Spottorno's *Omega* as a remote alternative, even though no one, beginning with the *editio princeps*, has ever seen it here before. *Sigma* instead of *Epsilon* for the third letter was one of two possibilities suggested in the *editio princeps*; the remnants appear to belong to a curvature, however, and would be much too high for the horizontal stroke of an *Eta*. As for the practically invisible trace of the last letter in this line, it is severely damaged by a turning to the right of the papyrus, probably caused by an early attempt at destruction.[15] It is hardly possible to suggest, let alone identify any letter at all. Personally, I should have preferred a mere dot, but O'Callaghan's *Alpha* (contrary to the *Sigma* of the *editio princeps*) is supported by a concrete textual suggestion, Mark 6:52-53. Thus, if the papyrological and palaeographical evidence of the complete fragment supports the identification, as seems to be the case especially after Eichstätt and Jerusalem, it must be allowed to stand. In principle, the same would be true, needless to say, of Spottorno's *Nu*; but, as we have seen, her alternative identification is doomed already on the basis of irrefutable evidence against other letters of her reading. Furthermore, she adds a sixth line to the fragment and sees an *Epsilon* in it. Original as this addition may be, it is hampered by the papyrus itself: there simply is not enough extant material to allow for a sixth line, let alone for a letter - any letter - in it.

As we have seen, Spottorno's alternative identification is ruled out by insurmountable palaeographical barriers. There may be scope for debate in one or two secondary cases, but decisive letters pass an unequivocal verdict on her attempt.

All this is further corroborated by a look at the actual passage which she suggests in place of Mark 6:52-53, Zech 7:4-5, and which should be, as we have seen, according to the text of her own reconstruction, 7:3b-5. To begin with, there would be no justification for the undoubtable and undoubted paratactical *kai* after a *spatium*. And, as Spottorno herself admits,[16] the text presupposed by her identification cannot be reconciled with any existing critical edition: neither Rahlfs (1979) nor any of the others corroborate what she suggests as the text of Zech 7: (3b)-5. Admittedly, she may have remembered a seemingly comparable problem in 7Q5 = Mark 6:52-53.[17] However, the singular variants in Mark make sense and could even be expected, as has been shown more than once,[18] whereas Spottorno's variants stem from an extreme and philologically unjustifiable eclecticism. Thus, she does not even try to find reasons for them.. For example, there is the omission of *tôn dynameôn* in 7:4; the impossibility of a spatium before *kai* in 7:4; the addition of *tês gês* between *hiereis* and *legôn* in 7:5; *tô pemptô* instead of *tais pemptais* and *tô hebdomô* instead of *tais hebdomais* in 7:5.

The sheer number of these variants invalidates Spottorno's attempt to improve upon 7Q5 = Mark 6:52-53. Her suggestion is to be rejected as impossible for palaeographical as well as philological reasons.

NOTES

1   V. Spottorno, 'Una nueva posible identificación de 7Q5', *Sefarad* 52, 1992, 541-543. Correctly, however, her suggestion involves 7:3*b*-5.

2   B. Mayer, (ed.), *Christen und Christliches in Qumran?*, Regensburg 1992. This volume contains the most up-to-date photographs of Qumran fragment 7Q5 on pp. 41, 242 and 243 (enlargement of *Nu* detail, cf note 5). Photographs of 7Q5 can also be found in *Bib* 53 (1972), J. O'Callaghan, *Los papiros griegos de la cueva 7 de Qumrân* (as in note 13), and in C.P. Thiede, *The Earliest Gospel Manuscript? Qumran Fragment 7Q5 and Its Significance for New Testament Studies* (as in note 8). The first published photograph of 7Q5 was part of the original *DJD* II edition (cf note 7), vol. 2, *Planches*, planche XXX, no. 5.

3   J. O'Callaghan, 'Papiros neotestamentarios en la cueva 7 de Qumrân?', *Bib* 53, 1972, 91-100. Authorized English translation by W.L. Holladay: *JBL* 91, 1972, Supplement, 1-14.

4   H. Hunger, '7Q5: Markus 6:52-53 - oder? Die Meinung eines Papyrologen', *Christen und Christliches*, 33-56, with 22 ill.

5   C.P. Thiede, 'Bericht über die kriminaltechnische Untersuchung des Fragments 7Q5 in Jerusalem', *Christen und Christliches*, 239-245, with 4 ill.

6   Detailed documentation and analysis in F. Rohrhirsch, *Markus in Qumran?* Eine Auseinandersetzung mit den Argumenten für und gegen das Fragment 7Q5 mit Hilfe des methodischen Fallibilismusprinzips', Wuppertal/Zurich 1990, 106-128.

7   *Les 'Petites Grottes' de Qumrân* ed. M. Baillet, J.T. Milik, R. de Vaux, OP *DJD* III, Oxford 1962, 142-146.

8   Cf C.P. Thiede, *The Earliest Gospel Manuscript? The Qumran Papyrus 7Q5 and Its Significance for New Testament Studies*, Exeter-Carlisle 1992, 40-41, note 31.

9   For the sake of comparison: 7Q5 = EpistJer 43-44 has twenty-two letters on five lines; Masada fragment 721 = Virgil, *Aeneid* 4:9, has fifteen letters in one line.

10   *DJD* III, 144.

11   O'Callaghan, *Los papiros griegos* p. 47.

12   Thiede, 'Bericht', 240.

13   J. O'Callaghan, *Los papiros griegos de la Cueva 7 de Qumrân*, Madrid 1974, infra-red enlargement of 7Q5 on plate VI, infra-red photographs of other 7Q-fragments on plates IV and V.

14   K. Aland, 'Neue neutestamentliche Papyri III', *NTS* 20, 1974, 357-381, here 375.

15   See Thiede, 'Bericht', 240.

16   Spottorno, 'Una nueva posible indentificación', 543.

17   Omission of *epi ten gen* in 6:53 suggested by stichometry; *Tau* instead of *Delta* in *tiapersantes* 6:53.

18   Most recently by Hunger, '7Q5: Markus 6,52-53 - oder?' and C.P. Thiede, 'Papyrologische Anfragen an 7Q5 im Umfeld antiker Handschriften', *Christen und Christliches*, 57-72. See also Rohrhirsch, *Markus in Qumran*, 73-83, and Thiede, *The Earliest Gospel Manuscript?*, 29-32.

18
Fragment 7Q5:
A Forensic Analysis in
Jerusalem

On Sunday the 12th April 1992 (a working day in Israel) Qumran Fragment 7Q5 was examined forensically in the Investigations Department (Division of Identification and Forensic Science) of the Israel National Police. The appropriate committee of the Israel Antiquities Authority had given permission for the transport of the glass plate with the 7Q Fragments. The transfer of the documents from the John D. Rockefeller Museum to the police laboratory in the Sheik Jarak district was carried out by the curator Joseph Zias. The person responsible for the work in the Division of Identification and Forensic Science was Brigadier Dr Joseph Almog, Director of the department. The examination was carried out by Chief Inspector Sharon Landau in the presence of the above named gentlemen and the author of this paper. The decisive phases of the analysis were recorded by a TV team from the Bavarian Television company, ARD.

The aim of the examination was to answer two questions:

1. Has the fragment 7Q5 been preserved in an unmanipulated state, without later (human) intervention or change?

2. Is it possible to discern from the remains of characters in the middle of line 2, which are generally assumed to be significant for the identification, whether or not they represent two characters - for example *Iota adscript* with *Alpha* following - or only one, that is *Nu*?

At the Qumran Congress of October 1991 at Eichstätt University numerous examples for *Nus* had been presented by the Vienna papyrologist Herbert Hunger, showing considerable variants within a manuscript written by a single writer, This is in part clearly demonstrated by a complete *Nu* in line 4 and a reconstructed one in line 2 of fragment 7Q5. Herbert Hunger went on to say that not only would *Nu* be possible in line 2, one may interpret the remains still existing today 'with confidence as *Nu*'.

The forensic study gave a quick and clear solution to question 1. It is absolutely certain that there has been no subsequent intervention in the text of 7Q5. The visible stock of characters corresponds with the visible remains of the original text. It remains open whether the heavy damage, especially to the right hand side of the fragment (tear and turn towards top right), is to be traced back to early human intervention. The hypothesis presented for cave 4, that the Romans found it in AD 68 or soon after and opened it; that the jars were smashed and the scrolls torn up, explains the existence of hundreds of small fragments in the cave and could reasonably apply also to cave 7 situated close by. It fits into this picture that only one smashed jar and few tiny scraps of papyrus were found here, of which at least one (7Q5), perhaps a further one (the two part 7Q4) show traces of deliberate destruction.

The ensuing examination of line 2 of fragment 7Q5 under the stereo microscope showed the clearly visible remains of a line running diagonally from top left to bottom right, starting at the top from that vertical line which is supposed to be either an *Iota adscript* or the left vertical stroke of a *Nu*.

Because of the discovery of the diagonal line the possibility of *Iota* is now ruled out. Although the stroke in its form now visible has not been preserved in full length, it is long enough to safely rule out a hypothetical alternative of a *Rho*. It clearly is the diagonal middle stroke of a *Nu*, as demanded by the identification of fragment 7Q5 as Mk. 6.52-53.

Thus a significant step has been made towards confirming the identification. The letter *Nu* in line 2 now belongs to the 'reliable letters' of the fragment; and a papyrological question important for critics and supporters alike is solved in favour of the Markan identification.

Nevertheless questions do remain. Beyond establishing the characters in line 2 as *Nu,* the forensic tests were also able to confirm Herbert Hunger's thesis of partially wide differences in the writing of identical characters within the same fragment, as in the two definite *Etas* of the fragment, establishing the possibility that the remains to the right of the tear in line 2 could well represent another *Eta* or its dislocated remains. However, even the Jerusalem laboratory was unable to make ink remains visible where they once must have existed without doubt, e.g. at the left vertical stroke of the *Kappa* in line 3, at the join of *Alpha* and *Iota* in the *kai* of this line or by the vertical on the right of *Nu* in line 2. Whilst the ink totally disappeared in some places, it can be made visible again in others, depending on how deeply ink *and* quill have penetrated the papyrus. Amongst other examples, the diagonal *Nu*-stroke clearly shows that the writer obviously put the pen down firmly at the top left, so that later in the upper part of the stroke a 'fault' became visible under extreme magnification. The examination of the fragments is to continue. In the case of 7Q5 the investigation will go on to employ much improved instrumentation, but it also applies to the other fragments of cave 7. The fact that the first forensic analysis of (part of) fragment 7Q5 has shown concrete results has strengthened the resolve of all those involved in this process.

Thanks are due to Dr Joseph Almog and Joseph Zias as well as to the staff of the Investigations Department of the Israel National Police and the John Rockefeller Museum/Israel Antiquities Authority for the generous readiness to help.

The forensic analysis of 7Q5 and its recording by Bavarian Television was part of the documentary 'Der unbekannte Jesus' (The unknown Jesus) which was shown on the first Channel (ARD) on 7.6.1992 in a sixty minute version, as well as in two forty-five minute programmes on 20.8.1992 (repeat 23.8.92) and on 27.8.92 (repeat 30.8.92) on the third Channel of Bavarian Television as well as on 1.9.and 6.9.1992 on Eins Plus.

19

An Unnoticed Fragment from Qumran: 7Q19 and the Origin of Cave 7

Since 1972 when the Spanish papyrologist José O'Callaghan suggested a New Testament identification for some of the fragments found in Cave 7,[1] much debate has taken place concerning the cave and O'Callaghan's interpretation of its history.

Recently a number of voices have been raised in support of both the fragments which O'Callaghan himself regarded as giving reliable evidence for the truth of this hypothesis - that is fragment 7Q4 identified with the First Letter of Timothy 3:16 to 4:3, and fragment 7Q5 identified with Mark's Gospel 6:52-53 - and such voices have been drawn not only from the ranks of New Testament scholars, but have contained papyrologists and Classicists[2] also.

Despite this recent development, questions remain. Was it a Christian cave? What about two other fragments in cave 7 which have been reliably identified for some time and which are of Biblical origin? That is to say 7Q1 which has been identified with Exodus 28:4-6 and 7Q2 which has been identified with Baruch(EPJer) 6:43-4.[3] The problem with the latter fragment is that 7Q2 like 7Q5 is very small, and suffers from a considerably larger and more complex number of deviations from the LXX standard text than does the 7Q5 fragment when compared with Mark 6:52-53.[4]

What is needed in order to transform this somewhat confusing situation, is for another fragment to be found amongst those in cave 7, which could provide additional support in favour or against an early Christian provenance for the material in the cave.

In the 1962 edition of cave 7, nineteen fragments were published, eighteen of which were papyri; number 19 was the print of a papyrus which had been preserved in reverse in the hardened floor. [5] As early as 1972 O'Callaghan had suggested that there might be New Testament passages included amongst the other fragments in addition to 7Q4 and 7Q5, yet he went on to state that the size of these fragments made it hard to determine this for certain. What he was primarily interested in doing at that time, was not to demonstrate such identification conclusively, but rather to show that the two fragments which he believed he had identified positively as being of New Testament origin, could well have been surrounded by other fragments of the same origin.[6] He referred explicitly to fragments 7Q6, 7Q7, 7Q8 and to 7Q9, and the latter could indeed be a productive manuscript to examine; it is soon to be investigated by the Forensic Laboratory of the Department of Investigation in the Israeli National Police (O'Callaghan had suggested Romans 5:11 as being the correct identification for this fragment); furthermore, he listed 7Q10 and 7Q15.

Fragments 7Q3, 7Q11, 7Q12, 7Q13, 7Q14, 7Q16, 7Q17, 7Q18 and 7Q19 remain for the time being unclassified. In the case of all but two of these fragments, this lack of classification is not surprising given their size and condition. However the case of 7Q3 and 7Q19 is different, as these fragments are of a similar size to 7Q2 and 7Q5. 7Q2[7] consists of twenty-two characters on five lines, which compares to 7Q3's thirty-one characters on four lines, 7Q19's thirty-five characters on six lines[8] and to 7Q5's twenty characters on five lines.

One attempt at identifying 7Q3 was made by M. Baillet who suggested that it might be a passage from Jeremiah (Chapter 43, verses 28-29), but he himself admitted that such an identification was not possible.[9] That he was right to be sceptical has been confirmed by subsequent scholars, and today the suggestion has fallen out of favour.[10]

Curiously, the comparatively large fragment 7Q19 has not been given its due attention, even though the first edition in *DJD II* had reproduced both the visible, reversed imprint, and a mirror-image photograph which made the text clearly visible.[11] As I am trying to show, it now appears to be possible that the fragment 7Q19 is an unknown early Christian text.

The existence of non-biblical theological texts at Qumran can and must be taken for granted. Such a premise has been proved over and over again by both Aramaic and Hebrew texts found in other caves on the site. Further evidence of the presence of non-biblical theological texts can also be gleaned from an examination of the six Greek manuscripts found in Cave 4. Of these six texts - four of which are on leather and two papyri - four can be identified with passages in the Pentateuch (one is a loose Exodus paraphrase), but one of the two papyri is an unknown Greek text. The fact that this text has not been identified is not a consequence of its size; 4Q 126 consists of no fewer than eight fragments, pieces 1 to 5 being roughly of the same dimensions as fragments 7Q2 and 7Q5. It is certain that it does not belong to either biblical or deuterocanonical literature.[12]

Fragment 7Q19 has the following letters and words:

]η[
]$\eta\lambda\chi$.[
]$\chi\tau\alpha\iota$ $\dot\alpha\pi\dot o$ τo[$\hat\upsilon$
τ]$\hat\eta$s $\chi\tau\dot\iota\sigma\epsilon\omega$[s
]$\dot\epsilon\nu$ $\tau\alpha\hat\iota$s $\gamma\rho\alpha\varphi\alpha$[$\hat\iota$s
]$\rho\alpha\nu$[

Now from what is present on lines 4 and 5 of this text (*tês ktiseôs, en tais graphais*), as well as from the probable verb ending in line 3, *ktai* with *apo tou*, it can be demonstrated that even allowing for variants, the text does not belong to either LXX, nor to the New Testament or the remaining extant Greek literature.

On the other hand despite its not being scriptural the text is clearly theological in nature, as it refers to creation in relation to the 'scriptures'. It is clear therefore that there are two possibilities for the text's classification. Either it is a Jewish text of the post-canonical period which refers back to the creation story in scripture, or it is an early Christian text with a comparable intention.

Now it can be established that there are no comparable examples of an author writing about the Old Testament in this way in the Greek-language Jewish Literature of the period before AD 68, the end date for all Qumran finds. For example whilst Philo does refer to 'the Scriptures' in the plural, he does so always adding the epithet 'holy' (*en hierais graphais* etc.) - see *De Abrahamo* 61, *Quis Rerum Divinarum Heres* 106, 159; *De Fuga et Inventione* 4; *De Specialibus Legibus* 1,214,II,104,134; *De Congressu quaerendae Eruditionis gratia* 34, 90; *De Optificio Mundi* 77; *De Decalogo* 8,37.

Even Josephus, who is writing too late for a strict comparison, confirms the Jewish-Greek use of language in this regard (see *Contra Apionem 2,45: tôn hierôn graphôn*).

An apparent exception to this rule occurs in Philo, *De Abrahamo* 236. Against the occurence in *De Abrahamo* 61, it reads only '*Tauta mën oun hai rhëtai graphai periéchousin*'. Yet as the context shows, in *Abraham* 235 - in contradistinction to *Abraham* 61 - the passage does not refer to the Bible or 'something theological', but rather to a piece of general worldly wisdom. The same goes for a similar passage in *De Vita Mosis* II, 40 (which is about the use of certain Greek and Chaldaic texts in translation). A similar picture emerges from an examination of post New Testament early Christian literature. In the *Letter of Clement*, the oldest of the writings of the Apostolic Fathers which was written no later than AD 96, the Old Testament scriptures are always referred to in the plural, again employing the epithet 'holy' alongside the word for scriptures (see *L of C* 45, 2; 53,1). This practice was later continued. Authors like Philo, Josephus and Clemens Romanus, always put 'hierais' (and other declensions) before 'graphas' (etc.).

Against this consistent practice, a different pattern emerges in the New Testament. Here the Old Testament scriptures are always referred to without adding the epithet 'holy'. An interesting example of this can be found in the Second Letter of Peter, chapter 3, verse 16 - *tas loipas graphas*. Only through exegesis has it been possible to show that Holy Scripture is referred to here - the reference is not made explicit in the text itself. An exception to this general practice is a passage in the Letter to the Romans chapter 1, verse 2. Here Paul writes *'en graphais hagiais'*. Yet this individual case is unique in its positioning of 'hagiais' after 'en graphai'. This inversion of noun and epithet, a 'Pauline' habitus,[13] is also conceivable in Qumran fragment 7Q19, particularly in conjunction with the article *'tais'*.

It is possible that in fragment 7Q19 line 5 the words *'en tais graphais'* could easily have been continued by either *'hagiais'*, or *'tais hagiais'*. Yet even if such a reconstruction remains speculation, it is still a fact that the kind of creation thinking found in this fragment is also a distinctive feature of Paul's milieu. One only needs to look at Romans 8:19 - *hê gar apokaradokia tês ktiseôs* - to be reminded of this.

In conclusion the evidence regarding fragment 7Q19 would appear to indicate that it certainly does not belong to Jewish Greek literature of this period. The probability therefore must be that it is in fact an early Christian document, written before AD 96,[14] and possibly the product of Paul's milieu or 'school'. Such a hypothetical classification would be affirmed by the other texts in cave 7 which probably came from Rome soon after Paul's Letter to the Romans. [15]

Following the important work done by E.Tov,[16] a certain consensus has been achieved with regard to the non-Essene origin of the Greek texts of caves 4 and 7. The above discussion concerning the current state of interpretation with regard to the evidence in cave 7 does not contradict this, but rather confirms how open the Essenes were to the Greek element in the culture of their environment, and how willing they were to take an interest in, and indeed to collect, documents written in Greek dealing with matters of faith. How far they also reflected upon the Christian theology of these writings is a different question of course.

NOTES

1   J. O'Callaghan, 'Papiros neotestamentarios en la cueva 7 de Qumrân?', *Biblica* 53, 192, 91-100; '1 Tim 3,16; 4,1.3 en 7Q4?' *Biblica* 53, 1972, 362-367; 'Notas sobre 7Q tomadas en el 'Rockefeller Museum' de Jerusalén' *Biblica* 53, 1972, 515-533, etc; a detailed summary is provided by his book *Los papiros griegos de la cueva 7 de Qumrân*, Madrid 1974.

2　For a summary of the debate see C. P. Thiede, *The Earliest Gospel Manuscript? The Qumran Fragment 7Q5 and Its Significance for New Testament Studies,* Exeter 1992; B. Mayer, (ed.), *Christen und Christliches in Qumran?,* Regensburg 1992; O. Betz/R. Riesner, *Jesus, Qumran and the Vatican. Clarifications,* London 1994, 114-123.

3　Some critics have used the non-Christian fragments 7Q1 and 7Q2 - which may well have been copied by Christian scribes, important as both texts were for early Christian theology - in an attempt to argue against the possibility that cave 7 was 'Christian'. A recent example, apparently written in ignorance of the latest publications, is R.H. Gundry's otherwise excellent monograph, *Mark: A Commentary on his Apology for the Cross,* Grand Rapids 1993, 343-344.

One has to accept that even 7Q2 = Baruch/Letter of Jeremiah 6:43-44 is an alien element at Qumran: this deuterocanonical text, preserved in Greek (!), has not been found in any other Qumran cave, neither in Greek, nor in Hebrew or Aramaic. But it does easily fit a Christian context - see the affinity to 1 John 5:21, etc.

4　For a detailed analysis, see chapter 16.

5　M. Baillet, J.T. Milik, R. de Vaux, (eds.), 'Les petites grottes de Qumran', *Discoveries in the Judaean Desert of Jordan II* (henceforth *DJD II*), Textes, 142-146, here 143-166.

6　J. O'Callaghan, 'The Identifications of 7Q', *Aegyptus* 56, 1976, 287-294.

7　As in note 5.

8　The first editors included two further, tiny and apparently unrelated pieces of hardened soil which they regarded as the *verso,* i.e. the back of the lost papyrus 7Q5. However, the existence of a *verso* can safely be excluded: 7Q, quite like all the other Qumran caves, contained exclusively scroll fragments with text on the front, the *recto* only. The possibility of an 'opistograph' or other exceptional instance, which can not be ruled out in theory, of course, would seem too far-fetched in a context of hundreds of scroll fragments - and this includes the 26 Greek texts from caves 4 and 7, with not a single second example.

9　M. Baillet, 'Les manuscrits de la Grotte 7 de Qumrân et le Nouveau Testament', *Biblica* 53, 1972, 508-526, here 516; *id.,* 'Les manuscrits de la Grotte 7 de Qumrân et le Nouveau Testament, Suite' *Biblica,* 54, 1973, 348-349.

10　A conclusive summary can be found in J. O'Callaghan, *Los papiros griegos de la cueva 7 de Qumrân,* Madrid 1974, 89-91, and *id.,* '7Q5: Nuevas consideraciones', *Studia Papyrologica* 16, 1977, 45, n. 10.

11   *DJD II*, as in note 5, vol. 'Planches', Oxford 1962, plate XXX.

12   See the critical edition of the Greek texts from cave 4, P.W. Skehan, E.
     Ulrich and J.E. Sanderson (eds.), *Qumran Cave IV: Paleo-Hebrew
     and Greek Biblical Manucripts, DJD* IX, Oxford 1992, here
     219-221.

13   In the so-called Pastoral Epistles which, irrespective of the debate about
     their author, clearly belong to the Pauline circle, we do not find the
     determined *graphai*, but the singular case of a vague *grammata*,
     which is preceded by *hiera* : 2 Timothy 3:15.

14   Archaeologically the contents of cave 7 must be dated to the period
     prior to AD 68. Palaeographically the fragment 7Q19 must belong
     to the same period as other Qumran writings such as 7Q4 and 7Q5,
     as it is written in the same late Herodian Ornamental style which
     was found up until the middle of the 1st century AD. For
     background information see H. Hunger, '7Q5, Markus 6.52-53 -
     oder? Die Meinung eines Papyrologen', in B. Mayer (ed.), *Christen
     und Christliches in Qumran?*, Regensburg 1992, 33-56, with plates.

15   The jug found in cave 7 bears a Hebrew inscription 'rwm', which J.
     Fitzmyer has interpreted as signifying the place of origin, Rome.
     See 'A Qumran Fragment of Mark?', in *America* 126, 1972,
     647-650. Attempts at refutation such as the work of H.-U.
     Rosenbaum have failed to shake this attribution (for a discussion of
     the evidence see C.P. Thiede, *The Earliest Gospel Manuscript? The
     Qumran Fragment 7Q5 and Its Significance for New Testament
     Studies*, Exeter 1992, 55).

16   E Tov, 'Hebrew Biblical Manuscripts from the Judean Desert: Their
     Contribution to Textual Criticism', in *Journal of Jewish Studies*,
     39/1, 1988, 5-37, here 19.